Three Generations, Two Languages

Multilingual Matters

Attitudes and Language
    COLIN BAKER
Citizens of This Country: The Asian British
    MARY STOPES-ROE and RAYMOND COCHRANE
Continuing to Think: The British Asian Girl
    BARRIE WADE and PAMELA SOUTER
Coping with Two Cultures
    PAUL A. S. GHUMAN
Education of Chinese Children in Britain and the USA
    LORNITA YUEN-FAN WONG
Equality Matters
    H. CLAIRE, J. MAYBIN and J. SWANN (eds)
European Models of Bilingual Education
    HUGO BAETENS BEARDSMORE (ed.)
Foundations of Bilingual Education and Bilingualism
    COLIN BAKER
Immigrant Languages in Europe
    GUUS EXTRA and LUDO VERHOEVEN (eds)
Language Diversity Surveys as Agents of Change
    JOE NICHOLAS
Language, Minority Education and Gender
    DAVID CORSON
Making Multicultural Education Work
    STEPHEN MAY
The Step-Tongue: Children's English in Singapore
    ANTHEA FRASER GUPTA

Please contact us for the latest book information:
Multilingual Matters Ltd,
Frankfurt Lodge, Clevedon Hall,Victoria Road,
Clevedon, Avon BS21 7SJ, England

MULTILINGUAL MATTERS 104
Series Editor: Derrick Sharp

Three Generations, Two Languages, One Family

Language Choice and Language Shift in a Chinese Community in Britain

Li Wei

MULTILINGUAL MATTERS LTD
Clevedon • Philadelphia • Adelaide

Library of Congress Cataloging in Publication Data

Li Wei
Three Generations, Two Languages, One Family: Language Choice and
Language Shift in a Chinese Community in Britain.
p. cm. (Multilingual Matters: 104)
Includes bibliographical references and index.
1. Cantonese dialect–Great Britain. 2. Chinese–Great Britain–Language.
3. Cantonese dialect–Social aspects–Great Britain.
I. Title. II. Series: Multilingual Matters (Series): 104.
PL1740.G7W45   1994
495.1'7–dc20   94-9959

British Library Cataloguing in Publication Data

A CIP catalogue record for this book is available from the British Library.

ISBN 1-85359-241-2 (hbk)
ISBN 1-85359-240-4 (pbk)

Multilingual Matters Ltd

UK: Frankfurt Lodge, Clevedon Hall, Victoria Road, Clevedon, Avon BS21 7SJ.
USA: 1900 Frost Road, Suite 101, Bristol, PA 19007, USA.
Australia: P.O. Box 6025, 83 Gilles Street, Adelaide, SA 5000, Australia.

Typeset by Editorial Enterprises, Devon.
Printed and bound in Great Britain by WBC Ltd, Bridgend.

Contents

Acknowledgments

The study reported in this book forms part of a larger, ongoing research project, funded by two ESRC grants (R000 22 1074 (1989–90) and R000 23 2856 (1991–94)). The fieldwork for the study was carried out by myself during my tenure of the Ridley Fellowship (1988–91) in the Department of Speech, University of Newcastle upon Tyne. Other financial support received in the course of the study included a personal donation from Mr S.H. Ng of Happy Travel (Newcastle).

Needless to say, the study could not have been possible without the co-operation and support from the community in question. I am privileged to know so many Chinese families in Tyneside who have accepted me as a friend. I am equally privileged to be able to work closely with Lesley Milroy, whose advice, criticism, and encouragement have been essential to the project.

A number of people have contributed to the study by discussing with me various points of the book. They include Peter Auer, Aidan Coveney, James Milroy, Suzanne Moffatt, Lisa Perkins and Peter Trudgill, all of whom read and commented on parts or all of the manuscript. Clyde Mitchell made available a number of his papers on social network analysis, which have proved crucial for the research design.

In April–May 1989, I visited the University of Hong Kong to avail myself of the expertise there on the transcription of Cantonese conversation. Luke Kang Kwong introduced me to some of the existing materials and generously allowed me access to a transcription system which he used for his own research. Siew-Yue Killingley in Newcastle also provided me with information on Cantonese and commented on my transcription in this book.

The statistical tests used in the present study have been assisted by Katie Reid. Doug Cudmore and his colleagues advised me with patience on word-processing and computing skills.

I owe a special debt of gratitude to Elma Steele who accommodated me in her house while I was working on the book. Extra-special thanks are due to my parents in Peking and my sister in Newcastle who have given me enduring love and encouragement. It is to them that this book is dedicated.

Romanisation and Transcription Conventions

Romanisation conventions for Cantonese

Symbol	IPA Equivalent	Symbol	IPA Equivalent
b	p	a	a
d	t	ai	ai
g	k	au	au
p	p'	aa	a:
t	t'	aai	a:i
k	k'	aau	a:u
l	l	e	ɛ
m	m	ei	ei
n	n	eu	œ
ng	ŋ	i	i
f	f	iu	iu
h	h	o	o
s	s	ou	ou
j	ts	oi	oi
ch	ts'	u	u
gw	kw	ui	ui
kw	k'w	eui	œy
y	w	yu	y
y	j		

The transcription of conversational data in this book follows normal procedures in Conversation Analysis (see Atkinson & Heritage, 1984: ix–xvi for a fuller description). The following are the most prominent conventions:

Convention	Meaning
(n)	a pause; n is the length of the pause in seconds
(.)	a slight pause less than a second
[	overlapping

Introduction

Despite the pioneering work of the Linguistic Minorities Project (1985), the demography and patterning of multilingualism and multiculturalism in Britain has yet to be fully documented. To date, societal-level censuses or surveys have provided the principal means for investigating the extent of linguistic and cultural diversity. Information gathered by such surveys is unquestionably useful, but has little explanatory value (for comments, see Martin-Jones, 1991). It fails to explicate, for example, the internal structuring of particular communities, and the norms and values that are inherent within them. It also fails to elucidate the salience of language use in and between communities whose mother tongues are not English. In this regard, the Chinese people in Britain, who constitute the third largest non-indigenous ethnic minority population in the country (after those of West Indian origin and from the Indian sub-continent) (HAC (Home Affairs Committee), 1985a), provide an interesting case in point.

It is almost a cliché now that the Chinese are among the least (if not the least) known and understood of Britain's ethnic minorities. So far, very few attempts have been made which go beyond the stereotypes that the Chinese are 'self-contained' and 'self-sufficient'. Public perceptions have largely ignored the heterogeneity of British Chinese communities, in terms of place of origin, migration and settlement pattern, social and economic position, and not least language. Without underestimating the attitudes of intolerance and indifference towards non-indigenous cultures which are still persistent in British society today, distinctively Chinese forms of cognition and rules for action have not facilitated research into this diverse group. Accurate and reliable information about Chinese communities in this country is simply not forthcoming, despite urgent calls by the Commission for Racial Equality (1979, 1988) and the Home Affairs Committee of the House of Commons (HAC, 1985a).

One of the greatest difficulties in initiating research has been in locating appropriate bilingual and bicultural investigators who have access to the target communities. The need for credence and trust is clearly paramount, as is the need for systematic investigations of the Chinese population in general and their linguistic behaviour in particular. It is here that the methods and practices of contemporary sociolinguistics have much to offer.

The work reported in this book forms part of a larger, ongoing sociolinguistic project, the aim of which is to provide empirical data on the language behaviours of different generations of Chinese residents in a defined area, namely, Tyneside in the north-east of England (Milroy & Li Wei, 1990, 1991). This area has been chosen primarily because of the extensive personal contacts which I, as the fieldworker, had established *prior to* the project, a prerequisite for community-based studies with ethnic minority populations.

The focus of the current study is on language choice, the principal behaviour through which bilingualism is expressed. Given the monolingual and unicultural tradition of Britain, the choice between English and other, often socially stigmatised, ethnic minority languages has taken on special symbolism. It is an 'act of identity' for individual speakers and a potent reminder of the competing cultural values for the British society as a whole. A study of language choice should therefore be of relevance not only to those who practise it in everyday life or encounter it through their professions (e.g. teachers and speech therapists), but also to policy makers whose decisions may affect our lives in a profound way.

As well as providing a substantial amount of systematically collected data on the bilingual behaviour of the Tyneside Chinese, a major concern of the current study is to develop a coherent model which accounts for the relationship between community-level language choice patterns and code-switching strategies by individual speakers (I take the latter as language choice at the *interactional* or *conversational* level), and for the relation of both to the broader social, economic and political context.

It is evident from the abundant research literature that a wealth of data on language choice and code-switching patterns from a large number of very different communities is readily available (e.g. Heller, 1988; Jacobson, 1990; Eastman, 1992; European Science Foundation, 1990a, 1990b, 1990c, 1991). Many insightful analyses have been offered. What seems to be generally lacking, however, is a *social* framework within which to interpret these rich data and varied analyses (Gal, 1987; Milroy & Li Wei, 1991; Li Wei, Milroy & Pong, 1992). Heller (1990) remarks that while John Gumperz, an important leader in the field, has always maintained that code-switching is constitutive of social reality, he has perhaps been less successful in linking this interactional level with broader questions of social relations and social organisation. While Gumperz himself may not have intended to make this micro-macro link, it is important that those who develop his procedures should attempt to do so. Otherwise, insightful interactional-level analyses of data sets which cannot be compared with each other will continue to proliferate without any corresponding advance in understanding similarities and differences in the language choice behaviours of different communities, or in explaining why rapid language shift is likely in one particular community but not in another.

Like Gal (1988, 1989), Heller (1990) and Woolard (1985), I take the starting point for any social model of language choice to be detailed sociolinguistic observations of interactional behaviours of individual speakers. But such everyday behaviour of social actors and larger scale institutional analysis should be seen as related rather than as dissociated, as tends to be the case in the bilingualism literature (cf. the approaches of Fishman and Gumperz, which are generally considered quite separately). Giddens (1984) has developed a social theory based on the relationships between these two levels, commenting that 'the study of day-to-day life is integral to analysis of the reproduction of institutionalised practices' (p. 282). In this book, I shall attempt to expand upon the *social network* approach developed by the Milroys in dialectal contact situations (L. Milroy, 1987a, b; J. Milroy, 1992; L. Milroy & J. Milroy, 1985, 1992) and aim to link micro-interactional behaviours of the speaker with macro-societal structures and social relations. The exposition is presented primarily with specific reference to the example of the Chinese/English-speaking community in Tyneside, although its applicability should reach Chinese communities elsewhere in the world as well as other immigrant bilingual situations.

The book consists of seven chapters. Chapter 1 reviews the existing models and approaches available in the study of bilingualism and language choice. Particular attention is paid to the relationship between social structures which are seen to be determining speakers' linguistic choices and interactional behaviour of the individual which contributes to the formation and transformation of these structures. A model based upon the concept of social network which integrates the two levels of analysis is outlined. Chapter 2 offers an ethnographic overview of the Chinese community in Britain, focusing on the internal organisation of the Hong Kong emigrants group which is chosen as the target group for the study. Chapter 3 discusses the methodology of participant observation and documents the fieldwork procedures of the study. Chapters 4, 5 and 6 present detailed analyses of data, concentrating in turn on patterns of language choice and language abilities of different generations of speakers from a sample of ten Tyneside Chinese families (30 male + 28 female = 58 speakers), social networks of the 58 speakers and their relationships with language choice patterns and bilingual ability, and conversational code-switching strategies. The book concludes in Chapter 7 with a summary of the major findings and a discussion of the implications of the social network model of language choice.

1 Perspectives on Bilingualism and Language Choice

Research in bilingualism and language choice has been carried out by investigators from a wide range of disciplines with diverse approaches and perspectives. Some of these approaches and perspectives are distant from the primarily *social* one with which I am concerned in this book. For example, there exists a large body of literature on neurolinguistic and psycholinguistic aspects of bilingualism, generally addressing such issues as lexical storage and retrieval processes, or hemispheric location of different languages often with references to aphasia and alexia.[1]

Within the broadly linguistic studies of bilingualism and language choice, different approaches and emphases can also be found. Muysken and his colleagues, for instance, have been working chiefly within the framework of generative grammar and focusing on the problem of specifying structural constraints on code-switching — the principal, micro-interactional manifestation of bilingualism (Muysken, 1990, 1991; DiSciullo, Muysken & Singh, 1986). Researchers who have worked with mixed language data are generally aware that there are constraints of some kind, such as major constituent boundaries, or semantic unit boundaries, on the switch point. Few, however, have actually succeeded in formulating constraints to which counter-examples have not rapidly been cited. Muysken and his colleagues have tried to capture the evident but elusive regularities in code-switching behaviour by positing various kinds of borrowability hierarchies and switched constituent hierachies. This work, however, is still at an early stage.

Perhaps the most extensive work on bilingual language choice from a linguistic perspective is carried out by Poplack, Sankoff and their associates, initially on Spanish–English code-switching data collected from New York City's Puerto Rican community, but more recently on the so-called Ottowa-Hull corpus, a computerised corpus of French–English material (Poplack, 1980, 1981, 1990; Poplack, Sankoff & Miller, 1988; Sankoff & Poplack, 1981; Sankoff &

Mainville, 1986; Sankoff, M'Barek & Montpetit, 1987; Sankoff, Poplack & Vanniarajan, 1991). Like Muysken, Poplack and Sankoff are interested primarily in the question of specifying structural constraints on code-switching, but they work overwhelmingly within a Labovian-style quantitative paradigm, and operate chiefly with notions of probability rather than with categorical constraints on switching.

Another major question which Poplack and Sankoff investigate is how *borrowing* might be distinguished from *code-switching*, and indeed where the borderline might be drawn between an established loan on the one hand, which eventually becomes codified as a dictionary entry, and a single word switch which may not be integrated morphologically or phonologically into the matrix language of the utterance (e.g. Poplack & Sankoff, 1984). This is in fact an interest shared by a large number of other investigators who often feel that such a distinction is needed chiefly because code-switching is generally analysed in terms of social motivation and meaning, whereas the insertion of lexical loans is not. More recently, Myers-Scotton (1992) argues that borrowing arises originally as code-switching and that at any point in time, borrowing forms and code-switching forms fall along a process continuum (see also Myers-Scotton, 1991).[2]

While these studies have undoubtedly contributed to our understanding of (in particular) the internal linguistic characteristics of bilingual speech, they seem to have drawn many researchers away from the fact that bilingual language choice is *essentially a social phenomenon*. Back in 1962, Mackey pointed out that:

> *Bilingualism* is not a phenomenon of language; but a characteristic of its use. It is not a feature of the code but of the message. It does not belong to the domain of 'langue', but of 'parole' (Mackey, 1962: 51, original italics).

The social significance of bilingualism has been well discussed in the literature (for general discussions see Appel and Muysken, 1987; Romaine, 1989; for a more recent discussion on 'bilingualism in/as social action' see Auer, 1990; 1991) and does not need to be repeated here. But the most important point about a *social* account of bilingualism is its capacity to provide a general, interpretative framework within which various data sets can be analysed and compared (Li Wei, Milroy & Pong, 1992). Myers-Scotton (1992: 417) argues that even with code-switching structures which seem to be very much cognitively determined, macro-level social forces as well as more micro-level socio-pragmatic motives may determine which permissible patterns are preferred.

There are of course different perspectives even among the primarily social studies of bilingualism and language choice. Here I shall review a selection of these studies. The aim of this review is to locate the present study of language choice of a British Chinese community within a broad theoretical framework.

Following Grimshaw (1987), I shall make a distinction between *macro-societal* and *micro-interactional* perspectives, which I believe has been fundamental to the way in which many investigators of bilingualism and language choice have conceived and located their work (see also Breitborde, 1983). This distinction corresponds generally to the dichotomies of structural versus interactional, or positivistic versus anti-positivistic, approaches in sociological research.[3] But rather than going into details of the sociological theorisation and debate underlying these dichotomies, I want to focus my attention on some specific models of bilingualism and language choice that have been proposed by sociolinguists. By doing so, I wish to argue that an adequate and coherent social account of bilingualism and language choice must be capable of explaining *both* micro-interactional practices of individual speakers and the macro-societal context in which these practices occur, *as well as their (inter)relations*.

It is necessary to note here that language choice may occur at several different levels, ranging from small-scale phonetic variables such as the ones studied by Labov (1966, 1972a) to large-scale discourse patterns such as address systems, conversation routines (e.g. greetings and partings), politeness strategies, and of course choices between languages. While acknowledging that the psycho-social dynamics underlying these different kinds of linguistic choices may be similar (Milroy, 1987b: Ch. 8; Fasold, 1984: 180–3), I am concentrating on the more visible process of bilingual choices.

The organisation of this chapter falls into three parts. In the first I shall discuss the macro-societal perspective which is concerned with societal-functional arrangements of different languages and which views language choice as being derived from and determined by higher-order social structures. The second part examines the micro-interactional perspective which contrasts the macro perspective with its emphasis on the individual speaker's capacity to produce and reproduce social norms and values through everyday interactional behaviours. In the third part I shall discuss the possibility of developing an integrated model using the concept of *social network*.

The Macro-Societal Perspective

Researchers of bilingualism generally agree that language choice is an 'orderly' social behaviour, rather than a random matter of momentary inclination. Where perspectives differ is in the conceptualisation of the nature of achievement and management of that orderliness. The macro-societal perspective is founded on the assumption that individuals' language behaviour is structured by social, situational context, and what activities individuals produce are seen to be the result of, or at the very least to be greatly influenced by, the organisation and structure of the society in which they live. To put it simply, the macro-societal perspective regards language choice as orderly because the social structures that govern the choices are orderly. Thus, factors affecting the societal arrangement of languages are the central concern of the macro perspective.

Within this broad perspective, it is possible to identify two main analytic models which I shall call the *complementary distribution model* and the *conflict model* respectively. They are distinguished not so much in terms of their view on the relationship between language behaviour and social structure, but on how languages are socially and functionally differentiated.

Complementary distribution model

Martin-Jones (1989a) attributes the first attempt to build a complementary distribution model of bilingual language choice to Weinreich (1953), who was concerned with the functional differentiation of languages in contact situations. Weinreich employed the term 'domain of language use', a term first used by the German linguist, Schmidt-Rohr (1932). The basic idea was that each of the co-existing languages or language varieties in a given society served a specific function, and the specialised functions of different languages or language varieties complemented each other, giving rise to cohesive and stable societal bilingualism and/or multilingualism.

Ferguson (1959) further pursued this functional differentiation of language by introducing the notion of *diglossia*, in which a binary distinction is made between High (H) and Low (L) varieties. Ferguson noted nine areas in which H and L would differ, including function, prestige, literacy heritage, acquisition, standardisation, stability, grammar, lexicon and phonology. The most important feature of diglossia is the functional specialisation of H and L. Table 1.1 lists some of the typical situations in which the two varieties are used.

As table 1.1 shows, in one set of situations H and only H is appropriate, while in another L and only L. The languages in a bilingual community are thus seen as falling into a neat pattern of complementary distribution with little or no overlap. Examples which have been cited to support the diglossia concept include Swiss German (L) and (Standard) High German (H) in Switzerland, classical Arabic (H) and colloquial Arabic (L) in Egypt, and Haitian Creole (L) and French (H) in Haiti.

One implication of Ferguson's conception of diglossia is that members of a bilingual community are seen as being constrained in their language behaviour, merely reflecting a set of predetermined society-wide norms. Rapid and frequent code-switching which has been shown to be a characteristic feature of conversational interaction in many bilingual communities seems almost impossible according to this model. As Eckert (1980: 1,054) points out, 'complementary

Table 1.1 Situations for High and Low varieties in diglossia

Situation	High	Low
Sermon in church or mosque	+	
Instructions to servants, waiters, etc.		+
Personal letter	+	
Speech in parliament, political speech	+	
University lecture	+	
Conversation with family, friends or colleagues		+
News broadcast	+	
Radio soap opera		+
Newspaper editorial, news story	+	
Caption on political cartoon		+
Poetry	+	
Folk literature		+

Source: Ferguson, 1972: 236

distribution of the co-existing languages virtually eliminates the possibility of random choice'. Consequently, researchers who have adopted Ferguson's notion of diglossia tend to concentrate on bilingualism at the macro-societal level, far removed from concrete, interactional behaviours of individual speakers.

Another problem with the diglossia concept concerns its inability to account for change over time. Ferguson insisted that diglossia was stable, capable of persisting for several centuries, although he did not explain why this could be the case. However, research repeatedly reveals that some bilingual communities (or groups within a bilingual community) apparently maintain their language less effectively than others and their patterns of language use change as time goes by (e.g. Gal, 1979; Dorian, 1981; Edwards, 1986). The diglossia concept as conceived of by Ferguson offers no account of the social and linguistic processes involved in language retention and shift in and across communities.

Over the years, attempts have been made to modify the complementary distribution model so that it can be used to analyse and explain different types of bilingual situation and language choice practice. In this particular regard, Fishman's contributions have been the most influential. Extending Weinreich's work, Fishman has tried to link the analysis of societal norms and expectation with language use in face-to-face encounters, using the concept of *domain* as a pivot (Fishman, 1965, 1972). Domain, as Fishman conceives it, refers to a clustering of characteristic situations around a prototypical theme which structures both the speakers' perception of the situation and their social behaviour including language choice. To give a simplified example, husband and wife (participants) talking about domestic affairs (topic) at home (setting) would constitute a 'family' domain, and the family domain would require the use of a special language or language variety which would differ from, say, that of the 'work' domain. Since Fishman's domain analysis underlies much of current work on bilingualism and language choice, it is necessary to examine it in some detail here.

Key to the concept of domain is the notion of congruence on two levels: (i) congruence among domain components, of which participant, topic and setting are deemed to be critical; (ii) congruence of domain with specific language or language variety.

Greenfield (1972) was among the first to implement domain analysis. In his study of the Puerto Rican community in New York City, Greenfield distributed a questionnaire in which subjects were given two congruent factors and were asked to select the third. For example, subjects were told to imagine themselves in a hypothetical situation where they were talking with their parents (participant) about domestic affairs (topic); they were then asked to select the most likely setting from among 'home', 'beach', 'church', 'school', and 'workplace' for such a communicative event to take place. In this particular case, 100% of Greenfield's subjects selected the expected congruent setting — home. In fact, with one exception (the selection of 'beach' as the appropriate location for 'friendship' domain) the expected congruent third factor was selected by at least 81% of the subjects (Greenfield, 1972: 23). Subsequently, Greenfield asked his subjects to indicate which language was most appropriate for a given domain. It was revealed that in New York City's Puerto Rican community Spanish was regularly used in the more 'intimate' domains such as 'family' and 'friendship', while English was the normal choice in domains where a status difference between participants was involved, such as 'religion', 'education' and 'employment'.

While Greenfield's study appears to confirm the theoretical validity of the domain concept, questions have to be asked as to how domains should be identified in practice, because nowhere in Fishman's work can we find a taxonomy or a set of principles for delimiting domains. Indeed, Fishman emphasises the need to establish relevant domains empirically, regardless of their number, and strongly rejects the idea of an invariant set of domains applicable to all communities (Fishman, 1972: 441). He argues, quite rightly, that the same domain may not be equally significant to different communities or to all members of a single community. Take the five domains — family, friendship, religion, education, and employment — which Greenfield (1972) studied, for example. Those who are unemployed are very unlikely to find talking to an 'employer' in a 'workplace' about 'how to do your job more efficiently' a meaningful domain. Older people may find the domain of education (participant: teacher–pupil; setting: school; topic: how to solve an algebra problem) irrelevant. Furthermore, speakers' perceptions of domains may differ depending on the backgrounds and social positions of the speakers in question. A British-born Pakistani graduate working as a computer programmer in a law firm will hardly have the same idea of an 'employment' domain as his immigrant parents working in a family-run corner-shop. However, without specifying the criteria whereby domains are to be identified, we would end up with endless listing, making comparisons within and between communities difficult, if not impossible.

A further problem relates to the congruence of domain components. Given the dynamic nature of contemporary social life, people constantly find themselves in situations where they may come across someone quite unexpectedly. For instance, a patient may accidentally meet her doctor in a supermarket and start talking about domestic issues such as cooking and looking after children. It is not at all clear how such 'incongruent' situations can be accounted for in Fishman's conceptualisation of domain.

This brings us to the question of interactive effect of various extralinguistic factors upon language choice. Many studies have shown that while situational factors such as setting and topic do influence speakers' language behaviour to a certain extent, the key determinant for language choice is the interlocutor (e.g. Gal, 1979). This point has been argued most explicitly and cogently by Bell (1984) who proposes that language variability at all levels is a matter of *audience design*, that is, 'people are responding primarily to other people' (p. 197). Non-audience factors such as setting and topic derive their effect on speakers' language behaviour by association with the audience, particularly the addressee. For instance, a setting such as a supermarket is normally associated with a more socially distant kind of addressee than a domestic setting, and the *danger of death* question (Labov, 1972b) mentions a topic associated with an intimate addressee and so on. In my own study of a Chinese-English bilingual student community in Newcastle upon Tyne, England, I specifically tested the interactive effects of interlocutor, topic and setting upon language choice. It was revealed that speakers made and varied their choices of language in accordance with the identity of the addressee, regardless of setting and topic (see further Li Wei, 1988; McGregor & Li Wei, 1991). Furthermore, many speakers reported that with certain types of interlocutors (e.g. fellow students within defined group networks), both Chinese and English would be used, which contradicts Fishman's (1972: 437) claim that: ' "Proper" usage dictates that only *one* of the theoretically coavailable languages or varieties *will* be chosen by particular classes of *interlocutors* on particular kinds of *occasions* to discuss particular kinds of *topics*' (Original italics).

Table 1.2 Relationships between bilingualism and diglossia

	Diglossia	
Bilingualism	+	−
+	1. Both diglossia and bilingualism	3. Bilingualism without diglossia
−	2. Diglossia without bilingualism	4. Neither diglossia nor bilingualism

It should be noted that the concept of domain was developed with particular reference to relatively stable and long-established bilingual communities where there tends to be clear and strict societal compartmentalisation of languages, and speakers in these communities habitually follow a set of behavioural norms predetermined by society. As Fishman himself has pointed out, when the analytic focus is on language choice as social dynamics (and this is frequently the case when we are dealing with language maintenance and shift situations), the domain concept is no longer of particular interest (Fishman, 1976: 64; see also Fishman, 1991).[4]

Another major contribution by Fishman to the complementary distribution model of bilingualism and language choice is his reformulation of Ferguson's notion of diglossia. Fishman has distinguished societal arrangements of languages from an individual's behavioural manifestation of bilingualism (Fishman, 1963, 1964, 1980). The aim here is to incorporate the factor of change in language use. Fishman suggests four possible combinations between societal diglossia and individual bilingualism, as shown in Table 1.2.

The first instance, both diglossia and bilingualism, occurs where individual bilingualism is not only widespread but also institutionally buttressed. This, Fishman believes, is imperative for language maintenance. The second case, diglossia without bilingualism, refers to different monolingual entities being brought together under one political-territorial rubric. At the societal level, more than one language receives institutional protection, although at the individual level there is only monolingualism. According to Fishman, relative stability can be maintained as long as societal compartmentalisation of language lasts. In the case of bilingualism without diglossia, the two languages compete for use in the same domains. This, Fishman argues, would give rise to language shift. He observes that:

> Without separate though complementary norms and values to establish and maintain functional separation of the speech varieties, that language or

variety which is fortunate enough to be associated with the drift of social forces tends to displace the other(s). (Fishman, 1971: 298)

One possible outcome of uninterrupted (i.e. uncompartmentalised) bilingualism-without-diglossia will be the last case - neither bilingualism nor diglossia.

It is obvious that Fishman, like Ferguson, associates diglossia with stability, and changes in patterns of language use are attributed to the breakdown of diglossia and of social consensus regarding appropriacy of language allocation. One question which Fishman has not asked, however, is how the functional differentiation of languages which led to diglossia came about in the first place. As Martin-Jones remarks:

> Diglossia is characterised as a natural and common sense reality. No account is given of the social origin of the functional division of labour between the H and L languages. The model merely represents this division of labour as a natural form of social and linguistic order, thereby implicitly reinforcing the legitimisation of the H language. (Martin–Jones, 1989a: 109)

The concern with the social origin of functional differentiation of languages has given rise to the second macro-societal model of bilingual language choice which I want to consider here, namely, the conflict model.

Conflict model

Studies of bilingualism and language choice which incorporate a conflict perspective were begun by Catalan linguists working in Spain (e.g. Ninyoles, 1969; Vallverdú, 1970), and were continued by researchers on varieties of Catalan and Occitan spoken in southern France (Bernardó & Rieu, 1973; Eckert, 1980; Gardy & Lafont, 1981; Kremnitz, 1981) (see further Martin-Jones, 1989a). The main themes of these studies are summarised by Martin-Jones (1989a: 118) as follows (see also Wardhaugh, 1987; Fairclough, 1988; Grillo, 1989):

(1) the ways in which divisions between linguistic groups are related to class divisions and to political and economic relations within the framework of the state
(2) the processes involved in the imposition of power and the reproduction of power relations
(3) the nature of conflicts and social struggles generated by relations of power.

In her account of the societal distribution of languages in the Pyrenees at Ariege, Eckert (1980) shows how the introduction of French through institutional structures such as local governments and schools led to symbolic oppositions between French and Gascon, the local variety of Occitan, and eventually a shift away from Gascon. At first Gascon was considered to be the 'inside' language, whereas French was the 'outside' language. But this symbolic evaluation gradually gave way to a 'private' versus 'public' opposition in the domains of language use and led to the legitimisation of French as the standard language. Ninyoles (1969) and Kremnitz (1981) have documented a similar stigmatisation process with respect to Catalan.

The chief argument put forward by these researchers is that the two languages involved in diglossia are unequal in terms of social status. One is 'imposed from above in the form of an administrative, ritual or standard language. By virtue of its political and economic status, this language becomes requisite for access to power and mobility within the society' (Eckert, 1980: 1,056), while the other is deliberately devalued and its domains of use are restricted. Eckert (1980) illustrates the inequality between the two languages in diglossia by showing how constraints on the 'appropriate' use of Gascon are not accompanied by similar constraints on the use of French. She points out that it is very often only the minority language which is deemed to be 'trespassing' on the domains of the dominant language.

Several British researchers who are concerned with minority languages in the Celtic periphery have also incorporated the notion of conflict in their work. Examples of such work include McKinnon (1977, 1984) on Scottish Gaelic and Williams (1979, 1987) and Williams & Roberts (1982) on Welsh. One point which has been emphasised by these researchers is that the functional differentiation of languages is symbolic of political, economic and social oppositions which exist in the communities in question. McKinnon (1984), for instance, discusses the use of English and Scottish Gaelic on the islands of Barra and Harris in the Western Isles in terms of a power versus solidarity opposition:

> A local language functions as a vehicle for community social solidarity and an intrusive language as the language of power epitomised in the form of economic activity, administration and communications which core society establishes in the periphery. (McKinnon, 1984: 495)

According to McKinnon, the use of Gaelic represents a form of protest against the intrusion of English in public life. Williams (1979, 1987) and Williams & Roberts (1982) show that Welsh speakers' demand for the extension of their language into institutional contexts such as state education and mass media is a direct manifestation of language conflicts in Wales.

The symbolic oppositions between different linguistic systems which these studies reveal are by no means confined to bilingual, ethnic minority communities. They also underlie the social stratification of, for example, English. Indeed, quantitative studies of standard versus non-standard English carried out by Labov (1966, 1972a, b) in America and Trudgill (1974, 1983) in Britain have employed the concept of *social class*, a key notion of Marxist conflict theory, in explaining both synchronic variation and diachronic change (see also Milroy & Milroy, 1991, 1992, 1993).

While the conflict model throws new light on the societal arrangement of languages, it shares with the complementary distribution model many of the basic assumptions about the relationship between social structure and individuals' language behaviour. They both endeavour to find out how social structure might be seen to shape and to delimit individual action. Their main difference seems to be that the complementary distribution model regards diglossia in which different languages or language varieties are socially and functionally compartmentalised as the necessary condition for language maintenance and social stability, whereas the conflict model emphasises the inequality and struggles between languages. Both models, however, see individuals' language choices as being determined and constrained by higher-order social structures. The macro-societal perspective on bilingualism and language choice contrasts sharply with the micro-interactional perspective to which I shall now turn.

The Micro-Interactional Perspective

The micro-interactional perspective on bilingualism and language choice draws upon interpretative traditions within sociological research. It views individuals' language behaviour *not* as a product of some abstract superstructure, but of what language users themselves decide is going on around them and of what they take the behaviour of others to mean. Any order or pattern of language choice is seen as the result of an ongoing interactional process. The emphasis here is on individuals' capacity to make use of the linguistic and social resources available to them in producing and reproducing social structures and social relations.

John Gumperz (see, for example, Gumperz, 1971, 1982) stands out as the most influential figure in the study of the interactional aspects of bilingualism.

Gumperz: Metaphorical code-switching

Gumperz anchors his work in concrete, observable behaviours of individual speakers. On the basis of extensive participant observation in a bi-dialectal community in Hemnesberget, Norway, he identified two types of code-switching practice — situational and metaphorical (Blom & Gumperz, 1972; for comments see Maehlum, 1990). Code-switching here refers to 'the juxtaposition within the same speech exchange of passages of speech belonging to two different grammatical systems or subsystems' (Gumperz, 1982: 59). Situational code-switching refers to the change of language which corresponds to changes in the situation, particularly participant, setting and activity type. For example, in

Sauris, Italy, speakers use a localised German dialect at home, but speak Friulian, an Italian dialect, in semi-public settings such as the local bar, and standard Italian at school and church (Denison, 1972). Similarly, an adult Berber-speaking Moroccan in The Netherlands speaks Berber with another Berber-speaking Moroccan, but changes to Moroccan Arabic when speaking to a non-Berber Moroccan (Appel & Muysken, 1987). As Blom & Gumperz (1972: 425) comment, 'the notion of situational switching assumes a direct relationship between language and social situation'. Subsequently, it is possible for an investigator to formulate predictive models of language choice at the community level. One such model is Rubin's (1968) 'decision tree' (see also Ervin-Tripp, 1969; Sankoff, 1972).

However, not all instances of code-switching correspond to changes in situational context. In some situations, speakers switch from one language to another in order to achieve special communicative effects, while participant and setting remain the same. Gumperz refers to this type of linguistic behaviour as 'metaphorical code-switching'. He regards metaphorical code-switching as symbolic of alternative interpersonal relationships. In modern society, individuals tend to be connected with each other in a complex way. Some people who hold posts in local governments, for instance, are friends of many of the residents who have to deal with them in their official capacities. In bilingual communities, choices of language are often seen as a 'metaphor' for the relationship being enacted. An example from Blom & Gumperz's (1972) study in Hemnesberget is that a resident approaches a clerk's desk and exchanges greetings and talks about domestic affairs using Ranamål, the local dialect, but switches to Bokmål, the standard variety, when conducting official business with the same person. According to Blom & Gumperz, the use of Ranamål here serves to highlight localised social network and solidarity, while Bokmål emphasises status (cf. Maehlum, 1990). Gumperz (1982) has elaborated on the social symbolism of metaphorical code-switching by making a distinction between 'we code' and 'they code'. He remarks that,

> The tendency is for the ethnically specific, minority language to be regarded as the 'we code' and becomes associated with in-group and informal activities, and for the majority language to serve as the 'they code' associated with the more formal, stiffer and less personal out-group relations. (Gumperz, 1982: 66)

It must be pointed out here that the 'we code' versus 'they code' dichotomy is quite different from the High versus Low distinction proposed by Ferguson (1959). The former symbolises alternative interpersonal relationships of language users, rather than the status of the languages or language varieties *per se*. The 'they code' does not necessarily have the literary heritage, stability and institutional support that the High variety in diglossia has. Nor does the 'we code' have to be non-written, non-standardised and restricted in lexicon as the Low in diglossia tends to be. The distinction between 'we' and 'they' codes is a product of a long-term interactional process, not of societal arrangements defined in advance and imposed upon language users as in the case of diglossia. Which language or language variety in a given community constitutes the 'we code' and which the 'they code' is a matter for the members of that community to decide through social exchange. It is rather unfortunate that in the course of application of Gumperz's model, the distinction between 'we code' and 'they code' has often been used as an *a priori schema* rather than a product of the interactional process of language choice.

Parallel to his consideration of the social symbolism of code-switching, Gumperz examines the conversational loci where speakers are likely to change from one language to another. But instead of analysing the linguistic-structural constraints on these loci as, for example, Poplack and Sankoff do (e.g. Poplack, 1980; Sankoff & Poplack, 1981), Gumperz has identified a number of discourse functions which code-switching are seen to fulfil. The functions typically include the following:

a) quotations
b) addressee specification
c) interjections
d) reiteration
e) message qualification
f) personalisation versus objectivisation. (Gumperz, 1982: 75–84)

Gumperz's approach to code-switching has inspired a great deal of research into the micro-interactional aspects of bilingualism. Here, I want to consider two studies which build upon Gumperz's work on the social meaning and discourse functions of language choice respectively. The first is Scotton's (e.g. 1976, 1980, 1982, 1983) 'markedness' theory of language choice, and the second is Auer's (1984a, b, 1988, 1991) sequential analysis of language alternation.

Scotton: The 'markedness' theory of language choice

Working with Swahili, English and a variety of East African languages used in Kenya, Scotton (1986) argues that bilingual (and of course multilingual) speakers have an innate theory of socially relevant markedness and indexicality. They use language choice to negotiate interpersonal relationships and they do so within a normative framework which does not restrict choices, but does limit interpretations. The centerpiece of the 'markedness' theory is a 'negotiation principle' which directs speakers to 'choose the form of your conversational contribution such that it symbolises the set of rights and obligations which you wish to be in force between speakers and addressee for the current exchange' (Scotton, 1983: 116).

Scotton suggests that there are four possible motivations for engaging in code-switching under the 'markedness' model of language choice:

(1) to make a sequence of unmarked choices in cases where situational factors change during the course of a conversation and therefore a new code becomes unmarked

(2) as an unmarked choice in cases in which it is expected that a person with the sociolinguistic profile of the speaker will wish to index the social identities associated with two or more codes in the same conversation and therefore the speaker switches between these codes to invoke simultaneous identities

(3) as a marked choice in cases where the speaker wishes to dis-identify with the unmarked rights and obligation set for an interaction and negotiate a change in the social distance holding between other participants and him/herself

(4) as an exploratory choice in cases where the speaker is unsure which norms apply in a given interaction, either because the interaction is novel or the speaker does not have full information about other participants (see further Myers-Scotton, 1992).

Scotton intends her theory to be capable of linking the social symbolism of languages on the one hand and conversational strategies of individual speakers on the other (Myers-Scotton, 1990, 1991), but as yet, not all the claims have been empirically confirmed, especially the ways in which languages become marked or unmarked. Furthermore, how speakers acquire the set of rights and obligations in social interaction has not been explained systematically. This of course is also true about Gumperz's model which we have discussed above. While he has gone some way to analyse the social values of language choice and discourse strategies of the choice makers respectively, Gumperz is less specific about how these two levels are interrelated to one another. I shall return to this point later.

Auer: Sequential analysis of language choice

A more recent development in the study of bilingualism and language choice from a micro-interactional perspective is the sequential analysis of code-switching carried out by Auer on data collected among Italian speakers in Constance, Germany (Auer, 1984a b, 1988). The original impetus of Auer's work comes from a dissatisfaction with Gumperz's classification of discourse functions of code-switching.

For Auer, enumerating functions of code-switching is problematic for a number of reasons. First, the conversational categories used for identifying the functions are often ill-defined. Frequently, a number of very different conversational structures are subsumed under one single category. For example, 'reiteration' can include a range of structures. Secondly, there is much confusion between conversational structure, linguistic form, and function of code-switching. 'Emphasis', for instance, may be a function of code-switching, whereas 'interjection' is a linguistic form whose conversational status and function are a different issue. Thirdly, the list of functions of code-switching can hardly ever be a closed one. Since code-switching is used in a creative manner, its functions are in principle infinite. Last but by no means least, the listing of conversational functions implies that code-switching should have the same conversational status in both language direction, i.e. from language A into B or vice versa. Although two instances of code-switching may fulfil the same conversational functions, the intended meanings of these instances by their speakers may not be identical because of different language directions of the switch (see further Auer, 1991: 326–33). Instead of trying to characterise speaker's linguistic choices according to a pre-established set of functional categories, Auer proposes that code-switching is most fruitfully analysed as a contextualisation cue.

The notion of contextualisation has been proposed by Gumperz (1982, 1992), which, in very general terms, refers to 'all the processes by which members construe the local and global contexts which are necessary for the interpretation of their linguistic and non-linguistic activities' (Auer, 1990: 80). For Gumperz and Auer, context is not something given *a priori* and influencing or determining linguistic detail, rather, it is shaped, maintained and changed by participants continually in the course of interaction (see also above). It has been demonstrated that conversational participants use cues at the verbal level (prosodic, phonological, morphological, syntactic, rhetorical) (see, for example, Local, 1986; Local, Wells & Sebba, 1984; Local, Kelly & Wells, 1986; French & Local, 1986) and the non-verbal level (gestural, kinesic and proxemic) (e.g. Duncan, 1969, 1972; Kendon, 1977) to contribute to the signalling of contextual presuppositions. Gumperz (1982) calls these cues 'contextualisation conventions' (or contextualisation cues). They have the following characteristics:

(1) They do not have referential (de-contextualised) meaning of the kind we find in lexical items. Instead, contextualisation cues and the interpretation of the activity are related by a process of *inferencing*, which is itself dependent on the context of its occurrence. The situated meaning of code-switching therefore cannot be stated unless a sequential analysis is carried out. The same cue may receive a different interpretation on different occasions.

(2) The way in which inferencing leads to contextual interpretation is twofold: by contrast or by inherent meaning potential. In the first, most simple case, contextualisation cues establish contrasts and influence interpretation by

punctuating the interaction. The mere fact of (usually abruptly) changing one (or more than one) formal characteristic of the interaction may be enough to prompt an inference about why such a thing has happened. In this process of inferencing, it is necessary to rely on information contained in the local context of the cue's occurrence. The only 'meaning' the cue has is (to paraphrase Jakobson's definition of the phoneme) to 'indicate otherness'. The direction of the change is irrelevant.

Yet, many contextualisation cues do more than that. They establish a contrast and thereby indicate that something new is going to come; but it also and at the same time restricts the number of possible plausible inferences as to what this might be. This is so because cues may have (received) an inherent meaning potential. This may be 'natural', e.g. when we observe a natural correlation between diminishing fundamental frequency on the one hand, and 'rest' or 'termination' on the other, or it may be conventionalised (as in the case of code alternation).

(3) Contextualisation cues often bundle together, e.g. there is a certain redundancy of coding which has specific interactional advantages. For the analyst, this redundancy provides methodological access to the conversational functions of one cue (e.g. code alternation), since, other cues supporting the same local interpretation can be used as 'external' evidence for the meaning of conversational code alternation. (Auer, 1991: 334–5, original italics)

Auer argues that code-switching can and should be analysed as a contextualisation cue, because it works in many ways just like other contextualisation cues on the prosodic or gestural level. But as a contextualisation cue, code-switching has some characteristics of its own. In particular, the sequential organisation of language choice provides a frame of reference for the interpretation of functions or meanings of conversational code-switching. Auer (1991) identifies a number of sequential patterns of language choice. The first pattern looks like this:

Pattern Ia: ...A1 A2 A1 A2 // B1 B2 B1 B2...

Here, a language-of-interaction (base language or unmarked language) *A* has been established; at a certain point, Speaker 1 switches to language *B*; this new language choice is accepted by speaker 2 as the new language-of-interaction so that beyond the switching point, only *B* is used. The pattern is usually considered as the prototypical case of conversational code-switching. A variant of this pattern would be:

Pattern Ib: ...A1 A2 A1 A2 A1 // B1 B2 B1 B2...

In this case, code-switching occurs within a single speaker's turn.

A different pattern of language choice which Auer identifies can be schematised as follows:

Pattern IIa: ...A1 B2 A1 B2 A1 B2 A1 B2...

In this pattern, Speaker 1 consistently uses one language but Speaker 2 consistently uses another language. Such patterns of language choice are not normally sustained in spontaneous conversation. After a short run of divergent language choices, one participant usually accepts the other's language, and the sequence continues with an agreed language as the language-of-interaction. The resulting pattern looks like this:

Pattern IIb: ...A1 B2 A1 B2 A1 // A2 A1 A2 A1...

In all these patterns, the change of language is accompanied by change of speakership. It is frequently observed, however, that bilingual speakers keep language choice open by switching between languages within a turn. The recipient of a turn which contains two languages may continue in this mode, giving rise to Pattern IIIa, or choose the language he or she thinks is appropriate or preferred, leading to Pattern IIIb.

Pattern IIIa: ...AB1 AB2 AB1 AB2...

Pattern IIIb: ...AB1 // A2 A1 A2...

Finally, code-switching may occur in the middle of a speaker's turn without affecting language choice for the interaction at all. Such momentary 'lapses' into the other language usually occur because a word, a phrase or another structure in language B is inserted into a language A frame. The insertion has a predictable end. Schematically, this pattern is represented as follows:

Pattern IV: ...A1 [B1] A1...

Auer calls this pattern 'transfer'.

Auer argues that the interpretation of function(s) or meaning(s) of code-switching is influenced by the sequential patterns of language choice as outlined here. He proposes a distinction between *discourse-related* and *participant-related* code-switching. Discourse-related code-switching contributes to the organisation of the ongoing interaction, while participant-related code-switching permits assessment by participants of the speaker's preference for and competence in one language or the other.[5] For example, the function of code-switching of Patterns Ia and Ib type is usually interpreted as contextualising some feature of the conversation, e.g. a shift in topic, participant constellation, activity type, and so forth, and is therefore 'discourse-related', whereas code-switching of Pattern IIa and IIb type is a negotiation of language-of-interaction and tells us something about participants' preferred choices; hence the designation 'participant-related'. However, this distinction is not always clear-cut, as Auer himself recognises. Take Patterns IIIa and IIIb for example: the turn-internal switches that occur in such an ambiguous turn may have a discourse function — such as in the case of other-language reiterations for emphasis, or topic/comment switching; but the fact of keeping the language choice open also provides information about the speaker and his or her conceptualisation of the situation. Therefore, switching of this turn-internal type is discourse-related and at the same time participant-related.

One reason for distinguishing discourse-related code-switching from participant related code-switching, as Auer explains, is that the discourse functions of code-switching have received a great deal of attention in the existing literature, while processes of language negotiation and preference-influenced or competence-influenced language choices are usually not subsumed under conversational code-switching, but are considered to be either determined by societal macro-structures or by psycholinguistic factors (see, for example, Ludi, 1987; McClure & McClure, 1988; Gardner-Chloros, 1991). As Auer's study of German–Italian code-switching demonstrates, participant-related code-switching should also be regarded as a contextualisation cue. What it contextualises, however, goes beyond discourse structures to include social attributes and relationships of the participants.

To study code-switching as a contextualisation cue requires an analytic procedure which focuses on the sequential development of interaction, because the meanings of contextualisation cues are conveyed as part of the interactive process and cannot be discussed without referring to the conversational context. This is best done by using the framework provided by Conversation Analysis (CA) (see Atkinson & Heritage, 1984; Levinson, 1983: Ch. 6). In Auer's view, the CA approach has at least two advantages. First, it gives priority to 'the sequential implicativeness of language choice in conversation, i.e. the fact that whatever language a participant chooses for the organisation of his or her turn, or for an utterance which is part of the turn, the choice exerts an influence on subsequent language choices by the same or other speakers' (Auer, 1984a: 5). Second, it 'limits the external analysts' interpretational leeway because it relates his or her interpretations back to the members' mutual understanding of their utterances as manifest in their behaviour' (Auer, 1984a: 6). CA is a fast developing, interdisciplinary approach whose application to bilingual data is new and not yet systematic. Many of Auer's concerns are methodological and therefore difficult to summarise on a theoretical level. I shall return to Auer's work and discuss the methods of CA specifically in relation to my own account of Chinese–English code-switching in Chapter 6.

Since the late 1970s, there has been a marked shift in social accounts of bilingualism and language choice to the micro-interactional perspective. This shift is certainly a necessary rebuttal of a more mechanistic version of language choice which tends to characterise individuals' behaviour as either conformity or non-conformity to closed systems of norms. At the same time, however, there seems to be a tendency to over-emphasise the degree of freedom speakers have in controlling their choices of language. Romaine (1984: 37) remarks upon the fact that language users are not 'free agents' — 'People are constrained by the expressive resources available in the language(s) to which they have access and by the conventions which apply to their use.' This brings us back to an issue raised by the conflict model which was considered in above, that is, the distribution of linguistic and social resources is not always equal with respect to all individuals in a given community. Consequently, language users can control their behaviours only with greater or lesser effectiveness, depending on the extent to which they have access to these resources (Martin-Jones, 1989a). Moreover, role relationships between individuals in a given community determine that their behaviours must be socially accountable to its members, in terms of the communicative norms and cultural values of that community. This is by no means to deny that individuals are capable of manipulating the resources already available to them in order to gain more resources and to develop new relationships, and thus gradually to transform the overall social organisation. It is important to recognise this dialectical relation between social structure and social action; that is, social structures provide the environment for social actions and social actions reproduce and change social structures (Giddens, 1984). What seems to be needed then is a model of language choice which accounts for both the social, situational contexts in which individuals' linguistic practices take place and the interactional process through which languages become socially meaningful. In the remaining part of this chapter, I shall discuss the possibility of developing such a model using the concept of *social network*.

The Social Network Perspective: Towards an Integrated Model

In a critique of Labovian-type quantitative sociolinguistics, Bell makes a distinction between *social* and *stylistic* dimensions of linguistic variation: 'The social dimension denotes differences between speech of different speakers, and the stylistic denotes differences with the speech of a single speaker' (Bell, 1984: 145). For many years, the social axis has been vigorously examined within the Labovian quantitative paradigm, which shows that linguistic variation correlates with variation in the speaker's age, sex, social class, and so on. The style axis, on the other hand, has been a central concern of qualitative, ethnographic research, which emphasises the sensitivity of language to situational context (e.g. Hymes, 1974; Bauman & Sherzer, 1974; Saville-Troike, 1989). Labov has tried to link social and stylistic dimensions of linguistic variation in his work, although he has not studied mechanisms of stylistic choice in any specific and convincing way. Research on bilingualism, especially those from the micro-interactional perspective, tends to be of the qualitative type, focusing on how speakers vary their choices of language according to situational variables such as interlocutors, topic and setting. Although these studies often point out that language practices are symbolic of group identities, they do not address the social dimension of linguistic variation systematically. For example, seldom do we find in Gumperz's work information on the speaker's age, sex, social class and so forth. In a series of studies in the East Harlem Spanish–English bilingual community in New York City, Poplack (1983) finds that while there are intra-speaker variations in language choice (e.g. speakers report adapting language choices to home, school and/or block), on the whole the most significant difference exists between individual speakers, especially between children in bilingual and monolingual classes. For example, none of the children in monolingual (i.e. English) classes report (nor were they observed) using predominantly Spanish in any of the three domains, which contrasts five reports (and eight observations) of Spanish-only use (out of a possible 27) from those in bilingual classes (see Table 1.3).

Inter-speaker variation of this kind is clearly important, not only because what appears to be the usual pattern for one speaker in a range of situations is rarely the same as any other given speaker's pattern, but also because differences in linguistic behaviours of various (groups of) speakers tend to reflect wider social relations and are constitutive of social structures.

There are several different ways of analysing the social (inter-speaker) dimension of linguistic variation. One approach which is commonly used in quantitative sociolinguistics is to choose an aspect of the speaker's social status such as age, sex, class, and so forth, and measure it independently of social interaction. This approach implicitly takes social status of the speaker to be the major determinant of his or her linguistic behaviour in social interaction. A different approach examines the identities of the people with whom the speaker regularly interacts, in addition to the speaker's own identity. This second approach is now known as the *social network approach*. It assumes that there is a dialectic relationship between speakers' linguistic behaviours and interpersonal relations; that is, speakers' language use is influenced and shaped by the types of social contact they have, and in the meantime it actively contributes to the social relations which speakers maintain. Thus, instead of focusing on some *ad hoc* categorisation of speakers, this approach starts with observable behaviours of individual speakers and investigates how speakers develop their social identities through interaction (see also Woolard, 1985).

In an account of language choice and language shift in a Hungarian–German bilingual community in Oberwart, Austria, Gal (1979) used an implicational scaling technique to conceptualise and display observed choices in a range of

Table 1.3 Reported and observed language used most frequently at home, on the block and in school according to placement in school program

	Reported			*Observed*		
	Home	*Block*	*School*	*Home*	*Block*	*School*
Bilingual class						
Iris	B[a]	S	S	Sb*	S	S
Indio	B	E	B	B	E	B
Connejo	S	B	B	B*	E*	B
Junaita	B	B	E	B	B	B*
Flaquita	B	B	B	B	B	B
Josie	B	E	B	B	B*	B
Doreas	B	B	B	B	B	B
Chico	B	S	S	S*	S	S
Mermineo	B	B	B	S*	S*	B
Monolingual class						
Maria	B	B	B	B	B	B
Pito	E	E	E	E*	E	E
Debbie	B	E	E	E*	E	E
Ramon	B	B	B	E	E*	E*
Gordito	B	B	E	B	E*	E
Linda	B	B	E	E*	E*	E

[a] Designations refers to language used most frequently:
    E = English S = Spanish B = Both or bilingual
*   Starred letters indicate a discrepancy in reported and observed language use
Source: Adapted from Poplack, 1983: 51

situational contexts as well as differences between speakers of differing social characteristics. Implicational scales rank both speakers and interlocutors — people with whom the speaker interacts — in terms of their language use. An example is given in Table 1.4.

In this implicational scale, speakers are ranked on the vertical axis and on the horizontal axis is a list of interlocutor types. The habitual usage of individual speakers can be read across each row, and by reading down each column it is possible to see the kinds of difference that exist across informants regarding language choice with a particular interlocutor. Speakers who use more German (G) than Hungarian (H) (relative to other speakers in the sample) are listed towards the top of the scale, and interlocutors with whom the speakers use more German than Hungarian (relative to other interlocutors) are listed to the right of the scale. Because speakers' ages are given next to their identifying numbers, we can see from the scale that younger people tend to appear at the top of the list and the very old at the bottom, which suggests an ongoing language shift from Hungarian to German across generations.

However, age alone does not always account for the language choice patterns displayed in the scale. For instance, Speaker 12 is aged 52 but is ranked higher than 11 others in the list who are younger than she, and the two youngest speakers, 8 and 9 (aged 3 and 4), rank lower than seven older others. Although the ranking of interlocutors on the horizontal axis seems to correlate roughly with age, with older people — grandparents and parents — appearing to the left of the axis and younger ones, including grandchildren, to the right, there are also some variations. For example, government officials are listed to the right of the axis regardless of age (they in fact appear to the right of the children's generation and those under 20 years old), in contrast to God who is located at the far left end of the list.

In order to explain these variations in language choice patterns which apparently cannot be fully explained in terms of the variable of age alone, Gal (1979) utilised the concept of social network — a collective of people with whom one interacts on a regular basis — and examined the identities of the speakers' network ties along a peasant to urbanite continuum. The basic hypothesis was that the two languages, Hungarian and German, symbolised opposing social values of rural and urban life and if Hungarian was used at all, it would be used among those who were more involved in the traditional peasant life and German by those who had moved away from such tradition. Results of Gal's analysis indeed show a positive correlation between a preference for the use of Hungarian and strong peasant ties (defined in this case by the percentage of contacts within a given time who own animals) and between a preference for German and urban-based contacts.

The application of the social network concept in studying language variation and change represents one of the most important developments in sociolinguistics in the last two decades and warrants some detailed discussion here.

Social network analysis

The concept of social network has been explored in a number of disciplines with various purposes. Social psychologists, for example, have used the concept as a means of analysing sources of stress, leadership, and information flow (e.g. Moreno, 1953; Guimarães, 1972; Erbe, 1977). Especially relevant to sociolinguistic research is the network analyses of human groups and human behaviour

Table 1.4 Choice of language by women in Oberwart (Observations)

Number of speakers	Age of speakers	Interlocutors												
		1	2	3	4	5	6	7	8	9	10	11	12	13
1	14	H	G		G	G	G	G	G	G	G		—	
2	14	H	GH		G	G	G	G	G		G		—	
3	25	H	GH	GH	G	GH	G	G	G	G	G	G	—	
4	15	H	GH		GH	—	G	G	G				—	
5	13	H	GH		GH	—	G	GH	G				—	
6	13	H	H		GH	—	G	G	G				—	
7	27	—	H		GH	—	GH	GH	—				—	
8	3	—	H		GH	—	GH	GH	—	GH	G	G	—	G
9	4	—	H		GH	—	GH	GH	—				—	
10	17	H	H		GH	—	GH	GH	G	GH	G	G	—	
11	39	—	H	—	GH	—	—	—	—				—	
12	52	—	H	GH	GH	—	GH	GH	G	GH	G	G	G	
13	23	H	H		GH	—	—	GH	—				—	
14	22	H	H		H	GH	GH	GH	—	GH	GH		—	
15	33	H	H		H	GH	GH	—	—	H	GH	G	G	
16	35	H			H		GH	GH		GH	GH	G		
17	40	H			H		GH	—		GH	GH	G		
18	42	H			H		GH	GH	—	GH	GH	G		
19	43	H			H		—	GH		H	GH	G		
20	35	H	H	H	H		H	GH	H	H	GH			
21	40	H		H	GH	—	H	GH	H	H	H		—	

Speaker	Age	1	2	3	4	5	6	7	8	9	10	11	12	13
22	40	H				H		H	GH	H	GH	—	G	G
23	50	H			H	H	GH	H	GH	G	G			G
24	61	—	H	GH	—	GH	GH	GH	GH	GH				
25	54	H	H	H	H	H	H	H	H	GH	H	GH		GH
26	55	H	H	GH	GH	GH	H	H	GH	H	GH			
27	61	H	H	H	H	H	H	H	GH	H	GH			
28	59	H	H	—	H	H	H	H	H	GH	H	H		GH
29	50	H	H	H	H	H	—	H	GH					
30	50	H	H	H	H	H	—	H	GH	H	GH	H		
31	60	H	H	H	GH	H	H	H	H	GH	—	GH	GH	
32	60	H	H	H	GH	H	H	GH	GH	GH		GH		GH
33	63	H	H	H	H	H	H	H	H	H	H	GH		GH
34	64	H	H	H	H	H	—	H	H	H	H	GH		GH
35	66	H	H	—	—	H	H	H	H	—	H	—		
36	68	H	H	H	H	H	H	H	H	H	H	H	—	H
37	71	H	H	H	H	H	—	H	H	H	H	H	—	H

Interlocutors: (1) God; (2) grandparents and that generation; (3) black market clients; (4) parents and that generation; (5) Calvinist minister; (6) age-mate pals, neighbours; (7) brothers and sisters; (8) salespeople; (9) spouse; (10) children and that generation; (11) non-relatives under twenty; (12) government officials; (13) grandchildren and that generation.

G = German, H = Hungarian

Source: adapted from Gal, 1979: 102

by social anthropologists (e.g. Barnes, 1954, 1969; Bott, 1957; Mitchell, 1969, 198; See Li Wei, 1994 for a summary).

In an earlier social network study, Mayer (1961) used the concept to distinguish three different categories of town-dweller in a South African city called East London. The first was made up of townspeople whose sets of personal relations were characteristic of townspeople everywhere. The other two categories were composed of migrants, distinguished particularly in terms of their differing network patterns. One category was composed of those members of the Xhosa people who for generations had resisted becoming converted to Christianity and by extension following European ways of life. They were called the Red migrants, because they traditionally smeared themselves with red clay during tribal initiation ceremonies. The social networks of this group tended to be dense; in simple terms this means that a given person's contacts all knew each other. The other category was made up of those Xhosa who had at some time in the past become Christians, been to school (thus school migrants), and adopted European ways of dress and diet and many European customs. Noticeably, the dense network ties which characterised the Red migrants were lacking in this group. Furthermore, Mayer found that the characteristics of network ties had some normative effect upon the behaviour of members of these different groups. For example, the close-knit cliques of the Red migrants exercised a tight social control over their members, ensuring that the traditionalist values to which they subscribed were faithfully adhered to. Each member was accorded a clear-cut structure of norms and activities and hence to some extent shielded from what has been called 'personal disorganisation', the breakdown of primary relationships and consequent disorientated behaviour (Mitchell, 1987). The school migrants who departed from dense networks, on the other hand, were experiencing alternately a number of inconsistent cultural influences and pressures. Mayer wrote:

> A migrant with a loose-knit network in town may start to apply, when with his clubmates, standards of conducts or etiquette which differ from the standards taught by his church associates, or his girl-friend; more probably still, any or all of these may differ from standards expected at home in the country. (Mayer, 1961: 289)

The capacity of a particular kind of social network to act as *a norm enforcement mechanism* was further pursued in Bott's (1957) study of conjugal role segregation in 20 families in London. She discovered a correspondence between the separation of each spouse's area of responsibility and their degree of independence of each other and the pattern of their social contacts: where the level of marital segregation was high and responsibility for tasks rigidly allocated, each spouse tended to have contracted long-standing networks ties with people who also knew one another (i.e. dense networks); where spouses were dependent on each other and did not allocate areas of responsibility as clearly, their networks were less dense, their contacts did not normally know each other. Moreover, Bott found that where the networks were dense, role relationships were usually multiplex, i.e. individuals interacted with each other in more than one capacity. These findings led Bott to suggest that there existed causal relationships between the characteristics of social network and everyday behaviour of the individual. She wrote:

> When many of the people a person knows interact with one another, that is, when the person's network is close-knit, the members of his network tend to reach consensus on norms and they exert consistent informal pressure on one another to conform to the norms ... But when most of the people a person knows do not interact with one another, that is, when his network is loose-knit, more variation of norms is likely to develop in the network. (Bott, 1957: 60)

It should be noted here that *density* and *multiplexity* pertain to the *structure* and *content* of the network respectively. Analysis of the structural aspects of social network, which, in addition to density, include anchorage, reachability and range (see further Mitchell, 1969: 12–20), has generated much of the literature on social network. Various analytic techniques have been developed, ranging from basic mathematical graphs and sociograms, to more sophisticated applications of matrix algebra and multivariate data reduction methods such as cluster analysis and block modelling. These techniques tend to minimise the content of the network which defines the meaning of interpersonal relationships. Mitchell (1986) argues that it is mistaken to separate the shape and pattern of the network from the intensity, frequency and durability of a relationship, describing these latter aspects of the network as 'interactional' features (for details see Mitchell, 1969). Bott's (1957) study clearly showed that there was a link between structure and content of network ties. Granovetter (1973; 1982) uses 'strong' and 'weak' to refer to two broad types of network ties. A 'strong' network would be dense in terms of structure, but the degree of intensity and frequency of contact involved in it would also be high.

Sociolinguistic applications of network analysis

The concept of social network has been introduced into sociolinguistics as an alternative to social class in identifying speaker groups. As has been mentioned earlier, the traditional approach is to distinguish groups of speakers in terms of their socio-economic status. There is little agreement on which factors should be taken into account in defining such status, although income, occupation, education, residence and life style are usually considered to be important contributory characteristics. All these characteristics can be ordered in accordance with the way they are evaluated by society at large — for example, a company manager would be rated higher than his office cleaner, and a college graduate higher than a non-graduate clerk. If everyone can be given a rating based on numerical values of a combination of these characteristics, society can be ordered into strata. The scale can then be segmented into upper, middle and lower classes, with as many subdivisions as the analyst wishes to make (Milroy, 1987a: 13–14; 1987b: 29–35). This way of differentiating groups of speakers does reflect social reality to a certain extent and is seen as a sensible way of ordering large amounts of variable linguistic data, such as those collected by Labov in New York City (1966, 1972a, b). But, as Milroy points out:

> we must not lose sight of the fact that the groups we end up with by segmenting our scale — such as 'lower class', 'working class', 'middle class' — do not necessarily have any kind of objective, or even intersubjective, reality … . Membership of a group labelled 'lower-middle class' does not necessarily form an important part of a person's definition of his social identity. (L. Milroy, 1987a: 14)

Milroy (1987a, b) argues that smaller-scale, more concrete categories are available which do reflect the fact that there are social units to which people feel a sense of belonging (see also Cohen, 1982). One such unit is *social network*.

In her study of three inner-city communities in Belfast, which formed part of a larger project on language variation and change in the city (Milroy & Milroy, 1977, 1978; Milroy & Milroy *et al.*, 1983), L. Milroy (1987a) examined the social distribution of eight linguistic variables, selected as indicators of the local vernacular. Instead of trying to explain it in terms of large-scale, abstract concepts such as social class, Milroy focused her attention on specific social relationships of individual speakers. Following careful participant observation, a six-point scale was constructed to measure the density and multiplexity (pertaining to 'structural' and 'interactional' properties respectively) of personal network ties, known as the 'network strength scale' (Milroy, 1987a: 141–2). Each individual was assigned a score at some point on the scale with respect to a number of indicators of these two network properties. The indicators were interpreted as conditions which, if fulfilled, suggested a relatively dense and multiplex network structure, and the network strength score was the sum of individual indicator scores. The relationship between network strength and language variation was examined by means of Analysis of Variance (ANOVA) and Spearman Rank Order Correlation procedures. The tests revealed a positive and significant relationship between network scores and language scores on five of the eight variables studied, as shown in Table 1.5. As scores on the network scale increase, so do linguistic scores. The results led Milroy to a conclusion quite similar to that of social anthropologists,

Table 1.5 Linguistic variables correlating with network scores

Variable	r	t	N	Level of significance
(a)	0.529	3.692	37	0 < 0.01
(th)	0.485	3.591	44	0 < 0.01
(Λ^2)	0.317	2.142	43	0 < 0.01
(ε^1)	0.255	1.709	44	0 < 0.01
(ε^2)	0.321	2.200	44	0 < 0.01

N = number of subjects tested for a given variable
Source: Adapted from Milroy, 1987a: 154

that is, 'personal network structure is in these communities of very great importance in predicting language use: a dense, multiplex network structure predicts relative closeness to vernacular norms' (1987a: 160).

The research design of the Belfast projects depended to a large extent on the assumption that linguistic changes take place in speech communities against a background of language maintenance, and 'the extent to which they are successful depends on the interplay of these two sets of social influences — those that encourage maintenance (or stability), on the one hand, and those that encourage change (or divergence), on the other' (J. Milroy, 1992: 10). Thus, following the anthropological model, the Milroys have distinguished between relatively weak and strong network links. Since strong network ties were shown to be 'a norm maintenance mechanism' (see especially, L. Milroy, 1987a; but also L. Milroy, 1982 and J. Milroy, 1992), weak ties were believed to be a major factor facilitating linguistic change, because they regularly provided bridges between different groups through which innovation and influence are diffused (for more detailed discussions on the role of 'weak' ties in transmitting innovation see Granovetter, 1973, 1982). However, weak ties are much more difficult to investigate empirically than strong ones, due to the fact that weak networks tend to exist in communities where the population is socially and/or geographically mobile and individuals contract large numbers of ties which are open-ended, seldom forming into closed clusters (J. Milroy & L. Milroy, 1985; J. Milroy, 1992).

A sociolinguistic application of network analysis which deals with linguistic change and generally weak network ties is Bortoni-Ricardo's (1985) account of dialectal adjustment of rural migrants to Brazlandia, a satellite city of Brasilia. Like Milroy, Bortoni-Ricardo rejected a stratificational analysis because it did not adequately discriminate between the individuals studied, all of whom were relatively poor. Bortoni-Ricardo's main hypothesis was that the change from rural to urban life involved a move from an insulated network, consisting largely of kinsfolk and neighbours, to an integrated urban network, where the links were less multiplex and associated with a wider range of social contexts. Bortoni-Ricardo devised two network indices to measure the changing patterns of the migrants' social relationships: the *integration index* and *urbanisation index*. The integration index expressed numerically certain relevant characteristics of the three persons with whom each migrant most frequently interacted — for example, whether or not they were kinsfolk, or whether the ties had been contracted in the pre-migration period. The score assigned to each migrant was intended to characterise progress in the transition from an insulated to an integrated type of network, and as such was a tool capable of investigating loose-knit types of personal network structure. The urbanisation index was designed to supplement this structural measure, representing the extent to which the members of each migrant's personal network were integrated into urban life. In the meantime, four linguistic variables were selected as indicators of the migrants' dialect diffuseness, a movement away from the norms of the Caipira dialect, and were analysed quantitatively as Labov (1966, 1972a) and L. Milroy (1987a) did with their data. Individual speaker's linguistic scores were then correlated with the two network indices in order to find out the relationships between language behaviour and social networks. Results revealed significant correlations between changes in network ties and dialect diffuseness.

It is important to remember that social networks are deliberately created by people for special purposes. This purposefulness of social networks has two important implications: first, it means that members of a given network will intentionally or unintentionally develop distinctive patterns of behaviour and will come to expect one another to conform to these patterns if they wish to remain members of the network; second, members of particular social networks are seen as actively contributing to the constitution of social relations and social structure through their interactive behaviour. This dialectic relationship between social network and social practice (including linguistic practice) has also been explored by social psychologists. An example is the 'accommodation theory' proposed by Giles and his associates (e.g. Giles, 1980, 1984; Giles & Smith, 1979; Giles & Coupland, 1991; Coupland *et al.*, 1988; Coupland *et al.*, 1990), who argue that speakers adjust their linguistic behaviour by using either 'convergent' or 'divergent' strategies to express aspiration towards and identification with a particular social group (see also Trudgill, 1986a). As Le Page (1978) puts it, 'Each speech act is an announcement: "to this extent I wish to be thought of as my own man, to this extent like A, to this extent like B, to this extent like C ..."' and so on' (see also Le Page & Tabouret-Keller, 1985).

This brings us back to the question of relation between social and stylistic dimensions of linguistic variation. Commenting on Labov's study, Romaine

(1980: 228) remarks that 'if a feature is found to be more common in lower classes than in the upper classes, it will also be more common in the less formal than the most formal styles, with each social group occupying a similar position in each continuum'. Bell (1984) expresses the relation between the two dimensions of linguistic variation in a more explicitly and systematic way. He writes: 'Variation on the style dimension within the speech of a single speaker derives from and echoes the variation which exists between speakers on the "social" dimension' (Bell, 1984: 151). As Bell explains:

> This cause-and-effect relationship holds on three levels. First, it operates synchronically for an individual speaker who, in specific situations, shifts style to sound like another. Second, it operates diachronically for individual speakers who, over time, shift their general speech patterns to sound like other speakers (e.g. after moving to a different dialect region). Third, it operates diachronically for an entire group of speakers which, over time, shifts its speech to sound like another group. (Bell, 1984: 151)

A diagrammatic representation of the derivation of intra-speaker variation (stylistic axis) from inter-speaker variation (social axis) can be seen in Figure 1.1.

The social network approach, as exemplified in the work of Gal (1979), Milroy and Milroy (L. Milroy, 1987a, b; J. Milroy & L. Milroy, 1985; J. Milroy, 1992; L. Milroy & J. Milroy, 1992), and Bortoni-Ricardo (1985), offers a framework in which the two dimensions (social and stylistic) of linguistic variation can be systematically investigated and interpreted, thus being capable of building a coherent model of bilingual language choice which accounts for both interactional behaviours of individual speakers and broader questions of social relations and social organisation.

Throughout the 1980s and into the 1990s the social network perspective has gained special popularity among sociolinguists who have long felt a need for a dynamic and coherent social model of linguistic variation and change. Methodologically, the network perspective has also been found useful, particularly for investigators of minority and other low-status sub-groups in the population. While there are theoretical objections to importing a social class model along with a number of unacknowledged sociological assumptions, an initial approach in terms of class may also be impractical because the class distribution of these sub-groups is usually quite uneven. A network approach is more feasible with groups who may be economically marginal, or powerless, and resident in homogeneous neighbourhoods and territorially well-defined neighbourhoods. Approaching a target community through personal network contacts not only facilitates the fieldwork process but also enables the investigator to observe communicative behaviours of members of the community which

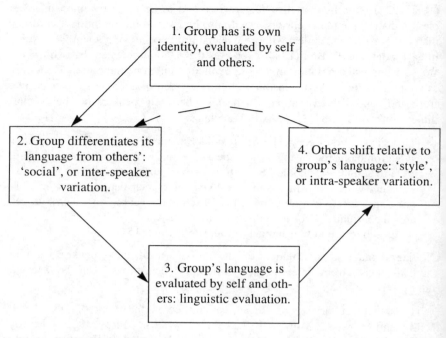

Source: Adapted from Bell, 1984: 152

Figure 1.1 The derivation of intra-speaker from inter-speaker variation

would not otherwise be accessible to the public.[6] This point will be discussed further in Chapter 3.

Summary

In this chapter, I have discussed three main perspectives on bilingualism and language choice. These three perspectives are characterised by their respective views on the relationship between social structures and the individual's linguistic practices. The macro-societal perspective regards language behaviour of the individual as conditioned by predefined societal arrangements, while the micro-interactional perspective stresses individuals' capacity to make their own choices. Neither of the two perspectives, however, addresses directly the question of relations between social structures on the one hand and language use on the other; rather, they seem to regard one as being reducible to the other.

A perspective which employs the notion of social networks emerges as being capable of bridging the macro and micro approaches as well as accounting for the interrelation between them. By focusing on the observable language behaviour of the speaker and his or her social relations, the social network perspective enables the analyst to investigate systematically the processes through which speakers in interaction utilise the resources of linguistic variability available to them and exercise influence and control over others' as well as their own language behaviour. In the present study, I have adopted the social network approach to investigate language choice practices in the Chinese communities in Britain which have hitherto not been systematically examined by sociolinguists. The next chapter gives a general descriptive account of the Chinese population in this country.

Notes

1. Examples of such work can be seen in Albert & Obler (1978), Grosjean (1982), Vaid (1986), and Hyltenstam & Obler (1989).
2. Examples of linguistic studies of language choice include Pfaff (1979), Sridhar & Sridhar (1980), Bentahila & Davies (1983), Woolford (1983), Joshi (1985), Singh (1985), Romaine (1986), Clyne (1987), Scotton (1987), Bokamba (1989), Heath (1989), Poplack, Wheeler & Westwood (1989), Schatz (1989), Tay (1989), Torres (1989), Nortier (1990) and Treffers-Daller (1990).
3. See further Knorr-Celtina & Cicourel, (1981), Giddens (1984), (1989); Eisenstadt & Helle (1985), Helle & Eisenstadt (1985), Silverman (1985), Cuff, Sharrock & Francis (1990).
4. Perhaps it is worth pointing out here that a study which has often been cited as an example of domain analysis in language change situations is Dorian's (1981) study of 'language death' of Gaelic in East Sutherland, Scotland. In fact, Dorian takes 'domain' to be a unitary factor in addition to interlocutor, topic and others, corresponding loosely to 'setting', rather than a clustering of situations around a prototypical theme.
5. Auer (1990: 80–1) explains participant-related and discourse-related code-switching in the following terms:

> Looking at code alternation [Note: Auer uses 'language (code) alternation' as a cover term for code-switching and transfer; see further Auer, 1984a] as a way to display one's own competence in and preference for a language, as well as a way to ascribe to other participants' and non-participants' competence- and preference-related predicates such as 'speaks language A very well', 'is fluent in language A and language B', ' has difficulties with language B', 'likes to speak language A', etc. i.e. ascriptions rather common in multilingual communities, implies treating bilingualism as a social datum, not as a mental disposition or ability. We are not inquiring into the actual bilingual competence of an individual, nor do we attempt to measure it; but we are interested in the ways in which members of a multilingual community display their own multilingualism to each other (cf. Auer, 1981).
>
> Discourse-related code alternation, on the other hand, ... may work as a contextualisation cue simply because of the contrast it is able to establish between two contiguous stretches of talk. It is a very convenient way of setting off what has been said in language A against what is going to be said in language B and works, in this respect, like prosodic and gestural cues. This contrast can be used for conversational tasks independent of the social meaning of the language involved, e.g. for setting off side remarks, marking new topics, switching between participant constellations, etc.

But code alternation may also work as a contextualisation cue because (in addition) it plays with the social values and attitudes associated with the languages in question, such as they have been established in the course of an individual's history of interaction by the recurring coincidence of language choice and particular conversational activities.

6. Examples of sociolinguistic applications of network studies include: Russell (1982) (Mombasa, Kenya); Schmidt (1985) (Australian aboriginal adolescents); Lippi-Green (1989) (Alpine rural community in Austria); Edwards (1986) (British Black adolescents in the Midlands); Labrie (1988) (Italians in Montreal), & W. Edwards (1990) (Detroit Black English speakers) and Schooling (1990) (Melanesians of New Caledonia).

2 Chinese Communities in Britain

Due to the lack of attention the Chinese in Britain have received, information about them is scarce, scattered and often contradictory. The Home Affairs Committee's (1985a) second report *Chinese Community in Britain* and Taylor's (1987) *Chinese Pupils in Britain*, originally presented as a report to the Committee of Inquiry into the Education of Children from Ethnic Minority Groups (Swann Committee, 1985) — provide the most comprehensive sources of reference to date. Empirical studies of Chinese emigration from Hong Kong and southeastern China to Britain by Baker (1966, 1968, 1979) and Watson (1975, 1977, 1982) also contain valuable information. In this chapter, I shall draw upon these and other existing materials, as well as my own participant observation within the Tyneside Chinese community in the northeast of England.

There are many issues concerning the Chinese — their cultural heritage, their beliefs and values, and their social organisation — which are of interest and importance and require book-length studies to do them justice. I can only discuss those aspects which are of direct and primary relevance to the present study. The sub-sections of this chapter concentrate in turn on the general composition of the Chinese population in the UK; the people and languages of Hong Kong; the history of Chinese settlement in Britain; the catering trade of the Chinese emigrants; the three-generation division among the British Chinese; the Chinese family system; language use, and lastly the Chinese community in Tyneside. These topics will be referred to in subsequent discussions of fieldwork methodology and data analysis.

Composition of the Chinese Population in Britain

Contrary to popular perceptions, the Chinese in Britain are *not* a homogeneous group. Three major groups of ethnic Chinese currently residing in the UK can be identified in terms of their social background. They are:

- emigrants from Hong Kong, particularly the rural New Territories, and other areas surrounding the South China Sea. They are long-term residents in this country and are British passport holders

- educational transients, who comprise mainly students from urban Hong Kong, Singapore, Malaysia, the Chinese mainland and Taiwan. The majority of them stay in Britain only for a relatively short time to receive (mainly higher) education and are not accompanied by their families
- urban professionals (e.g. doctors, solicitors, bankers, architects, accountants, nurses, teachers, and academics), who have received western-style education and training in their youth, and many of whom have right of abode in Britain.

In addition, there are refugees from Viet Nam, who came to be resettled in the UK via Hong Kong in the early 1980s. A considerable number of these refugees are believed to be of Chinese ethnic origin, or, for various reasons, speak some form of Chinese as their mother tongue (HAC, 1985b). However, they are generally perceived as a distinct group, namely, the Vietnamese. Whether and how they interact with the three Chinese groups identified above is unclear.

Lack of information extends to the sise of the various Chinese groups. In 1985 the Office of Population Census and Statistics offered a tentative figure of 122,000 (see details in Roper, 1988). This figure does not include the educational transients and urban professionals whose precise numbers are unknown. The present study concentrates on the emigrants group, which is by far the largest cohesive Chinese group in Britain.

Since at least two-thirds and probably as many as 80% of this emigrants group are believed to have originated from Hong Kong (including the British-born Chinese whose parents came from Hong Kong), it is necessary to consider briefly the history, people, and languages of this colony, as background information on the Chinese emigrant population in Britain.

The Hong Kong Background

History of Hong Kong

Before the nineteenth century, Hong Kong was hardly a notable place, occupied by a handful of farmers, fishermen and pirates. As a result of the first Anglo-Chinese Opium War (1832–40), Britain obtained Hong Kong Island (29 square miles) by the Nanking Treaty in 1843. During 1858–60, a second Opium War was fought and was ended with a treaty whereby Britain acquired the Kowloon Peninsula and Stonecutters Island. In 1898, under the Peking Convention, an additional 325.5 square miles north of Kowloon was leased for 99 years. This piece of land is the so-called New territories. After initial opposition by the Chinese, the New Territories became an integral part of the crown colony. Today, Hong Kong comprises an area of some 404 square miles, including 236 islands (see the map in Figure 2.1).

Figure 2.1 Hong Kong: Hong Kong Island, Kowloon Peninsular and the New Territories

People of Hong Kong

At least 98% of the population in Hong Kong are of Chinese ethnic origin. They comprise several different groups, including:

- the Cantonese Punti (native), who are generally thought to be descendants of pioneering northerners who gained control of southern China centuries ago;
- the Hakka (guest), who arrived in Hong Kong much later than the Punti group and scattered in the poorer, hilly areas of the New Territories;
- the fishermen, who spent most of their lives aboard the junks and boats in Hong Kong's many harbours.

There are also smaller groups of Chiu Chow and Hokkien origins, together with people from the midlands and the north of mainland China. The Cantonese Punti, however, are the predominant group.

Languages of Hong Kong

Hong Kong has become officially an English-speaking territory after British colonisation. Very few Chinese people, however, actually use English in day-by-day interaction. English is largely confined to law, government, international trade, and some aspects of education and the media (Luke & Richards, 1982; Gibbons, 1987).

As for the Chinese language, it is useful first of all to make a distinction between the spoken and written form. Spoken Chinese comprises a large number of related varieties, known to the Chinese as *Fangyan* (regional language). Traditionally, the Chinese Fangyan are classified into seven groups in terms of geographic distribution and linguistic-structural affiliation. The seven Fanyan groups are:

(1) *Beifang* (northern), the native language of about 70% of the Chinese population
(2) *Yue*, the majority of its speakers are in Guangdong province, the southern-most mainland province of China, with the capital city of Guangzhou (Canton) as its centre. Large numbers can also be found among overseas Chinese diaspora
(3) *Kejia* (Hakka), whose speakers came from small agricultural areas and are now scattered throughout southeastern China
(4) *Min*, spoken in Fujian (the mainland province on the western side of the Taiwan Strait), Taiwan and Hainan Islands. It is often further distinguished into Northern Min and Southern Min
(5) *Wu*, spoken in the lower Changjiang (the Yangtze River) region, including urban, metropolitan centres such as Shanghai
(6) *Xiang*, mainly spoken in south central region
(7) *Gan*, spoken chiefly in the southeastern inland provinces.

Major linguistic features and historical development of the seven Fangyan groups are discussed in Li and Thompson (1987), Ramsey (1987), and Norman (1988).

Within each Fangyan group, there are sub-varieties which may equate with what are normally called dialects in English. For example, Cantonese as it is known in the West is a dialect within the Yue Fangyan group and Hokkien within Min.

One prominent feature of spoken Chinese is the unintelligibility between one Fangyan and another. This unintelligibility is often regarded by the Chinese as a social group boundary marker distinguishing people of different origins. Among the Hong Kong Chinese, for example, Cantonese is spoken by the Cantonese Punti as their native language; others speak Chiu Chou, Hakka, Hokkien, Hokklo, Beifang, Shanghainese, and other dialects and sub-dialects.

In addition to these regional varieties, there is a spoken Chinese form known as *Guoyu* (literally: national language), which has evolved from *Guanhua*, a hybrid, standardised spoken form used during the Qing Dynasty (1644–1911), and which has been officially endorsed and promoted as the lingua franca in China since the 1920s. It is now widely used, in modified forms, in mainland China, where it is known as *Putonghua* (or 'common speech'), Taiwan, and Singapore (where it is known as *Huayu*), and is taught to non-native-Chinese speakers as the 'standard' Chinese language. Some older generations of Chinese in Hong Kong who emigrated from mainland China (and subsequently to other parts of the world) are able to understand and speak Guoyu to varying degrees. More recently, there are growing numbers of Hong Kong-born Chinese learning Guoyu, in response to the forthcoming changes in the colony's political status. Guoyu is better known in the English-speaking world as *Mandarin*. For convenience, the term Mandarin will be used here to refer to this particular spoken Chinese variety.

It is estimated that nearly 70% of the Chinese population in Britain use Cantonese as their first language, 25% Hakka, 5% some form of Beifang, and a very small number speak other varieties (1985a). It is not clear to what extent Mandarin is known and spoken by the British Chinese. My personal experience within the Chinese community in Tyneside suggests that about a quarter of the adult population have some knowledge of Mandarin.

It is important to point out that only Mandarin has a corresponding written form, which is shared by all literate Chinese whatever Fangyan they may speak. Written Chinese is one of the few contemporary languages in the world whose history is documented in an unbroken tradition extending back to the second millenium BC, and has been a major cultural symbol distinguishing the Chinese from all other peoples. The Chinese traditionally lay great emphasis on the written language. Chinese schools at all levels devote a considerable amount of time to literacy — in the Chinese context, the reading and writing of ideographic characters.

One reason for such emphasis seems to be due to the unique and complex relationship between the Chinese phonological system and the written script. Chinese is a monosyllabic and tonal language. Every written Chinese character represents a syllable with a tone (Norman, 1988; Li & Thompson, 1987). There are over 48,000 written characters in the standard Chinese dictionary *Zhonghua Da Zidian* (1916). Yet according to Mandarin pronunciation, there are only 300-odd sounds with five different tones:

(1) Yinping (high-level)
(2) Yangping (rising)
(3) Shangsheng (falling-rising)

(4) Qushen (falling)
(5) Qingsheng (light or unstressed).

That is to say that there are numerous homophones in Chinese. The pocket-size Chinese dictionary *Xinhua Zidian* (1980), for instance, lists 131 different written characters with the same pronunciation of *yi*, among which 39 are pronounced with the falling tone. Their differences can be made clear only in context and through separate written characters. Consequently, literacy is widely regarded by the Chinese as an important indicator of a speaker's linguistic competence.

There have been two main varieties of written Chinese: *Wenyan*, which was used in literary classics and formal documents of ancient China, and *Baihua*, a written form of colloquial speech (whose corresponding spoken form is Mandarin). Normally the Chinese learn to read and write in Baihua. Wenyan is now studied as an example of the Chinese cultural heritage.

Since the 1950s, there have been a series of mass campaigns in mainland China and in Singapore to popularise Mandarin. The rationale behind these campaigns is to remedy communication difficulties caused by the differences in regional speech varieties. One of the principal strategies used in the campaigns is to introduce a phonetic spelling system based on the Roman alphabet. This system is known as *Pinyin*. It has been designed to represent the written characters as they are pronounced in standard Mandarin, so that non-native-Chinese speakers or speakers of non-standard Chinese dialects could learn a standard pronunciation. There is as yet no agreed Romanisation system for other spoken varieties of Chinese, and given the popular perception among the Chinese that there is only one Chinese language, it seems unlikely that efforts will be made to design such systems.

The differences among the Hong Kong Chinese in terms of ethnic origin and spoken language which we have seen here have significant implications for the structure of Chinese communities in Britain, and in turn for sociolinguistic field-work. I shall discuss these implications the section on the 'Chinese Family System' below and in Chapter 3. For the moment, I want to consider the history of Chinese migration and settlement overseas, particularly in Britain.

Chinese Migration and Settlement Overseas

Mass migration has long been a regular part of Chinese history. Until the early twentieth century, overseas Chinese settlements had mainly been in Southeast Asia. Apart from Hong Kong and Taiwan where the Chinese make up over 99% of the indigenous populations, countries such as Singapore, Malaysia, Indonesia, Thailand, and the Philippines all host large Chinese communities (e.g. at least 76% of the total population in Singapore and nearly one-third of the population in Malaysia are ethnic Chinese) (Osbourne, 1983; Taylor & Turton, 1988; Zhu, 1991).

Chinese migration to regions outside Asia is a relatively recent phenomenon. In the mid-nineteenth century poor peasants and artisans plus a few small merchant traders went from southeastern provinces of mainland China (mainly Cantonese, Hokkien and Hakka speaking areas) to North America and the Caribbean (Kwong, 1979; Li, 1982; Daniels, 1988; P.S. Li, 1988). This movement continued well into the twentieth century with people fleeing the Japanese occupation and subsequent civil wars between the nationalists and the communists, although the sise of emigration has greatly reduced due to immigration restrictions of receiving countries (Sung, 1967; Hsu, 1971; P.S. Li, 1988).

Western Europe became a destination for siseable Chinese settlements only after the Second World War. The bulk of the Chinese in this part of the world come from Southeast Asia, partly as a result of the established colonial links between the two regions. They are sometimes called 'second-hand' overseas Chinese, because they migrated from China to Southeast Asia generations ago and transferred to Europe in the last two centuries. It is popularly believed that Britain hosts the largest Chinese population in western Europe, followed by France, The Netherlands, and West Germany (HAC, 1985a; see also Pieke, 1988).

It is important to note that although political turmoil in mainland China has undoubtedly contributed to mass migratory movement, the principal reason for the continuous population drift seems to be economic pressure. Wu & Wu (1980: 129) report a 1934 survey of 905 families in the Swatow area in Guangdong province. Of these, 633 (69.95%) families apparently emigrated for economic reasons (see Table 2.1).

The fact that emigration was the only chance of survival has significant implications for the subsequent activities and organisation of the Chinese overseas, which I shall discuss further in the section entitled 'The Catering Trade' below. I turn now to look specifically at the history of Chinese settlement in Britain.

Chinese settlement in Britain

It has been said that the Chinese settlement in the UK has gone through three distinct phases (HAC, 1985a):

- pre-War (WWI) arrivals
- post-War (WWII) arrivals (till mid-60s)
- reinforcement (till mid-70s).

We'll look at these phases in turn.

Table 2.1 Principal reasons for emigration from near Swatow, 1934

Reason given	No. of families	% of emigration
Economic pressure	633	69.95
Previous connections abroad	176	19.45
Losses from natural calamities	31	3.43
Plan to expand specific enterprise	26	2.87
Bad conduct	17	1.88
Local disturbance	7	0.77
Family quarrel	7	0.77
Other	8	0.88
Total	905	100.00

Source: Wu & Wu (1980: 129)

Pre-War arrivals

The pre-War arrivals consisted mainly of seamen who had been recruited aboard European freighters from southeastern provinces of China including Hong Kong (still under Chinese government at that time) (HAC, 1985a). With the expansion of trade with China following Britain's success in the two Opium Wars (1832–40 and 1858–60), employing Chinese seamen became a regular practice. By the 1880s, Chinese seamen could be found in most of the major port areas of Britain, such as Bristol, Cardiff, Liverpool and London (HAC, 1985a).

At the same time, members of the Chinese aristocracy began to come to Britain (some trace their earliest arrival to the eighteenth century, e.g. O'Neill, 1972). But there could be no greater contrast between this small number of intellectual elite and the large groups of seamen and labourers. Contacts between them were extremely limited, if they existed at all (Taylor, 1987).

During the inter-war years, the Chinese population in Britain declined considerably. Pre and post-War demolition for urban redevelopment led to the dispersal of the two largest Chinese settlements in London and Liverpool away from the original dockland areas (Broady, 1955; Ng, 1968; May, 1978; O'Neill, 1972). Due to the imbalanced ratio of Chinese men and women in this country at the time, many seamen subsequently married non-Chinese women and distanced themselves from other Chinese people, both physically and socially (Ng, 1968). Thus, the pre-War Chinese had not been able to make their mark as a cohesive social group in Britain.

Post-War arrivals

The post-War (from the 1950s) arrivals which began in the 1950s have been attributed largely to the decline in traditional agriculture in Hong Kong (Watson, 1977; HAC, 1985a). Until after the Second World War, Hong Kong had been heavily dependent upon rice farming. Post-War changes in the international rice markets resulted in the undercutting of Hong Kong produce costs by Tai and other imports. Small-scale farmers who occupied the less fertile land were no longer able to make a profit. As they were qualified only for the most menial and low-paid industrial jobs, most of them were not prepared to work in the emerging urban Hong Kong (England & Rear, 1981; Lau, 1982).

It so happened that there was an economic boom in Britain in the late 1950s and early 1960s, and a change of eating habits of the indigenous population away from the traditional British cuisine. The displaced Chinese farmers were thus presented with a unique opportunity to leave Hong Kong and seek catering jobs in the UK. It is believed that over 90% of the Chinese who came to Britain during the decade between 1956 to 1965 were from the rural areas of Hong Kong, and have since engaged in some form of food trade (HAC, 1985a) (see further below).

The emergence of independent but autocratic governments in mainland China, Taiwan and some Southeast Asian states meant that the number of people allowed to emigrate from these regions during the 1950s and 1960s was very small indeed. As a result, Hong Kong emigrants constitute the predominant group within the Chinese population in this country.

Reinforcement

The growing popularity of Chinese cuisine in Britain called for expansion of trade and reinforcement of the workforce. Between the mid-1960s and the mid-1970s, there was a marked increase in the number of Chinese emigrating from Hong Kong to Britain.

Unlike during previous phases, the arrivals during this period were highly organised. The increasingly restrictive immigration laws of Britain required that admission into the UK should be at the invitation of a relative or a specific employer to a particular job. Kinship ties thus provided an important channel for emigration. More elaborate emigration networks based on common birthplace or shared dialect were also at work (Watson 1975, 1977). Usually, travel documents and work permits were arranged by the families in the UK; employment in Chinese eating establishments was promised; passage money was provided as an advance of wages (Cheung, 1975). It seems somewhat ironic though that the British immigration laws which were imposed to restrict increases in the number of immigrants have in reality contributed to the delay in returning home of the first post-War arrivals, in order that their relatives who wished to emigrate could use their contacts.

While the decision by many Chinese to send for their families seemed to be based largely on economic grounds, there were other factors which may also have contributed to emigration from Hong Kong in the late 1960s and early 1970s. Baker & Honey (1981) suggest, for example, that the political unrest in mainland China, provoked by Mao's Cultural Revolution (1965/6–76), gave added impetus to the trend of emigration. It appears though that those who left Hong Kong for political reasons tended to be educated, urban professionals, rather than unskilled farmers. Moreover, the established links between Britain and Hong Kong provided many Chinese young people there with an opportunity to come to Britain for education and training. They of course form a distinctive group of their own, namely, educational transients (see above).[1]

Between them, the post-War emigrants (between mid-1950s and mid-1960s) and their reinforcement (between mid-1960s and mid-1970s) account for two-thirds of the long-term residential Chinese population in Britain today (HAC, 1985a).

Since over 90% of the Chinese emigrants in Britain are associated with some aspects of the catering trade, it is useful to consider in some detail this special economic niche that the Chinese occupy.

The Catering Trade

Reasons for concentration in catering

The overwhelming concentration in catering by Chinese emigrants in Britain can be attributed to a number of factors. First of all, employment opportunities for immigrants have generally been restricted. Work permits for jobs in which they might be in direct competition with the 'indigenous' British are known to be extremely difficult to obtain. For their part, the immigrants are usually aware of the potential consequences of appearing over-ambitious and competitive. Subsequently they opt for family-based businesses and self-employment. Secondly, family-based, small-scale businesses serve well the purpose of emigration which is to seek economic survival and eventually independence (as discussed above), and traditional Chinese cultural values which are based upon high levels of loyalty and commitment within a complex kinship system (see further below). Thirdly, the Chinese emigrants from the New Territories of Hong Kong are generally unskilled in professions other than farming and fishing and speak little English. They can only go into an occupation where no formal qualification is needed and where diligence alone can succeed. Fourthly, the Chinese have a traditional love of cuisine. They usually celebrate various folk festivals with an elaborate family dinner and home-made food is frequently given to each other as presents. Fifthly, the Chinese food trade has met a growing need for diversification in the British catering industry, as tastes were becoming more catholic and society more affluent. A combination of these factors, and perhaps others, has resulted in the concentration of Chinese emigrants in Britain in the catering trade (Watson, 1977; Taylor, 1987).

Types of catering

The catering businesses run by Chinese emigrants in Britain range from first-class restaurants to neighbourhood take-aways. Chinese restaurants are usually owned by multi-family partnerships. Managers, cooks, waiters and others could all be shareholders. It is generally understood that the ultimate goal for individual partners is to achieve independent proprietorship, and shareholders may therefore pull out of the partnership to establish their own business should opportunities arise (Watson, 1977).

By the end of the 1960s, many junior partners had accumulated enough savings to be able to set up their own trade. Chinese take-aways (or 'carry-outs' in Scotland) thus came into being. For a relatively small capital outlay, the Chinese take-away shops provided independent living accommodation and employment, which suited the newly united families (HAC, 1985a; Taylor, 1987).

Unlike large restaurants, the take-aways generally operate on small profit margins. Success of the business depends heavily on the commitment of all members involved. In order to avoid high wages, overtime payments, other potential drains on resources, and conflicting interests, Chinese take-aways are usually single-family-based. Men, women and children of the same family all contribute towards the business. There are traditionally no objections among the Chinese about employing women and children in the family trade (Cheung, 1975; see further below).

As the trend has been moving towards independent proprietorship, the number of Chinese take-aways has increased considerably since the 1970s, and they are dispersed to all parts of the British Isles. It is now almost impossible to find a town, especially in England, with a population of 5,000 or more which does not have at least one Chinese eating establishment (Watson, 1977; HAC, 1985a).

Supporting businesses

Since the mid-1960s, there has been a steady growth in a network of supporting businesses run by the Chinese which provide services for the catering families. Such businesses include grocery stores, food-processing factories, barber's shops, book/audio-visual cassette rental stores, and gambling halls —

Table 2.2 Proportions of ethnic minority populations living in metropolitan counties in the UK in 1985

Caribbean	80%	in Metropolitan Counties
Bangladeshi	75%	in Metropolitan Counties
African	71%	in Metropolitan Counties
Pakistani	71%	in Metropolitan Counties
Indian	65%	in Metropolitan Counties
Chinese	51%	in Metropolitan Counties

Source: Adapted from Roper, 1988: 5

the recreation centre for Chinese men. Like Chinese restaurants and take-aways, these supporting businesses tend to be family-based, and many of their owners have once been caterers themselves. More recently, a small number of Chinese professionals — doctors, accountants and solicitors in particular — have also begun to provide services for the caterers.

Implications for settlement and social life

Implications of the catering trade for the settlement pattern and social life of Chinese emigrants in Britain may be seen in their geographic dispersal and extensive working-hours. In order to provide services for the maximum number of potential customers, Chinese caterers do not live in identifiable settlements. The so-called *Chinatowns* in larger cities such as London, Liverpool and Manchester are established for business (and increasingly tourism) rather than residential purposes. The Chinese thus present a sharp contrast with other ethnic minority communities in Britain who tend to cluster in specifiable urban areas. Table 2.2 above illustrates the relative dispersal of the Chinese compared to other ethnic minorities. As it shows, nearly half of the Chinese population live *outside* metropolitan areas.

Competition for customers with small businesses run by other (especially South Asian) communities leads to the extension of working hours. Some Chinese restaurants and take-aways keep open for up to 14 hours a day, almost every day of the year. With such long working hours and the fact that whole families, including women and children, are involved in the daily running of the business, Chinese caterers generally have little time for leisure and socialising.

One point which needs to be raised here is that the Chinese are traditionally seen as dedicated and diligent workers. They have been regarded by many as ideal labourers, who are likely to produce more than any other ethnic group under the same working conditions. Their dedication to hard work has often been attributed to the Confucian work ethic, which is ultimately based on filial piety (see further below). Yet, in a study of Chinese family businesses in Southeast Asia, Redding (1990) argues that the question of work ethic is one of circumstances as much as people. Indeed, environment determines that in order to survive Chinese emigrants in Britain, like many other immigrant communities, have no other choice but to work exceptionally hard. We must also not forget that the majority of Chinese emigrants left their homeland precisely because of economic pressure (see above). Any effort which may lead to financial independence and wealth is therefore considered natural, in fact ideal. It is perhaps for this reason that the employment of women and children in the Chinese catering trade has not met with much opposition (Taylor, 1987).

The dispersed settlement and lengthy working hours of the catering Chinese families present special problems for would-be investigators. I shall discuss some of these problems in relation to my own fieldwork in the Tyneside Chinese community in Chapter 3.

The Emergence of a Three-Generation Population

Since the mid-1970s, the influx of Chinese emigrants into Britain has begun to slow down. The 1981 British Nationality Act has made it difficult even for dependents to gain access to the UK. The long-term residential Chinese population in Britain has grown mainly by the emergence of a British-born generation. They are now estimated to constitute about a quarter of the Chinese population in this country (HAC, 1985a; Taylor, 1987). Thus, a Chinese population consisting of three generations has come into existence. These three generations are:

- first-generation emigrants, mainly those who came to Britain in the 1950s, but also including the pre-War emigrants who have not intermarried with non-Chinese
- sponsored emigrants, who came either as immediate kin of the first-generation emigrants or through personal contact with people already established in this country
- the British-born.

This grouping is not always isomorphic with the three generation cohorts of parents, children and grandchildren (for example, many grandparents are in fact sponsored emigrants, and some British-born Chinese have now become parents), but provides a useful reference point for studying the social organisation and social behaviours of the Chinese in the UK. So far I have focused my attention mainly on the first two generations, i.e. the first-generation emigrants and sponsored emigrants. I shall now consider briefly the British-born Chinese generation in particular.

The British-born Chinese

Information about the British-born Chinese is sketchy. Studies of Chinese children and adolescents in Britain to date have tended to focus on those who were born in the Far East, or the few who, for various reasons, have been sent back to Hong Kong to receive part of their education (e.g. Jackson & Garvey, 1974; Garvey & Jackson, 1975; I. Jones, 1979; Nuffield Foundation, 1981; Ng, 1982; Rowe, 1988). There has been a particular tendency to concentrate on the few who are judged to be low achievers in schools. The majority of the British-born Chinese, on the other hand, have been exposed to British culture and the English language from a very young age. They are generally perceived as assimilated or at least 'better adjusted' to the British way of life and sharing similar characteristics with their British peers and thus are not perceived as presenting a problem to mainstream society (Taylor, 1987).

Significantly, however, the British-born generation is perceived by the Chinese communities themselves as a major cause of concern. They are seen as lacking respect for traditional culture (e.g. authority structures of the family; see further below), which is often expressed through their Anglicised social behaviour (e.g. speaking English) (Ng, 1986, 1988; Social Service Department, City of Newcastle upon Tyne, 1985–88; see further). Derogatory names such as 'bananas', meaning 'yellow outside, white inside', have been used to refer to this generation (e.g. Macphedran, 1989). Although reports of the communication difficulties between the British-born and previous generations of Chinese emigrants are becoming more numerous (e.g. Swann Committee, 1985; Taylor, 1987; Wong, 1992), there remains a serious gap in empirical and systematic research into this particular generation. As the British-born Chinese are growing as a proportion of the Chinese population, much more attention in future research needs to be focused on this group and inter-generational relationships, in order to provide information which might help to improve the quality of life for the Chinese people in Britain in the 1990s.

Having outlined the history and socio-economic background of different groups and generations of the Chinese in Britain, it is now time to ask the following questions: To what extent do the Chinese constitute a community?, and Why is the popular perception of the Chinese as a homogeneous group so strong?.

Chinese migrants as a 'community'

'Community' is a sociological concept which may be defined as 'a cohesive and self-conscious social group' (Watson, 1977: 195; see also Cohen, 1986). The concept is somewhat difficult to apply in the case of the Chinese emigrants in Britain. We have already considered differences in place of origin, language, and phase of settlement in the UK. All these differences form a basis for group boundaries, which in turn inform the behaviour and attitude of their members. In a study of the Chinese in Liverpool, O'Neill (1972) finds that the first-generation Cantonese speakers see the later-arriving Hakka-speaking emigrants as 'flighty and unreliable and not showing due respect', while they themselves are perceived as 'old-fashioned'. The Liverpool-born Chinese, on the other hand, seem to be more concerned with their relationships with the host community, compared with the Hong Kong-born generations who are more aware of regional differences according to their place of origin. Ng (1986, 1988) and So (1989) report their observations among the Chinese in the Tyneside area that the New Territories emigrants are perceived by the students and professionals groups as uneducated, uncivilised, and lacking in intelligence, while the emigrants view the students and professionals as over-privileged, self-centred, and lacking in respect for tradition (see also Pong, 1991). Stereotypes such as these, coupled with the secular nature of Chinese culture which lacks strong religious ties compared with, for example, communities of Indian or Pakistani origin, have undoubtedly contributed to the difficulty of viewing the Chinese as a single, united community (see also D. Jones, 1979; Shang, 1984). It is important that these divisions and stereotypes are taken into account when field research is being planned.

None of these internal differences, however, can be compared to the dichotomy between Chinese and non-Chinese, a dichotomy established from the very beginning of Chinese history and maintained by the Chinese people wherever they are. In his study of the Chinese in London, Watson (1977) claims that while traditional group differences based on place of origin, socio-economic status and language are clearly perceived as significant, the Chinese often find it to their advantage to unite themselves, or at least to appear to be united, against their common rival, which is the non-Chinese generally (see also Taylor, 1987). Redding (1990) suggests that the majority of the Chinese people living overseas have not psychologically left China, or at least not left some ideal and perhaps romanticised notion of Chinese civilisation. Indeed, the name given to the emigrants by the Chinese themselves, *Huaqiao*, signifies a short-term visitor, a sojourner. The fact that many families have sojourned for centuries does not alter the expectation that they will eventually be returning to the motherland, even perhaps in their afterlife. The 'synthesising mind' (Rin, 1982) of the Chinese people which has been kept alive by the legacy of China and Chinese culture has been one of the most distinct features of their ethnic identity (see also Sachdev *et al.*, 1987; Sachdev *et al.*, 1990; Dikoter, 1990; Allinson, 1991).

What is particularly interesting, however, is that despite their deeply rooted sense of opposition between Chinese and non-Chinese, the Chinese appear to be the most acceptable ethnic minority in Britain. In the 1950s and 1960s when racial conflicts became a feature of British society, the Chinese managed to avoid overt discrimination. Watson (1977) reports that when English landlords posted 'No coloureds' signs in their windows, Chinese students were generally exempt from that category.

The superficially harmonious relationship the Chinese have managed to maintain with others owes a great deal to their belief that everyone has a specific role in society and in order to have peace one must know one's precise social position and behave accordingly. Thus, while few of the emigrants have illusions about their socially defined role as caterers or waiters, they have made no specific effort to change it. They tend to see themselves as living and working in someone else's country, even though many of them have decided to settle down permanently (Watson, 1977; Redding, 1990). This peculiar form of cognition characteristic of the Chinese emigrants is directly attributable to the Chinese family system and the authority structure which is inherent within it (Watson, 1977; Baker, 1979). I shall now discuss in some detail this structure, as its influence on interpersonal interaction is considerable.

Chinese Family System

The family as the focus of Chinese way of life has been recognised and stressed by the Chinese people from earliest times. Confucian philosophers throughout history, who dominate Chinese ideology, have refined and extended family consciousness through a carefully worked out hierarchy of relationships which informs the individual's daily behaviour. In this section, I shall first look at different types of family, and then move on to consider the authority structure embodied in the 'extended' family ideal. I shall then discuss the impact of the family system on the life of the individuals involved.

Types of family

A distinction needs to be made between the *extended* family, the ideal Chinese family type, the *simple*, and the *stem* families (Baker, 1979; see also Freedman, 1958, 1966; Watson, 1982).

The simple family, sometimes called nuclear, is founded by the marriage of a man and a woman, and enlarged by their children. When the children grow up, they usually move out of the parental home, maintaining the family as the territory for the parents.

Sometimes, grown-up children may continue to live with their parents even after they get married and bring their spouses into the family. In Chinese society, it is traditionally the eldest son, or the only son, of the family who brings his wife into the parental home. When the married son and his wife produce their

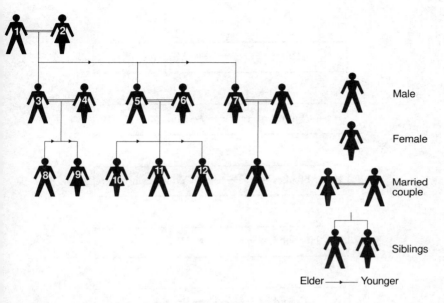

Figure 2.2 An 'extended' family: 1 and 2 are the grandparent generation; 3, 4, 5, 6, and 7 belong to the parent generation, and 8, 9, 10, 11 and 12 belong to the child generation; 5, 6, 10, 11, and 12 form a 'simple' (nuclear) family; 1, 2, 3, 4, 8, and 9 form a 'stem' family; 1, 2, 3, 4, 5, 6, 8, 9, 10, 11, and 12 form an 'extended' family. 7 is married to some other family's son and is therefore considered to be outside the immediate family.

own child, there will then be three generations co-residing. Baker (1979) calls this type of family the stem family. It is a vertical extension of the simple family, and is usually a transitional type. Sooner or later the parents will die, leaving behind a simple family once more. Between them, the simple family and the stem family types account for the vast majority of Chinese families (cf. Wong, 1979; Lau, 1981).

If, however, more than one son brings his wife into the family after marriage, a different family type will then emerge. This type of family, with several married sons living with their parents, is known as the extended family, the ideal family type in Chinese society. It expands on the basis of the stem family horizontally (see Figure 2.2 for a diagrammatic illustration).

Unlike simple or stem families, the extended family cannot be materialised without several sons, each of whom must be prepared to bring a wife home who will bear children. It becomes apparent then that wealth, or the lack of it, is an

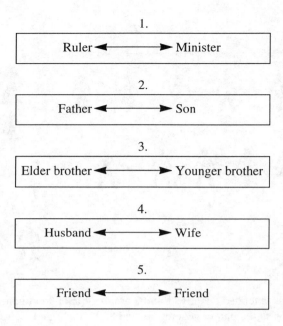

Figure 2.3 *Wu Lun* (Five Relationships)

important factor determining the realisation of the extended family ideal. For a family in poverty, there could be little hope of raising sufficient sons to begin the necessary expansion. Childhood mortality, which may be a direct consequence of under-nourishment, over-work, inability to afford medical care and other conditions attendant upon poverty, also limits the possibility of the extended family. Even for the comparatively wealthy, personality clashes and conflicting interests in control over family property may lead to the break-up of a large family into smaller units. Furthermore, the extended family is a property-owning co-operation based on land. It is traditionally tied to one specifiable locality. Any physical move away from the original territory would mean a break with the family system (see further Baker, 1979). As a result, the extended family is in actual fact rare. For the Chinese emigrants living overseas, there is little hope that an extended family could ever materialise.

Authority structure of the family

The 'extended' family, although an ideal rather than a common reality, embodies an authority structure which influences the Chinese perceptions of rules for social relationship and social interaction. From at least as early as the fifth century BC, that is about the time of Confucius, there has existed a list of important relationships by which man's life should be ordered. This list is known as *Wu Lun* (Five Relationships) and is presented in Figure 2.3.

In this list, three intra-family relationships are specified. They are the relationships between father and son, elder brother and younger brother, and husband and wife. These relationships are arranged on a superior versus inferior hierarchy, and represent, in order of priority: generation, age, and sex. They are intended to give guidance as to where one stands in the family and society, and to whom one owes duty, respect and obedience. We can illustrate how this system works with a diagrammatic representation of an example family of grandfather, grandmother, three married couples, and their unmarried children (see Figure 2.2).

In this family, everyone owes obedience to the grandfather (1), because he is superior in generation, age and sex. Everyone except the grandfather owes obedience to the grandmother (2), because she is senior in generation and age. The wife of the eldest son of the grandparents (4) owes obedience to her father-in-law and mother-in-law because of generation and age, and to her husband on sex grounds. The second son of the grandparents (5) owes obedience to his elder brothers' wife (4), his elder brother (3), his mother (2) and father (1). The married daughter of the grandparents (7) is traditionally considered to be outside the immediate family, but still owes obedience to her brothers' wives, her brothers and her parents, in addition to her husband, his siblings (depending on age and sex) and his parents. The youngest son of the second couple (12) has to obey all the others, except perhaps his aunt's son (see Baker, 1979, for a more detailed discussion on this topic).

These relationships are not to be taken at face value only. They are extendable to include much wider groups of both kin and non-kin. For instance, the father and son relationship may be taken to govern the father and unmarried daughter, mother and son/unmarried daughter, and uncle/aunt and nephew/niece relationships, while further extension includes relationships between senior and junior generations. In a similar vein, The elder brother and younger brother relationship holds good for the various permutations of brother and unmarried sister, elder and younger cousins, and may be extended to cover the relationship between age and youth. The husband and wife relationship represents of course the relationship of the two sexes. Redding (1990) argues that the family system forms the basis of a 'networked society' which characterises China and Chinese settlements overseas. The chief characteristic of a networked society, as Redding describes it, is that every member is held tightly in check by the duty, respect and obedience which he or she owes to another. Even though an individual may take on different social roles in different contexts (e.g. one may be a take-away owner at one time, but leader of a community organisation at another), his or her position in the family-relationship hierarchy remains the same and is perceived to be so. In fact, very often one's family role determines whether or not one can assume a specific position in the community at all. The complexity of the Chinese family system and the authority structure that is embodied in it has significant implications for sociolinguistic fieldwork. I shall explore this question further in Chapter 3.

Implications for social life on the micro level: An example of address terms

The authority structure of the family manifests itself as a model of social life in various ways. Here, I would like to consider an example of the use of address terms in daily interaction, which reflects the significance of the Chinese family system.

It is customary among the Chinese that within the family those older or senior in generation to the speaker are always addressed by the appropriate kinship term, e.g. father, uncle, elder brother, and so on, while those younger or junior are usually called by their personal names. Parents often refer to their children as 'the eldest', 'the youngest', specifying their individual positions in the family. Outside the family, a man of roughly the same age as the speaker is generally called 'brother'. An older man would be addressed as 'father's younger brother', while a much older man would be called 'father's elder brother'. A similar distinction according to age could be shown by using either 'elder brother's wife' or 'father's younger brother's wife' to a woman, while 'father's older sister' could be used as a polite way of addressing a female stranger. The honorific prefix *lao* (old) and *xiao* (little/young) are also often used. If one is not very well acquainted with the speaker, then he/she is referred to as '*lao*-something', because it gives the addressee honour by emphasising his/her seniority. For people in employment, their position in the profession could be used together with their names as address terms, such as 'Accountant Li', and 'Shop-owner Wang'. Such systems of address terms are obviously influenced by the hierarchy of relationships of the family, and in the meantime the authority structure which is inherent within the family is reinforced (see also Yum, 1988, for a general discussion on the impact of the Chinese family system on communication patterns).

Implications for social life of Chinese emigrants in Britain: Inter-familial organisations and community language schools

The general pattern of social life of the Chinese emigrants in this country seems to be family-based and usually centres around the catering businesses.

Leisure and recreation for the Chinese normally mean weekend gatherings in restaurants for families — gambling for men, mahjong tea for women, and Chinese language classes for children. Apart from celebrating major folk festivals, such as the Spring Festival (the Chinese New Year), the Chinese have shown little enthusiasm for organised events. There is a notable lack of centralised leadership at both regional and national levels (Watson, 1977; Taylor, 1987).

As the community grows, so do the attendant problems and the consequent need for counselling. For the Chinese emigrants in Britain, seeking help has not proved to be easy. On the one hand, provision of services for ethnic minority groups in this country is far from adequate (this in fact was one of the main reasons for the HAC to commission a report on the Chinese in Britain, 1985a); and on the other, Chinese people traditionally rely on self-help within the family.

Yet, emigration has made it impossible for family members to live close enough to offer support when needed. Alternative, inter-familial organisations thus have come into being. A typical example of such organisations is the surname/townsmen association. Among the Chinese, there is a common assumption that all people with the same surname have descended from the same ancestor, thus being related to one another. Since the Chinese kinship organisations are traditionally tied to land and specific territories, people originating from the same hometown tend to believe that they are in some way related as well. As the Chinese saying goes, 'he who comes from my hometown is my relative'. The surname/townsmen associations are established with such assumptions as substitutes of kinship ties which the emigrants can no longer maintain (see further Baker, 1979).

In most cases, however, members of surname/townsmen associations cannot prove a common ancestry or any blood relationship. Consequently, these associations do not usually have a centralised leadership. Although male members who are senior in generation and age are often nominated as leaders of these associations (another example of the implications of the authority structure of the extended family ideal), important decisions are normally made collectively, and the everyday running of the associations becomes the duty of the relatively better educated Chinese-English bilinguals for practical reasons.

Since the 1970s, a new kind of community organisation has begun to emerge, namely, the Chinese language schools. They are currently estimated to be around 100 in total number across Britain (Chann, 1988). Chinese language schools are based even less on concrete family connections than the surname/townsmen associations. They have been set up in order to tackle a specific problem, that is, the maintenance of Chinese language and culture among the British-born generation.

Table 2.3 Chinese adults' competence in English

Chinese language speakers	N	Respondents answering fairly or very well	
		Understand and speak %	Read and write %
Bradford	50	10	6
Coventry	43	44	30
London	137	47	42

Source: Adapted from Linguistic Minorities Project, 1985. Cited in Taylor (1987: 139). Table 27

As has been described earlier, the majority of the Chinese emigrants in this country came from the rural New Territories of Hong Kong. These emigrants had had little formal education before they left for Britain, and spoke very little, if any, English. Their subsequent engagement in the family-based catering trade, which entails long working hours, has given them few opportunities to learn and use English. Cheung (1975) reports that for most Chinese caterers there is hardly any social contact between themselves and the society at large, apart from the waiter–customer relationship. It is possible for a Chinese kitchen staff never to exchange a word with English-speaking people. Watson (1977) has made a similar observation that Chinese waiters learn only enough to handle the menus and that fewer than 20% of them are able to hold a simple conversation in English. The Adult Language Use Survey in three southern English cities, part of the Linguistics Minorities Project (1985), suggests that the Chinese speakers' skills in English are in fact among the poorest claimed by all ethnic language speakers (see Table 2.3).

In contrast to these earlier emigrants, the British-born Chinese generation, which now constitutes over a quarter of the whole Chinese population in this country (HAC, 1985a), have acquired English through education and peer interaction. Some have begun to use English most of the time. A study of 31 Chinese families in Liverpool, one of the largest and oldest Chinese settlements in Britain, carried out by Fong in 1981 (cited in Taylor, 1987: 143) finds, for example, that 55% of the children use both English and Chinese with friends, and 30% speak only English (see further below). Problems of communication caused by changing patterns of language use across generations have become a major concern for the Chinese families. As the British education system is strongly oriented towards English monolingualism (Edwards & Alladina, 1991; Martin-Jones, 1989b) and Chinese children rarely make up more than 5% of the local school populations (due of course to their dispersed settlement pattern, which in turn was determined by the catering trade) (Watson, 1977; Taylor, 1987), a support system within the community in the form of language schools seems (at least for the moment) the only solution. It is in this context that the Chinese language schools have come into existence. They are gradually becoming an integral part of social life of the Chinese in this country (see further Li Wei, 1992, 1993).

I want to turn my attention now to patterns of language use within and between different generations of the Chinese emigrant population in this country.

Language Use: Existing Evidence

Existing information concerning language use among the Chinese people in Britain is extremely limited and is mostly derived from societal-level surveys and censuses which cover many other ethnic groups as well. Again, the reports by the HAC (1985a) and Taylor (1987) provide the most comprehensive source of reference. There are a small number of case studies of Chinese children's language use patterns (see Taylor, 1987, for references). These studies are mostly implemented in the context of language teaching and tend to focus on the difficulties of Chinese children acquiring English (if the studies are carried out by non-Chinese researchers) or learning and maintaining their mother tongue (if done by Chinese). Despite their diverse methodological perspectives and analytic focuses, most of the existing studies point to inter-generational variations in language use as a prominent feature of the Chinese communities in this country. The Commission for Racial Equality carried out a survey in 1979 (cited by Tsow, 1984) in which two groups of Chinese parents were interviewed: 138 of them had children who were aged up to 11 and were not attending Chinese community schools, and 195 had children aged 8 and over attending Chinese schools, The first group of parents were mostly from non-catering families who had lived in London for ten years or more. The 195 parents whose children attended Chinese schools were from catering families or other lower socioeconomic backgrounds. The languages spoken at home by these two groups of parents are shown in Table 2.4.

As Table 2.4 shows, Cantonese is used predominantly and most frequently by both groups in family communication, although a greater proportion (43%) of the non-catering parents of non-school-attenders reported using some English at home and 14% claimed it as their most frequently spoken language.

Tsow (1984) also cites a separate sample of 312 children aged 8–14 as shown in Table 2.5, who were attending Chinese language schools (these are not the

Table 2.4 Languages spoken at home by parents of children attending and not attending Chinese language classes

	Spoken by parents of non-attenders/attenders		Spoken most frequently by parents of non-attenders/attenders	
	N = 138 %	N = 195 %	N = 138 %	N = 195 %
English	43	35	14	9
Cantonese	80	80	67	69
Mandarin	4	2	3	
Other Chinese	35	37	18	

Source: Adapted from Tsow, 1984. Cited in Taylor, 1987: 144

Table 2.5 Languages spoken at home by pupils attending Chinese language classes

	Total	Birthplace Hong Kong and elsewhere	Length of time in the UK (years)			
			UK	1–2	3–9	10+
Base: all	312	148	164	49	188	75
	%	%	%	%	%	%
Cantonese	72	85	60	82	76	56
English	62	46	76	33	64	75
Mandarin	1	1	1	—	1	1
Other Chinese	26	19	32	22	24	32

Source: Adapted from Tsow, 1984. Cited in Taylor, 1987: 145

children of the parents sample described in Table 2.4). Some 62% of these children claimed to speak English and 38% claimed English as their most frequently used language. Moreover, as Table 2.6 shows, 51% of the UK-born group spoke English most frequently at home (for further discussion see Taylor, 1987: 144-6)

Further evidence of contrasting patterns of language use by speakers of different generations is provided by Ng (1982), who interviewed 251 adolescents (134 females, 117 males; aged 12–17) from ten Chinese community schools. Some

Table 2.6 Languages spoken most often at home by pupils attending Chinese language classes

	Total	Birthplace Hong Kong and elsewhere	Length of time in the UK (years)			
			UK	1–2	3–9	10+
Base: all	312	148	164	49	188	75
	%	%	%	%	%	%
Cantonese	48	66	32	63	48	36
English	38	23	51	16	40	47
Other Chinese	14	10	18	16	13	18

Source: Adapted from Tsow, 1984. Cited in Taylor, 1987: 146

93% claimed that their parents spoke to them in a Chinese dialect (118 were Cantonese speakers, 107 spoke Hakka or one of six other Chinese dialects). Fewer (86%) claimed to use Chinese in speaking with their parents, with about 14% claiming to speak to their parents in English. Amongst siblings and friends, Chinese was less commonly used. 41% reported that they spoke to their brothers or sisters in English and 48% were spoken to by their siblings in English; 46% spoke English to their Chinese friends and 37% were spoken to by their Chinese friends in English.

Two other studies also reveal similar inter-generational differences in language behaviour. O'Neill (1972) observed that among the 30 Chinese families whom she studied in Liverpool in the late 1960s, the parents typically lived in a Chinese cultural environment, with kin and Chinese friends, and spoke very little English; the children, on the other hand, were typically English in their orientation and spoke little Chinese. More recently, Wong (1992) has reported that while the majority of children in the community school in London which she studied could manage to speak to their parents and grandparents in the mother tongue, about 20% tended to use a mixture of English and Chinese. When they talked to their siblings or friends, more than half indicated that they used some Cantonese but more English, with a further 6% using English alone.

All these data suggest that the pattern of language use is changing across generations within the British Chinese population, with strong indications that the use of English is beginning to dominate interactions among the British-born generation. It is the aim of the present study to investigate the social and linguistic mechanisms underlying the variations and change in the language behaviours of different generations.

In the final section of this chapter, I shall provide a brief description of the Chinese community in the Tyneside area in the northeast of England, where the study reported in this book was carried out.

The Tyneside Chinese Community

The location of the present study is the city of Newcastle upon Tyne with the surrounding urban areas straddling the borders between County Durham and Northumberland (see Figure 2.4). This conurbation is conveniently referred to as Tyneside, but more strictly is the former metropolitan county of Tyne and Wear. There are two main reasons for choosing this particular location: first and foremost, I, as the fieldworker, had lived in Newcastle for three years prior to the formal start of the study and had established extensive personal contacts within the Chinese community in the region which are a prerequisite of detailed, community-based sociolinguistic research (L. Milroy, 1987b; see further Chapter 3). Second, the area hosts a large Chinese population who as yet have not been internally centralised. This demographic pattern contrasts with those characteristic of, for example, London, Liverpool and Manchester, and thus may be more representative of the Chinese communities which are scattered in different parts of the country (see above).

As in many other parts of Britain, there has been no systematic study of the Chinese in Tyneside. Information obtainable from official channels is scarce and often unreliable. For example, the 1986 Household Survey carried out by the City of Newcastle upon Tyne, the most comprehensive demographic survey conducted by the city council to date, included four categories of 'origin of the head of the household' — 'European', 'Asian', 'Afro-Caribbean', and 'Others'. Chinese heads of household were classified as one of the many 'Others'. Results of surveys such as this are unlikely to be of value for detailed studies of particular groups such as the Chinese (for a discussion see Moffatt, 1990). The demographic information presented in this section is therefore gathered by means of participant observation and informal interviews with senior Chinese residents in the Tyneside area, which were conducted by myself as the initial exploratory stage of the research (see Chapter 3).

Demography of the Chinese in Tyneside

The Tyneside Chinese number somewhere between 5,000 and 7,000 persons. They are the second largest ethnic minority population in the region, after those of South Asian origin, but are a relatively 'young' group compared with those in the south and south-west of England. Before 1948, there were no more than 30 Chinese people, including children, living in the whole of the northeast (Ng, 1986). Although the first Chinese restaurant was opened in Newcastle upon

Figure 2.4 British Isles and Tyneside

Tyne in 1949 and subsequently eight laundries run by the Chinese came into existence, it was not until the early 1960s that the Chinese began to settle on Tyneside in significant numbers.

The 1960s was a period of change for the Tyneside Chinese. Laundries were gradually replaced by eating establishments — first small fast-food shops, then large restaurants. At that time, the majority of the Chinese were not accompanied by family members. Their businesses were often run on the basis of partnership.

The arrival of family members during the late 1960s and early 1970s facilitated the emergence of Chinese take-aways in the region. Within a period of about ten years, some 300 take-aways had been set up. Unlike large restaurants, the Chinese take-aways are generally single-family-based and are scattered in various parts of the area. In 1989 there were estimated to be 27 Chinese restaurants, at least 300 take-aways, four groceries and supermarkets, and one food-processing factory on Tyneside.

Since the 1970s, there has been no more large-scale Chinese migration into the region. A generation of British-born Chinese has begun to emerge. They now constitute nearly a quarter of the Chinese population in Tyneside.

Apart from the long-term residents, there are some 1,000 students from Hong Kong, mainland China, Singapore, Malaysia, and other parts of the world, currently studying in the region's higher education institutions (Li Wei, 1988; McGregor & Li Wei, 1991). There are as yet very few Chinese professionals in the region. In the city of Newcastle upon Tyne, there are three accountancies, two travel agencies, and two acupuncture clinics run by the Chinese.

Community organisations

Until the mid-1970s, there was no community-level social organisation for the Tyneside Chinese. The first Chinese inter-familial organisation was established by a group of senior emigrants from a small island called Ap Chau next to Crooked Island in Crook Harbour to the north-east of Hong Kong (see Figure 2.1). It carries the name of True Jesus Church, an evangelical church which also exists in Hong Kong. The True Jesus Church in Newcastle upon Tyne is in fact a townsmen association. All its members could trace their origin to the fishing community of Ap Chau; many have the surnames of Ho, Liu, Shek or Tang. The chief function of the church seems to be to provide an opportunity for the families to gather together, and the activities in which its members participate each Sunday do not resemble those of the church-going population of Britain generally. Usually they gather on Sunday afternoon for a short service, during which a bilingual teenager is invited to translate the sermon. Then the children, around 150 of them, will have their Chinese language lessons. Some adults learn English, while others talk among themselves, have tea, or go shopping in the Chinese shops. Sometimes the church provides food (often donated by one of the Chinese restaurants in the region) for its participants at either the beginning or the end of the afternoon. More recently, the church has admitted a small number of children to its language classes whose parents are not from Ap Chau but who have contributed financially to the church activities.

The majority of the Tyneside Chinese, however, are not from Ap Chau; they are Cantonese Punti from various parts of Hong Kong and Guangdong province of mainland China (see above). Two community organisations were set up during the 1970s to look after the interests of these people — the North-East Chinese Association and the Wah Sun Chinese Association. These associations organise festival celebrations and occasional trips to Scotland and southern England. Membership of the associations is loosely controlled. Anyone (including those from Ap Chau) can join either or both of them. There is no fixed membership fee. People contribute in various ways when participating in events organised by the associations. Neither association has a formally elected leadership. Those who are relatively better educated, experienced, and enthusiastic are entrusted with the general administrative duties. More recently, the two associations have established a women's group and an elderly people's club for female and senior members of the Chinese community to meet on a regular basis and exchange news and gossip.

With the support of the Hong Kong Government Office in London and the local authorities, the Chinese on Tyneside have set up a language school in the city of Newcastle, which enrols some 300 British-born Chinese children. They meet every Sunday afternoon for three hours and learn Chinese language as well as traditional calligraphy, painting, and folk dancing. The teachers are mainly students from Hong Kong and mainland China (see further Li Wei, 1992, 1993).

Language environment

The Tyneside area has its local English dialect which is popularly known as *Geordie*, a name applied also to anyone who comes from the region. The main phonological and syntactic features of Geordie are discussed in detail by Hughes & Trudgill (1987), Wells (1982) and Beal (1993).

In addition to English, there are a number of European as well as non-European languages spoken mainly by migrant and ethnic minority communities. A small survey of nine classes within five schools in the West End of Newcastle gives some indication of the proportion of native English-speaking population and speakers of mother tongues other than English (see Table 2.7). Inter-ethnic communication is normally in English.

It is estimated that around 80% of the Chinese residents on Tyneside speak Cantonese as their first language; at least 15% speak Hakka, and the rest speak other regional languages of Chinese such as Beifang and Min (including, for example, Hokkien). About 25% of the total Chinese population in the region can understand and speak some Mandarin. The use of Chinese, of whatever variety, is largely confined to family communication. Public representation of the Chinese language is minimal. Only very recently (since 1988) the Chinese community has been given permission to display signs and notices in Chinese in Stowell Street in Newcastle, the so-called Chinatown of the northeast of England. BBC Radio Newcastle offers a 15 minute slot every Sunday afternoon in which the Chinese community can broadcast news and information in their own language. Newcastle's Central Library has a new and small collection of Chinese publications, including the popular European Chinese daily *Sing Tao*. It also provides a rental service for Chinese music tapes and videos of Chinese films. The two universities in the region — Newcastle and Durham — both offer degree courses of which Mandarin Chinese forms an integral part. There are as yet no mainstream schools teaching Chinese as part of the curriculum.

Table 2.7 Mother tongue languages spoken by children in nine classes within five schools in the West End of Newcastle

Language	Number of Speakers
English	113
Panjabi	85
Bengali	24
Urdu	11
Arabic	6
Cantonese	3
Malay	3
Hindi	2
Farsi	2
French/Ewondo	2
Vietnamese	1
'Chinese'	1
Turkish	1
Norwegian/German	1
Yoruba	1
Total	256

Source: Adapted from Moffatt, 1990: 65

According to the teachers of the Chinese community school and the students from Hong Kong and China, there is no significant difference between the Chinese the local residents speak and that spoken in the Far East. However, a small number of words (mainly nouns) and phrases which seem characteristic of the local Chinese community have been observed. Some of them are obviously influenced by a period of contact with English. Compare, for example, Hong Kong Cantonese *saisanfong* (bathroom) with Tyneside Cantonese *bafong* (derived from ba(th) + *fong* (room)). Similarly, compare local Cantonese *toijau* (literally: table + wine) with the usual Hong Kong Cantonese *jau* (wine). Despite the emergence of forms such as these, there does not seem to be a coherent localised variety of Chinese which we could call 'British Chinese'. The most visible and socially meaningful language phenomenon appears to be the choice between English and Chinese or a mixture of both (see also So, 1989; Pong, 1991).

The heterogeneous composition of the Chinese in Britain, together with their culturally specific internal organisation and traditional values, provide a fascinating and challenging research opportunity. Great care needs to be taken in order to collect data on the sociolinguistic patterns of the British Chinese. In the next chapter, I shall discuss the fieldwork procedures of the present study of language choice and language shift in the Tyneside Chinese community.

Note

1. Following the Sino-British Joint Declaration of 1984, China will resume her sovereignty over Hong Kong in 1997. The implications of this historic change for the Chinese communities both in the colony and in Britain are not yet clear. The British government is to grant a limited number of middle-class families from Hong Kong the right of abode in the UK after 1997. The Chinese communities in Britain have voiced their uneasiness about this decision.

3 Participant Observation in a Chinese Community

In Chapter 1, I outlined three main theoretical perspectives on bilingualism and language choice. These three perspectives can further be differentiated in terms of the fieldwork procedures they employ and the types of data they use for analysis as outlined below.

The macro-societal approach tends to favour reported data, usually gathered at the community level, which summarise probable behaviours of large numbers of people. The underlying assumption is, as has been discussed in Chapter 1, that language choices are determined by situational context and that speakers are usually conscious about any change in setting, topic, participant and so on. Therefore, it is feasible for researchers to ask speakers (especially bilinguals) to report their linguistic choices in different situations. The most common procedures involve the use of sample surveys and censuses, interview schedules, or written questionnaires, and often require the use of quantitative measures and statistical analysis.

The micro-interactional approach, on the other hand, focuses on the meanings of language choice and the discourse strategies whereby speakers make use of the different languages in the community repertoire. Researchers adopting this perspective rely primarily on information collected at the level of face-to-face interaction. Participant observation is the principal data-gathering method, and tape-recordings (audio or video) are made of conversation as it occurs in actual social encounters. Fine-grained analyses are carried out, normally without quantification and statistical tests. Informal interviews eliciting information about language attitudes are sometimes conducted to supplement the conversational data. Both the macro-societal and micro-interactional perspectives concentrate mainly on the stylistic dimension of linguistic variation, that is, the same speakers' choices of language in a range of situational contexts.

The social network perspective uses observational data and tape-recordings of conversation, as does the micro-interactional approach. But in addition, information about the social characteristics of speakers and their social contacts is gathered, often through a combination of participant observation and in-depth, ethnographic interviews. Care is taken to ensure that the language data collected from different (groups of) speakers are in some way comparable. This is because the network approach examines inter-speaker (or social) variation as well as intra-speaker (or stylistic) variation in language use. In other words, the social network approach analyses not only *language-in-use* but also *speaker-in-community*.

The present study adopts the social network perspective on language choice. Participant observation has been used to collect data, which is supplemented by information gathered through ethnographic interviews. In this chapter I shall discuss in detail the fieldwork procedures of the present study. Special attention will be given to field relationships between the investigator and the informants and implications of the relationships for the linguistic data which is being collected and which will ultimately be analysed. The chapter will proceed in four sections. In the first two I outline the main features of the methodology of participant observation and discuss the difficulties and need for providing an explicit and systematic account of it. I give a step-by-step report on the fieldwork procedures of the present study in the third section, and in the fourth part I discuss the effects of participant observation on the language behaviours of the informants as well as of the fieldworker.

Features of Participant Observation

Book-length discussions of the strengths of participant observation are provided by Spradley (1980), Agar (1980), and Jorgensen (1989). As far as fieldwork procedure is concerned, the methodology of participant observation contrasts survey research in that data collection and analysis are carried out *consecutively* in the latter but *concurrently* in participant observation. Typically, survey research follows a linear process, which begins with defining a research problem (or problems) and formulating hypothesis. Following that, a research instrument (e.g. a questionnaire) is designed. The fieldworker then goes and collects information from a specific group of subjects sampled according to predefined procedures. Afterwards the data are coded and often computerised. Only then does the analysis begin, with the machine-readable data being manipulated according to some statistical procedure. The conclusions drawn from the analysis usually take the form of statistically valid generalisations on the behaviours of the individuals sampled.

In participant observation, on the other hand, the investigator (participant observer) begins with some general problem in mind, learns something in the field (data collection), tries to make sense of it (analysis), then goes back to see if the interpretation makes sense in the light of new experience (more data collection). The interpretation is refined (more analysis), and so forth.

The methodology of participant observation allows the investigator a flexible approach in obtaining data and is especially appropriate when the phenomenon of interest is somehow obscured from the view of the public or when there are important differences between the views of insiders and outsiders (see further Jorgensen, 1989). It may therefore be considered a promising method of studying ethnic minorities such as the Chinese in Britain which are little known publicly (see further below under 'Stages of Fieldwork').

Although participant observation has been widely adopted as a useful data collecting method in sociolinguistic research, documentation of the actual procedure often lacks explicitness (L. Milroy, Li Wei & Moffatt, 1991). There is usually little detailed, systematic description as to how the fieldworker entered the target setting, what questions have been asked, and how they have been asked, and what effects the relationships between the fieldworker and people in the field have upon the data being collected and ultimately analysed. At this point, I will consider some of the main difficulties in providing systematic and explicit accounts of participant observational research.

Describing Participant Observation: Some Problems

Characteristically, participant observers eat, work, and relax with the people they are studying; they take part in social activities just as everyone else in the field does, and they come to understand the problem they are studying through personal involvement. This experiential wealth tends to present methodological problems to participant observers.

First of all, it is not always predictable what one may find at a specific point in time and whether the finding needs further exploration. Therefore, one cannot plan every detail ahead. Participant observers constantly define and redefine their research questions according to the situation as it is actually happening (Spradley, 1980).

Second, personal experiences are especially difficult to communicate. As we know, in order to understand a message, a certain amount of shared background knowledge is needed. For example, if two people have gone to the cinema together and one of them later comments on it, the other can draw upon the experience to interpret these comments. On the other hand, if one has gone to the cinema alone, and wants to talk about it, he or she has to provide a certain number of details before any comments can make sense to other people. The need for shared experience in effective communication is referred to by ethnomethodologists as indexicality (Garfinkel, 1967). While survey methods are relatively easy to 'de-indexicalise' (for example, questionnaires and censuses can be reproduced as appendices to a research report), personal experiences are not. Sometimes what participant observers regard as significant may turn out to be totally irrelevant to some others, while what they consider as trivial may in fact be most interesting to others.

Third, participant observers tend to have their individual territories in which social relationships with the people they are studying are developed through long-term personal involvements. Such territories are often personalised and imply sets of rights and obligations (L. Milroy, 1987a). It would be extremely difficult, if not impossible, for another researcher to replicate a participant observational study in the way survey researchers often do to check each others' reported results (Agar, 1980). In fact, participant observers seldom attempt to replicate each others' studies. Consequently, a reflective account of how the many conversations, observations, and interviews are conducted during the participant observation is not a high-priority task.

Fourth, participant observers tend to support or argue with each other by presenting new empirical findings from different situations. Their debates are different from those among survey researchers, which can usually be traced to the defects of specific questions asked and the way they are asked. Participant observers are more concerned with the substance of the information they are gathering than with the general procedures by which it is obtained.

In view of comparative analysis, sociolinguists who use participant observation as their main data-collecting method are becoming increasingly aware of the importance of being explicit and systematic about their fieldwork procedures (e.g. L. Milroy, Li Wei & Moffatt, 1991). Agar (1980), who sees the traditional methodological implicitness of participant observation as a more general problem of ethnographic research, argues that much more attention should be paid to the role of the investigator in field research, his or her relationships with the people in the field, and the effects on the data being collected and ultimately analysed. This will mean that information generated from various case studies can be in some way comparable or is capable of being related to wider contexts. Poplack (1983, 1988) has elaborated on the way different methods of data collection can lead to quite different findings on code-switching behaviour, sometimes even of the same speakers. Gal (1988) also has discussed the question of data comparability, emphasising the need to embed small-scale ethnographic descriptions within a wider social, political and historical context.

It is also worth commenting here that at a more practical level participant observers are under pressure to increase their methodological explicitness in order to gain public credibility. Given the current socio-political climate in Britain (and no doubt in other countries too), scientific research cannot receive institutional support unless it systematises itself according to certain prescribed criteria. As Agar (1980: 10) points out, if a grant-giving agency has to choose between a survey which asks the wrong questions very explicitly and an observational study which has the right questions in the mind of the fieldworker but does not tell how they are asked and of whom, it is more likely to be the survey that gets the financial support (see also Bilton *et al.*, 1987: 502–7).

This does not at all mean that participant observers should stop using the traditional approach outlined above. Indeed, participant observation offers a unique perspective which no other methods can replace. L. Milroy (1987b: 78) summarises three chief advantages of this procedure with reference to sociolinguistic research:

- The very high quality of the data in terms of capacity to provide a good sample of everyday language.
- The insight it is capable of yielding into the social and communicative norms of the community. Under this head is included not only information on informal social ties and organisation, but also the fields of study generally described as 'the ethnography of speaking' and 'interactional sociolinguistics'.
- The possibility of explaining why a speaker's language occupies a particular position in a wider social structure.

The essential point here is that participant observers must try to give explicit and systematic accounts of how the fieldwork is done so that their findings could have a wider applicability. I shall attempt in the following section to provide such an account of the fieldwork procedures used in the present study of language choice in the Tyneside Chinese community. Particular attention will be paid to the difficulties encountered during the fieldwork and the steps undertaken to overcome them.

Stages of Fieldwork

The fieldwork for the present study formally started in November 1988 and lasted for about 18 months (L. Milroy & Li Wei, 1990). However, contacts with the community began much earlier and are still maintained. It was decided that participant observation was the most appropriate fieldwork method for two reasons:

- Chinese communities in Britain are largely unknown with regard to their internal structuring and their norms and values. Participant observation permits flexibility in accessing the target community and offers an 'insider' view of it.
- The present study aims to discover language choice patterns and social contacts of a Chinese community at the micro-interactional level. Participant observation allows the researcher to document and interpret social behaviours in naturally occurring contexts.

The observation proceeded in three stages: descriptive, focused, and selective,

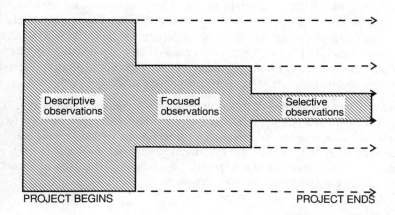

Descriptive observations

Focused observations

Selective observations

PROJECT BEGINS   PROJECT ENDS

Source: Adapted from Spradley, 1980
Participant observation begins with wide-focused *descriptive observations*. Although these continue until the end of the field project, as indicated by the broken lines, the emphasis shifts first to *focused observations* and later to *selective observations*.

Figure 3.1 Stages of participant observation

along the lines suggested by Spradley (1980) (see Figure 3.1). What this amounts to here is that I began with wide-focused observation, aiming to get an overview of the demography of the Chinese communities in Britain and those in Tyneside in particular. Much of the discussion in Chapter 2, especially that in the last section, is based upon information obtained during this stage of the field-work. Two specific findings from the descriptive observation phase are crucial for the subsequent stages of the fieldwork. First, the family is the primary and central unit of social organisation. Second, there seem to be certain differences in patterns of socialisation and language use by different generations of speak-ers, especially between the emigrants and the British-born.

On the basis of these findings (already discussed in some detail in Chapter 2), I decided to use the family as the starting point and basic unit for the second stage of participant observation. Attention was focused on speaker variations in language choice patterns with different types of interlocutors and on social net-work ties of members of different generations. Ten families with members from the three generation cohorts were selected (30 males + 28 females = 58; see Appendix I for details). In addition to direct observation, informal interviews were conducted to gather information on social network ties of the people under investigation (see further below).

Then, having identified the general patterns of language choice on a relatively gross level, the scope of the fieldwork was further narrowed to allow selective observation of specified linguistic behaviour at the interactional level in a more or less comparable setting. At this stage, I concentrated on code-switching in inter-generational conversations. Some 23 hours of tape-recordings of spontaneous conversation involving different family members were made (see further below).

As we can see, this fieldwork procedure involves a dialectic process of data collection and data analysis. The choice of what to observe depends on what has been observed and understood. Descriptive observations of the social context continue even when the scope of the investigation becomes narrower and more focused. I shall now consider some specific issues arising from the fieldwork procedure, beginning with gaining entry to families.

Gaining access to families

The decision to use the family as the starting point and basic unit for investigation requires careful choice of entry strategies, because the family is a 'backstage' of social life which is usually invisible and closed from the view of the general public. Goffman (1959, 1963) distinguishes social life into visible 'frontstage' and such concealed 'backstage' aspects. Generally speaking, entry to visible 'frontstage' situations is open to anyone willing to become a participant. The 'backstage' aspects of social life, on the other hand, are usually concealed from the view of all but the most trusted members. Accurate and dependable information about such situations cannot be gathered unless the investigator becomes an 'insider' (see also Jorgensen, 1989). Gaining access to 'backstage' situations is one of the most difficult and demanding aspects of participant observation.

Jorgensen (1989) identifies two basic entry strategies, *overt* and *covert*. When permission to study is sought openly, the strategy is overt. This direct approach raises few ethical problems, and when permission is granted can yield relevant information within a short time (see also Whyte, 1984). However, it is not always possible to negotiate overt entry, and once the fieldworker is denied access, it may not then be possible to gain subsequent entry. For example, Pong (1991) reports that when she first telephoned the Chinese families whom she wanted to interview for her study of language attitude and use, she was invariably refused permission because they did not know her personally. Her 'official' introduction letters did not help her in any way; rather, they led the families to link her with government-sponsored agencies. She then tried to contact families through leaders of community organisations. Again, she met with marked reluctance to co-operate, because many people rarely took part in organised events outside their immediate families. Eventually, Pong obtained the help of a

Chinese health worker who had personal contacts with individual families. Together they visited the families and offered help of various kinds over a period of time. Only then could she obtain the necessary consent to conduct a questionnaire survey.

The alternative entry strategy is covert, in which case the fieldworker assumes some participant role provided by the setting first and begins formal research when some kind of informal and mutually beneficial relationship is established with the people in the field. Some researchers become involved with a community as a matter of personal interest, only later deciding to conduct participant observational studies. An example of a semi-covert entry strategy is provided by Milroy (1987a) who assumed the role of a second-order member of the localised social networks (see also Boissevain, 1974). She rapidly became enmeshed in the exchange and obligation relationships with the people whose language behaviour she was studying. Many families regarded her as someone with whom they could talk through personal problems arising from the conflicts in working-class Belfast. In return she obtained a substantial amount of high-quality vernacular data. A similar approach was used by Kerswill (1985) in his study of the Strils dialect in Bergen, Norway.

Any kind of covert approach, however, is viewed by some as totally unethical, because it violates the principle of 'informed consent' (see Bulmer, 1982). Since people in the field are not told of the research objectives, they are unable in advance to agree or to refuse to participate in the research. To counter this criticism, some researchers have argued that unlike survey research, participant observation does not have human 'subjects'; rather, situations in which human beings are involved are observed under otherwise natural conditions. People are not manipulated or controlled in any way as in other kinds of (sometimes intrusive) research procedures (Agar, 1980). Furthermore, participant observers are generally careful to respect the dignity and anonymity of the people being observed, often performing services in exchange for information (see also Spradley, 1980). L. Milroy (1987a), for example, offered miscellaneous help with transport or with filling in complicated official forms to the families she was studying, and made sure that sensitive information recorded on tape was wiped off even before leaving the house. Although the covert approach is therefore a rather contentious issue, most researchers agree that it is often essential for acquiring truthful information in publicly invisible and closed situations. It has been adopted in sociolinguistic investigations of rural, working class and ethnic minority communities with impressive results (for further discussions see Milroy, 1987b).

The decision to choose an overt or a covert entry strategy involves more than a choice of theoretical stance. It has to take into account the characteristics of the target setting as well as norms and values of the people in the field. In rural, or urban working-class and ethnic minority communities, for example, a clear distinction is often maintained between 'members' (or insiders) and 'non-members' (outsiders) (Edwards, 1986). Researchers of urban, educated backgrounds from the majority ethnic group are likely to encounter suspicion, if not open hostility, and an overt entry approach is generally not preferred (Nuffield Foundation, 1981). However, such researchers may have difficulty in adopting a covert approach because their socially defined role (and sometimes their distinctive physical appearance) makes it impossible for the people in the field to accept them as an 'insider'. Moffatt (1990), for example, reports in her study of a Pakistani community in Newcastle upon Tyne that as a white, British, monolingual investigator, she could not become an 'insider' of the target community, although she points out that her 'outsider' status actually gave her more freedom to come and go into homes than, for example, a young male Muslim 'insider'.

The present study has adopted a covert approach, making use of roles readily provided by the social context. During a period of three years of residence on Tyneside prior to the formal investigation, I had become friendly with a number of Chinese families who invited me to meals and asked me to look after their houses when they went on holidays. Since I had a degree in English (in fact I was the only Chinese with such a qualification in Newcastle at the time), I was often asked by Chinese adults to help with English language problems — for example, on visits to their doctors and solicitors. Local Chinese businesses and community organisations also asked me to translate letters, leaflets and other documents. At weekends I taught in a Chinese language school in Newcastle where the British-born children were learning their ethnic language. All these contacts enabled me to establish a firm footing within the local community. When I subsequently decided to conduct a study of language choice patterns of different generations in the Chinese families, I was generally given full co-operation and support.

Politics of field relationships

The relationship between the fieldworker and the people in the field is often political in character and is affected by many factors (Punch, 1986). While it usually is not easy to establish and sustain genuine rapport with people of disparate social backgrounds and positions, under certain circumstances people find it to their advantage to underplay differences and emphasise whatever they have in common. The acceptance of me as a friend by the Chinese families on Tyneside is an interesting case in point.

As has been described in Chapter 2, various internal divisions exist within the Chinese population in Britain: Hong Kong Chinese versus mainland Chinese versus Singaporan and Malaysian Chinese; rural emigrants versus urban students versus professionals; Cantonese Punti versus Hakka versus fishermen, and so forth. While all these divisions are recognised by the Chinese in the UK, some are apparently perceived to be much more significant than others. For example, the dichotomy between those from rural and those from urban parts of Hong Kong is regarded as one of the most important divisions among the Chinese communities in Britain. The rural, New Territories emigrants are mostly from agricultural or fishing backgrounds. Many of them experienced considerable hardship in the 1940s and 1950s before emigration and could not find employment in industrialising Hong Kong; indeed many left their homeland for that reason. In Britain, the majority of these rural emigrants are involved in the catering trade. In order to earn a reasonable living and achieve better education for their children, they have to work extremely hard in the family-based restaurant and take-aways. In comparison, students from urban Hong Kong and other parts of Southeast Asia are normally from families which are wealthy enough to send them to study abroad. They do not appear to appreciate the hard-working life style of the Chinese emigrants in Britain. Consequently, there is an evident lack of empathy and interaction between the rural emigrants and urban students and professionals from Hong Kong (see also Chapter 2).

Perhaps more significantly, however, the emigrants tend to regard the students and professionals as potential economic and social rivals. With high qualifications and professional skills, some students are likely to seek employment in Britain after completing their studies. Although few of them intend to join the catering trade and compete directly with the emigrants, their increasing number may give rise to hostile attitudes towards the Chinese as a whole in British society, which may in turn affect the welfare of the emigrants. Here, it has to be said that the recent decision by the British government to grant some high-rank Hong Kong Chinese professionals the right of abode and the public debate aroused by this decision has probably not helped the situation in a positive way.

The Chinese from mainland China, on the other hand, seem to be more acceptable to the emigrants. The majority of mainland Chinese in Britain, particularly young students, arrive with very limited funds. In order to support themselves, they often seek occasional jobs in restaurants and take-aways run by the Chinese emigrants from rural Hong Kong. They generally seem to have a better understanding of the life and experiences of the emigrants than their counterparts from urban Hong Kong. Furthermore, their numbers are small and due to immigration restrictions few of them stay in Britain for any lengthy period. They therefore do not appear to present a threat to the social and economic position of the New Territories Chinese emigrants. Consequently, the emigrants seem to be more at ease with mainland Chinese than with urban, educated students and professionals from Hong Kong (see also Pong, 1991). This appears to have affected my position when I first arrived in Newcastle upon Tyne in 1986. Many Chinese emigrant families invited me to their homes and offered me lodging, daily necessities and odd jobs in their family-run restaurants and take-aways chiefly because I came from mainland China and was thought to be in need of their help.

Linguistic background of the fieldworker

Another factor which may affect field relationships is the linguistic background of the fieldworker. In the existing sociolinguistic literature there is very little detailed documentation of the linguistic background and competence of the fieldworker and its effects on field relationships, although it is generally accepted that if the linguistic competence of the fieldworker is compatible with that of the people being studied, fieldwork should be smoother and more successful. Native competence certainly helps the fieldworker to reveal some of the minute linguistic details, particularly of non-standard language varieties (e.g. Trudgill, 1974). But the number of field linguists who can claim such competence is relatively small. In fact, the majority of existing sociolinguistic studies are carried out by non-native speakers (either of languages or dialects). Moffatt's (1990) study of Punjabi/English-speaking children in Newcastle upon Tyne shows that even monolingual fieldworkers can carry out systematic studies of code-switching and code-mixing successfully, provided they adopt the appropriate procedures.

As has been described in Chapter 2 over 80% of the Chinese residents in the Tyneside area are Cantonese speakers or were born to Cantonese-speaking parents; the rest speak Hakka or some form of Beifang and other regional Chinese languages. This clearly causes difficulties for recruiting appropriate fieldworkers, since a monolingual speaker of any of these varieties may not be able to carry out a study covering different sub-groups. Moreover, in order to include the British-born Chinese in the study, a good command of English is also necessary.

A possible solution to the problem is of course to use a team of fieldworkers with different linguistic backgrounds. Edwards (1986), for example, reports a study of a Black English community which employed more than one fieldworker. While team work has the advantage of being able to divide labour in such a way as to gain more access to the target communities, it also presents potential problems. The most significant is the problem of comparability of data, since differences in gender, age and ethnicity of the fieldworkers may lead to different perspectives on the phenomenon being investigated. While such different perspectives are themselves valuable information, they may create problems in interpreting data. Due to the availability of appropriate fieldworkers and constraints on finance and time, the fieldwork of the present study

Table 3.1 Linguistic background of the speaker sample:

	Male	Female
First Chinese language:		
Cantonese	29	26
Hakka	1	2
Second Chinese language:		
Cantonese	1	0
Hakka	2	4
Mandarin	8	6
Others	3	4

was carried out by myself, with occasional assistance from local Chinese residents and Hong Kong students for specific tasks (e.g. checking transcripts of conversational data, recording information about social networks of individuals and families).

As Table 3.1 shows, the linguistic backgrounds of the ten families who were studied are especially complicated. Of the sample of 58 people, 55 are native Cantonese speakers, of whom seven are monolinguals (two males and five females). The remaining three claim to speak Hakka as their first language, of whom two (both are female) are monolinguals. A further six of the 55 Cantonese-speakers also speak some Hakka. There are no native speakers of Beifang dialects, but 14 (13 native Cantonese and one Hakka speaker) claim to have some knowledge of Mandarin. Seven (six native Cantonese and one Hakka speakers) also have some knowledge of other spoken Chinese varieties. It is obvious that there was no way that I could master all these language varieties in time for the study. In the event, I spoke Cantonese, Mandarin, and English, and very often a mixture of all these, according to the addressee's linguistic background and preference (see further below).

It is also worth pointing out that as a Mandarin speaker my efforts to learn and speak Cantonese in the field were taken as a gesture of friendship and solidarity. I was told that in the past the families had come across very few Mandarin speakers who wanted to do this. The general attitude among native Chinese speakers is that Cantonese is no more than a regional spoken variety, whereas Mandarin is the standard, pan-Chinese language (see also Chapter 2). It is therefore quite acceptable, and in some cases desirable, for native Cantonese speakers to learn to speak Mandarin, while it is usually considered 'a waste of time' for a Mandarin speaker to learn Cantonese.

An additional point here is that as a non-native speaker of Cantonese, I could spend more time listening to the family members talk among themselves without directly engaging myself in the conversation. This gave me more freedom and opportunities to observe and record spontaneous speech.

Gender issues in field relationships

One further factor which may affect field relationships and ultimately the linguistic data that is being collected is the gender of the fieldworker. While in many situations, female fieldworkers present a less threatening image than males, in others their gender may seriously limit what can be observed (Warren, 1988). Moffatt (1990) reports, for example, that in Pakistani communities male outsiders, regardless of age and ethnicity, would not be allowed into the house without the presence of male members of the family. A male fieldworker could therefore not be able to conduct interviews or make observations in a domestic setting as Moffatt was able to do. Yet, both So (1989) and Pong (1991) report particular difficulties for female fieldworkers working within the Chinese community, because Chinese culture traditionally attaches much more importance to males than to females and women are not normally considered competent for non-domestic work. Although it is difficult to claim that being a male fieldworker has had any overt advantage for my investigation, my experience was unlike that of So and Pong in that the families expressed no doubts of my academic ability, even though few of them actually understood the nature of the current study.

While social status, linguistic background, gender, and other factors clearly affect field relationships, much depends also upon the personality of the fieldworker. There is no ideal candidate for field research. Successful field relationships require the investigator's sensitivity to the ongoing situation and willingness to overcome difficulties.

Tape-recordings of conversation

As a basis for examining the discourse strategies underlying speakers' choice of Chinese and/or English, approximately 23 hours of spontaneous conversation were tape-recorded (Stage III of the fieldwork). A Superscope Professional Cassette Recorder CD-330 was used for making these recordings. This relatively cheap recorder was considered to be adequate, because the focus of the linguistic analysis was primarily on the alternation between two languages in conversation and did not require fine phonetic details. To ensure that the data was reasonably characteristic of normal, everyday behaviour and comparable, I tried to concentrate on a single situation, namely, family meal-time (including periods immediately before and after the meal). This particular situation was chosen because it was a self-contained and highly valued event, where both inter-generational and intra-generational communication took place. However, other settings were not entirely excluded. In fact, recordings were made in a range of situations whenever and wherever appropriate. Detailed analysis of samples of the tape-recorded conversational data is presented in Chapter 6.

In seeking permission to make the tape-recordings, I met no objections from the families. This was partly due to the cordial field relationships that had been built over a long period of social interaction, partly because most Chinese families were used to making tape-recordings of themselves. Many families often make tape-recordings and send them to their relatives in the Far East as substitutes for written letters, which helps overcome problems caused by illiteracy. Indeed, the general public is now quite familiar with tape-recording equipments and much less self-conscious than at the time of Labov's (1966) New York City study. Trudgill (1986b), for example, found a very clear difference in people's responses to being recorded when he revisited Norwich after a period of 18 years from his first study.

An additional point to be made here is that developments in audio technology in the last 20 years have had some significant (but sometimes unnoticed) effects on sociolinguistic fieldwork. Modern radio microphones make it possible to systematically record natural conversations even in the absence of the investigator. This method was used some time ago by Reid (1978) in Edinburgh and Wells (1985) in Bristol, and more recently it has been used in Newcastle by Moffatt (1990) to collect bilingual data from young Pakistani children.

Information on social network ties

In addition to the conversational data described above, information was sought about the participants' social network ties. This information was obtained both by participant observation in various situations and informal ethnographic interviews. These interviews comprise a series of friendly, casual conversations, and are distinguished in a number of ways from structured interviews that are traditionally used in survey research:

- There was no written list of questions. Instead, I prepared a schedule which included the types of information I wanted to obtain.
- There was no planned setting or timetable for the interviews. They took place wherever and whenever appropriate to all parties concerned — at home, in restaurants, streets, shops, and schools.
- They involved both dyadic and multi-party conversations.
- I did not take on the role of interviewer, but of a conversational partner. I answered as well as asked questions.

Although time-consuming, this method proved highly successful. The people whom I interviewed did not feel that they were under pressure. In some cases, they provided detailed accounts of their family background, life in Britain and social contacts without being pressed (for more general discussions of the technique of ethnographic interview see Spradley, 1979; McCracken, 1988). The information given by the families, which forms the basis for the discussion in Chapter 5, was first recorded in a personal diary form, to be later summarised and classified.

Ethical issues

I have already touched upon the question of ethics when adopting a covert participant observation procedure. Unlike, for example, medical researchers, sociolinguists do not have recourse to an agreed ethical code. Some of the general issues concerning the use of candid recording, preservation of anonymity and access to tape-recordings have been discussed in detail by L. Milroy (1987b: 87–93), but they are not all as straightforward in practice as they may appear. There is, for example, a general consensus among sociolinguists that permission to tape record conversational interaction should be sought in advance. Yet, as Milroy (1987a, 1987b) reports in her Belfast study, sometimes the original participants would leave in the course of an extended recording session and other people would join in. Although the recording equipment is not concealed, and is monitored openly by the fieldworker, it is not always clear whether all participants are equally aware of being tape-recorded in situations like this, and it is not usual to interrupt proceedings in order to renegotiate permission to record.

But a more difficult question facing sociolinguistic fieldworkers, especially long-term participant observers, concerns the exchange and obligations relationships with the people they are studying. Very often in casual, friendly conversations, participants will tell stories about themselves and other people which would not normally be told to outsiders. They would expect the fieldworker, whom they regard as a close friend, to keep such stories confidential. During the informal interviews about social network contacts, my informants told me a great deal about relationships between individuals and families within the Tyneside Chinese community. They obviously trusted me not to relate such information to anyone else.

Sometimes during a recording session, certain unexpected events might force the fieldworker to make a decision on the spot as to whether it is appropriate to continue recording. For example, on one occasion while I was making a recording in a family, a quarrel broke out between the spouses. I immediately stopped the recorder and wiped out parts of the tape.

To ensure anonymity of the families and their social contacts whom I studied, I used numbers, letters or pseudonyms. Tape-recordings are carefully vetted for sensitivity of content (e.g. profits of businesses, payments made to chefs in restaurants, and employment of Chinese students in family-run businesses). Access to the original tapes is restricted to the people immediately involved in the research project. Where appropriate, I have let the families see some of the transcripts, figures, and tables which I present in this book.

So far I have looked at ways of gaining access to a target setting, building up appropriate field relationships, and carrying out tape-recording and interviews. In the remainder of this chapter, I want to consider the effects of field relationships upon the linguistic data which is being collected.

Field Relationships and Linguistic Data: The Observer's Paradox Revisited

One of the central concerns of field linguists has always been how to ensure that the linguistic data being collected is reasonably characteristic of speakers' normal language behaviour. Ethnographic linguists such as Hymes (1974) and Gumperz (1982) have repeatedly emphasised the sensitivity of language to situational context, of which the interlocutor (including addressee, auditor, overhearer, and eavesdropper) is a critical component (see also Bell, 1984; Giles & Coupland, 1991). This seems to call both for field methods which reduce the prominence of the investigator, and for analytic procedures which account for his/her interactional role.

The role of the observer has been discussed a great deal by Labov (1966, 1972a, b, c) in terms of the so-called 'observer's paradox', which springs from the effects upon language of direct observation and may be characterised as follows: while the vernacular (i.e. the casual language of everyday interaction) is the focus of the researcher's interest, the act of systematic observation and recording radically alters the character of what is observed. One of the major tasks of a fieldworker who wishes to obtain reasonable quantities of vernacular data may therefore be seen as that of moving towards a resolution of the observer's paradox.

The observer's paradox was originally phrased with reference to the then popular data collecting method of interview in monolingual communities. Labov generally tackled the problem by attempting to redefine the role of the observer, for example, as a conversationalist instead of an interrogator (Labov, 1981). For those who have adopted the micro-interactional approach and have used participant observation to collect conversational data, there seems to be an implicit assumption that the observer is enmeshed in localised social relationships and therefore the effect on linguistic data that is being collected becomes minimal (e.g. Gumperz, 1982). When the role of the observer/analyst is discussed by interactional sociolinguists, the concern seems to be chiefly with demonstrating a relationship between a participant's communicative strategies in a conversational context and the analyst's interpretation (e.g. Auer, 1984a, b). However, an account of the role of the fieldworker and the effects of his or her relationships with the people under investigation needs to be in place before any interpretation of the meaning of specific linguistic behaviour makes sense. Without a clear specification of fieldwork procedures, it is difficult to carry out a comparative analysis of the behaviour of different social groups or of comparable groups in different locations (see also Edwards, 1986).

The observer's paradox afflicts investigations of bilingual communities in a particularly acute form where the sense of ethnicity is strong and the investigator is not an 'insider'. The issue is discussed more thoroughly by Milroy, Li Wei & Moffatt (1991). In the existing sociolinguistic literature on bilingual, ethnic minority communities, a considerable amount of discussion has been devoted to means of reducing the interference of 'outsider' observers with the language behaviour of the people under observation (see, for example, Linguistic Minorities Project, 1985; L. Milroy, 1987b). Although relatively little has been said about the 'insider' observer's effects on linguistic data, examples from the present study suggest that he or she affects the language behaviour of the participants in no less significant way than 'outsiders'. The following is an extract of a conversation between myself and a Chinese woman in her forties, which illustrates that while my personal ties within the local community provided me with smooth access to the family setting which would otherwise be submerged from public view, they constrained in an interesting way my own language use as well as that of the people I was observing.

(1) 1 **Informant:**   *Sik gai a.*
                          (Eat chicken.)
   2 **Fieldworker:**   mm.
   3   (5.0)
   4 **Fieldworker:**   Haven't seen Robert Ng for a long time.
   5   (2.0)
   6 **Fieldworker:**   Have you seen him recently?
   7 **Informant:**   No.
   8 **Fieldworker:**   Have you seen Ah Ching?
   9 **Informant:**   ... (2.0) (To daughter) *Ning ngaw doei haai lai.*
                          (Bring my shoes.)
   10   (To fieldworker) *Koei hoei bindou a?*
                          (Where was she going?)

I was conversing with the informant in Chinese up to Line 2. The pause following my minimal response suggests the end of an interactional episode (L3). At this point, I attempted to introduce a new topic (i.e. the whereabouts of a mutual friend — NB. all personal names in the transcript have been changed to protect the informants' anonymity), and at this topic boundary I switched from Chinese to English (L4). Since the informant gave no response, I reinitiated the topic in English with an interrogative (L6). The response from the informant this time was negative and minimal (L7). I then asked her about a different person (L8). After a short pause, she selected another addressee and code-switched (from English to Chinese) (L9). This strategy excluded me temporarily from the conversation, before she turned back to address me in Chinese (L10).

There are of course various possible reasons for the informant's apparent reluctance to speak English to me, but the most important one here seems to concern the communicative norms governing intra-generational conversation among adults. Inter-generational conversations between adults and children are usually in both Chinese and English, although most adults prefer to speak and to be spoken to in Chinese only. Intra-generational conversation, on the other hand, especially among adults, is most often exclusively in Chinese. Since I was accepted by most families as a friend of the parent generation, my use of English was expected to be confined to conversation with the British-born generation. My use of English to a Chinese adult violated this communicative norm. Consequently, I was met with little co-operation.

What is particularly interesting is the 'change of addressee' strategy accompanied by code-switching which the informant used to handle the situation. This strategy is in fact quite common for Chinese adult speakers who are apparently reluctant to converse in English but who, to preserve interactional equilibrium and the 'face' of the addressee, do not wish to switch back into Chinese with undue abruptness. We can schematise this strategy as follows:

A: Initiation in English
B: No response/dispreferred response in English
A: Re-initiation in English
B: Change of addressee accompanied by a switch to Chinese;
Switch back to A in Chinese

A change of addressee (for whatever reason), along with other kinds of inter-actional boundary, appears to be a common site for code-switching. The consequence of such a discourse strategy is that as a Chinese I could not sustain an exchange in English with a Chinese adult without affecting our relationship (see Eades, 1982, and Briggs, 1986, for more general discussions of discourse strategies of the fieldworker).

It should be pointed out that the relationship between myself and the Chinese adult in the above example was one of equality, in that neither party was of significantly higher status or more powerful than the other. Thus, the informant had to consider preserving the 'face' of the addressee in deciding what discourse strategy to employ (see also Brown & Levinson, 1987). When the relationship between the participants is unequal, quite different strategies may be used, as the following extract shows:

(2) 1 **Mother:**   *Oy-m-oy faan a? Ah Ying a?*
                       (Want some rice?)

   2   (2.0)

   3 **Mother:**   *Chaaufaan a. Oy-m-oy?*
                       (Fried rice. Want or not?)

   4   (2.0)

   5 **Daughter:**   I'll have some shrimps.

   6 **Mother:**   *Mut-ye? (.)   Chaaufaan a.*
                       (What?)   (Fried rice.)

   7 **Daughter:**   *Hai a.*
                       (OK.)

This extract is taken from a conversation between the same female informant in extract (1) above and her 12-year-old daughter. Here, we see that the daughter does not respond to her mother's offer of rice (line 2). The mother asks again and emphasises that it is fried rice as opposed to ordinary boiled rice (L3). The daughter delays her response to the offer (L4) and then requests an alternative to rice (L5). Rather than accepting the daughter's request, the mother repeats her offer of fried rice (L6). The daughter then accepts (with apparent reluctance) the mother's offer (L7).

Remarkably, the daughter chooses to use English to mark her 'dispreferred' response (see further Chapter 6 and Levinson, 1983) in line 5, but then has to switch to Chinese for her final acceptance, whereas the mother insists on the use of Chinese all along. Here, a culturally defined politeness norm is at work. In Chinese culture, direct questions with certain functions (such as offering) made by a person of higher status to a lower status other is generally expected to meet with compliance. Thus, when the mother asks her child whether she wishes to eat rice, a positive response is preferred. The child's response, 'I'll have some shrimp', violates this politeness norm, to the evident irritation of her mother. Furthermore, the daughter's use of English contradicts the mother's choice of language. But the mother is able to use her authority, derived from her generation and age (see Chapter 2), to insist on the daughter's acceptance of her offer and on her switching to Chinese to comply with her own language choice, which contrasts with her strategy of code-switching in extract (1) above where she was addressing me who was of equal status with her.

Although there is nothing particularly unusual about these examples, they do illuminate the effect of interpersonal relationships upon the linguistic data which is being collected and ultimately analysed. An adequate specification of the role of the fieldworker, of his or her relations with the people in the field, and of the overall fieldwork procedures, is clearly needed for the linguistic data to be appropriately interpreted.

I have in this chapter emphasised the need to provide more explicit and systematic exposition of participant observation and field relations so that the linguistic data collected can be interpreted within a clear context, and have tried to offer a detailed account of the fieldwork procedures employed in the present study. I shall now turn my attention to data analysis.

4 Patterns of Language Choice and Language Shift

Scotton (1986) remarks that the analysis of individuals' interactive acts needs to be contextualised within an analysis of the communicative norms of the community in which these individuals live. In other words, an overall model of language choice needs to be in place *prior to* a discussion of conversational code-switching. The purpose of this chapter is to describe language choice patterns of the Chinese emigrants in Britain, using the sample of 58 people from ten Chinese families in the Tyneside area. Code-switching strategies will be discussed after a general picture of language choice patterns of the community is obtained.

The chapter consists of three sections. In the first I examine language choices by members of three generations — grandparents, parents, and children — focusing primarily on speakers' choices of language(s) according to different interlocutors. On the basis of this discussion, a number of language choice patterns are generalised and speakers are grouped according to the linguistic behaviours they display in the second section. The aim of this analysis is to establish whether speakers who make the same choices also share similar characteristics on the social dimension. In the third section I discuss, speakers' ability to use Chinese and/or English for different communicative purposes and go on to relate variations in the language ability of individual speakers to observed patterns of language choice.

Language Choice by Three Generations

The data in this section is drawn from long-term participant observation in a range of situational contexts. Instead of analysing extra-linguistic factors such as topic and setting individually, I shall, following Bell's (1984) audience design theory, concentrating on speakers' language choices in response to different interlocutors, assuming here that non-audience factors are subservient to audience types (see also L. Milroy, 1987b: Ch. 8). Details concerning age, sex, employment, emigration background and duration of residence in the UK of the sample of 58 speakers are provided in Appendix I. Both intra-speaker and inter-speaker variations in language choice by speakers from three generations are examined and are shown in six matrices (see Tables 4.1–4.6), with male and female speakers listed separately. In these matrices, speakers are ranked on the vertical axis, and on the horizontal axis is a list of both family and non–family interlocutors — people with whom the speaker interacts. The list of family members refers to specific individuals in the family (empty cells indicate lack of such relations), while those listed under 'non-family member' are interlocutor types. I have chosen six types of non-family interlocutors who are categorised according to generation and sex. As explained in Chapter 2, in the Chinese cultural context generation and sex usually imply and embody social status. For example, males of the parent generation are normally considered socially higher than females of the same generation and the child generation (either male or female), but lower than the grandparent generation (male or female). The interlocutor types used in the following matrices could therefore be understood as representing higher or lower status relative to the speaker's own social position. Each row of letters in these tables represents the language choices of one speaker, and each letter represents the language(s) chosen — C for Chinese and E for English. If both languages are used, it is indicated by the two letters appearing together. Individual speakers' choice patterns can be read across each row of letters in these tables, while any difference that exists between speakers regarding language choices with a particular (type of) interlocutor can be read down each column.

I shall start with language choices of the ten married couples who constitute the core of the sample, i.e. the parent generation; moving on to consider the choice patterns of the grandparent generation and then the child generation. Each table is followed by a brief description of the variations in language choice patterns of that particular generation. A summary of the overall patterns of the 58 speakers will be given and discussed after each generation has been examined separately.

Parent generation

Table 4.1 presents observed choices of language(s) by ten male speakers of the parent generation (ranked according to age in vertical axis). The numbers in the far left column indicate the families they belong to. Eleven interlocutors are listed here under two categories: 1–5 are family members and 6–11 are non-family members. Within each category, the ones listed on the left are of relatively higher social status (determined by generation and sex) than the ones to the right. Thus males are placed to the left of females and parents are to the left of children.

The table shows that only Chinese is used with female members of the grandparent generation, whether or not they are family members (interlocutors 2 and

Table 4.1 Language choice by ten male speakers of the parent generation

Speakers		Family Members					Non-Family Members				
No.	Age	1	2	3	4	5	6	7	8	9	10	11
6	56	C	—	C	CE	CE	C	C	C	C	CE	CE
9	53	—	C	C	CE	—	C	C	C	C	CE	CE
7	49	—	C	CE	CE	CE	CE	C	CE	CE	CE	CE
3	47	—	C	C	CE	—	C	C	C	C	CE	CE
8	44	CE	C	CE	CE	CE	CE	C	CE	CE	CE	CE
10	44	CE	C	CE	CE	CE	C	C	C	C	CE	CE
2	41	—	—	C	CE	—	C	C	C	C	CE	CE
4	40	—	C	CE	CE	CE	CE	C	CE	CE	CE	CE
5	37	—	C	C	CE	CE	C	C	C	C	CE	CE
1	35	C	—	C	CE	—	CE	C	CE	CE	CE	CE

Interlocutors:
1 = Grandparent, male 2 = Grandparent, female 3 = Spouse (wife) 4 = Child, male 5 = Child, female 6 = Grandparent generation, male 7 = Grandparent generation, female 8 = Parent generation, male 9 = Parent generation, female 10 = Child generation, male 11 = Child generation, female

7). Both Chinese and English are used to children of both sexes whether or not they are family members (interlocutors 4 and 5 are family members, and 10 and 11 are non-family members). Two out of ten speakers (speakers 8 and 10) use both Chinese and English with the male grandparent of the family, while four speakers (7, 8, 10, 4) use both Chinese and English with their wives. Four speakers (7, 8, 4 and 1) use both Chinese and English with non-family members of their own generation (the parent generation), and no one uses only English with any of the interlocutors.

Table 4.2 summarises in the same way observed language choices by the wives of the ten male speakers of the parent generation. Like their husbands, these women use only Chinese with female grandparents, whether or not they are family members (interlocutors 2 and 7). Only Chinese is used also with male members of grandparent generation outside the family (interlocutor 6), in contrast to the four male speakers who use both Chinese and English with male, non-family members of grandparent generation. Two out of ten speakers (speakers 10 and 8) use both Chinese and English with the male grandparents of the

Table 4.2 Language choice by ten female speakers of the parent generation

		Interlocutors									
Speakers		Family Members					Non-Family Members				
No.	Age	1	2	3	4	5	6	7	8	9	10	11
6	52	C	—	C	CE	CE	C	C	C	C	CE	CE
9	50	—	C	C	CE	—	C	C	C	C	CE	CE
3	46	—	C	C	CE	—	C	C	C	C	CE	CE
10	45	CE	C	CE	CE	CE	C	C	C	C	CE	CE
7	42	—	C	CE	CE	CE	C	C	C	C	CE	CE
8	40	CE	C	CE	CE	CE	C	C	CE	CE	CE	CE
2	38	—	—	C	CE	—	C	C	C	C	CE	CE
4	37	—	C	CE	CE	CE	C	C	CE	CE	CE	CE
5	35	—	C	C	CE	CE	C	C	C	C	CE	CE
1	32	C	—	C	CE	—	C	C	C	C	CE	CE

Interlocutors:
1 = Grandparent, male 2 = Grandparent, female 3 = Spouse (husband) 4 = Child, male 5 = Child, female 6 = Grandparent generation, male 7 = Grandparent generation, female 8 = Parent generation, male 9 = Parent generation, female 10 = Child generation, male 11 = Child generation, female

family, i.e. their fathers or fathers-in-law (interlocutor 1); these women are wives of the two men who also use both Chinese and English with male grandparents (see Table 4.1). However, these two female speakers use only Chinese with male members of the grandparent generation outside the family, which is in agreement with the language choice pattern of other women of their generation but differs from the pattern of some of their male counterparts. Four speakers (10, 7, 8, 4) use both Chinese and English with their husbands, and two of them (8 and 4) use both Chinese and English with non-family members of their own generation, both males and females. All speakers, like their husbands, use both Chinese and English with the children, whether or not they are family members, both males and females (interlocutors 4, 5, 10, 11). No one speaks only English to any of the interlocutors.

Comparing the language choice patterns of male and female speakers of the parent generation, the main difference lies in the choice with non-family members of the male grandparent generation and with non-family members of their own generation of both sexes. More men than women use both Chinese and

Table 4.3 Language choice by male grandparents

Speakers		Interlocutors										
		Family Members					Non-Family Members					
No.	Age	1	2	3	4	5	6	7	8	9	10	11
6	73	—	C	C	C	C	C	C	C	C	C	C
10	68	C	CE	CE	CE	CE	C	C	CE	CE	CE	CE
1	66	—	C	C	C	—	C	C	C	C	C	C
8	65	C	CE	CE	CE	CE	C	C	CE	CE	CE	CE

Interlocutors:
1 = Spouse (grandmother of the family) 2 = Parent, male 3 = Parent, female 4 = Child, male 5 = Child, female 6 = Grandparent generation, male 7 = Grandparent generation, female 8 = Parent generation, male 9 = Parent generation, female 10 = Child generation, male 11 = Child generation, female

English (as opposed to Chinese only) with these interlocutors, and women's language choice patterns conform more to those of their own group (i.e. women of the parent generation) than to those of their husbands.

Let us now look at the language choice patterns of the grandparent generation who are the parents (or parents-in-law) of the ten married couples.

Grandparent generation

There are four male and seven female members of the grandparent generation in the sample. Table 4.3 presents observed language choices by the four male grandparent speakers. The format of the matrix remains largely the same as Tables 4.1 and 4.2, except interlocutor 1 now indicates spouses of the grandparents; 2 and 3 the parent generation, who are of course the ten married couples; and 4 and 5 the child generation. The six interlocutor types under the 'non-family members' category have also changed, in relation to the speaker's generation.

As Table 4.3 shows, two speakers (6 and 1) use only Chinese with all interlocutors, while the other two (speakers 10 and 8) use only Chinese with their wives (i.e. grandmothers of the families), and members of their own generation (grandparent generation) who are not family members. These same two speakers (10 and 8) use both Chinese and English with the parents and children of the families, and with members of the parent and child generations outside the family. No one uses only English with any of the interlocutors.

Table 4.4 Language choice by female grandparents

							*Interlocutors*					

Speakers		Family Members					Non-Family Members					
No.	*Age*	*1*	*2*	*3*	*4*	*5*	*6*	*7*	*8*	*9*	*10*	*11*
9	72	—	C	C	C	—	C	C	C	C	C	C
3	70	—	C	C	C	—	C	C	C	C	C	C
7	67	—	C	C	C	C	C	C	C	C	C	C
4	65	—	C	C	C	C	C	C	C	C	C	C
10	63	C	C	C	C	C	C	C	C	C	C	C
8	61	C	C	C	C	C	C	C	C	C	C	C
5	58	—	C	C	C	C	C	C	C	C	C	C

Interlocutors:
1 = Spouse (grandfather of the family) 2 = Parent, male 3 = Parent, female 4 = Child, male 5 = Child, female 6 = Grandparent generation, male 7 = Grandparent generation, female 8 = Parent generation, male 9 = Parent generation, female 10 = Child generation, male 11 = Child generation, female

In contrast, all the seven female grandparents in the sample use only Chinese with all interlocutors, as Table 4.4 shows; no one uses any English at all.

As well as displaying language choice patterns of the speakers of the grandparent generation, these two tables (4.3 and 4.4) help to clarify one aspect of the language choice patterns of the ten married couples, as seen in Tables 4.1 and 4.2, that is, speakers use both Chinese and English with those who themselves use both languages (e.g. male grandparents 8 and 10) and they would speak only Chinese if the interlocutors are themselves Chinese monolinguals (e.g. female grandparents). This pattern confirms Bell's (1984) argument that speakers design their speech according to their audience.

Next examined are the language choice patterns of the child generation, comprising 27 speakers of whom 16 are male and 11 female.

Child generation

Table 4.5 presents observed language choices by the 16 male children. Six family relations are listed here: 1 and 2 indicate grandparents of the families (male to the left of female), 3 and 4 parents, and 5 and 6 siblings. 7–12 are non-family interlocutors of both sexes of the grandparent, parent and child generations.

Table 4.5 Language choice by male children

		Interlocutors											
Speakers		Family Members						Non-Family Members					
No.	Age	1	2	3	4	5	6	7	8	9	10	11	12
9a	24	—	C	CE	CE	CE	—	CE	C	CE	CE	CE	CE
6a	22	C	—	CE	CE	CE	CE	CE	C	CE	CE	CE	CE
9b	22	—	C	CE	CE	CE	—	CE	C	CE	CE	CE	CE
3a	21	—	C	CE	CE	CE	—	CE	C	CE	CE	CE	CE
3b	19	—	C	CE	CE	CE	—	CE	C	CE	CE	CE	CE
7a	18	—	C	CE	CE	CE	CE	CE	C	CE	CE	E	E
9c	18	—	C	CE	CE	CE	—	CE	C	CE	CE	CE	CE
6b	17	C	—	CE	CE	CE	CE	CE	CE	CE	CE	CE	CE
8	16	CE	C	CE	CE	—	CE	CE	C	CE	CE	E	E
10	16	CE	C	CE	CE	—	CE	CE	CE	CE	CE	E	E
2a	15	—	—	CE	CE	CE	—	CE	C	CE	CE	CE	CE
7b	15	—	C	CE	CE	CE	CE	CE	CE	CE	CE	E	E
5	14	—	C	CE	CE	—	CE	CE	CE	CE	CE	E	E
2b	12	—	—	CE	CE	CE	—	CE	C	CE	CE	CE	CE
4	11	—	C	CE	CE	—	CE	CE	C	CE	CE	E	E
1	10	C	—	CE	CE	—	—	CE	CE	CE	CE	CE	CE

Interlocutors (relations to the speaker):
1 = Grandparent, male 2 = Grandparent, female 3 = Parent, male 4 = Parent, female 5 = Brother 6 = Sister 7 = Grandparent generation, male 8 = Grandparent generation, female 9 = Parent generation, male 10 = Parent generation, female 11 = Child generation, male 12 = Child generation, female
The small letter after the number indicates the order of the child in the family, e.g. 9a is the first child of Family 9, 9b the second and 9c the third.

We can see from Table 4.5 that only Chinese is used with grandmothers (interlocutor 2) by all speakers, while three speakers (6a, 6b and 1) use only Chinese with their grandfathers. They are from two families (6 and 1) whose grandfathers use only Chinese with all interlocutors (see Table 4.3). Two speakers (8 and 10), on the other hand, use both Chinese and English with their grandfathers. They are from two families (8 and 10) whose grandfathers use both Chinese and English with all interlocutors except the grandmothers and members of the grandparent generation outside the family (see Table 4.3). This pattern is consistent with that of their parents who also use both Chinese and English to the grandfathers in the two families. All speakers use both Chinese

Table 4.6 Language choice by female children

		Interlocutors											
		Family Members						Non-Family Members					
Speakers													
No.	Age	1	2	3	4	5	6	7	8	9	10	11	12
9a	22	—	C	CE	CE	CE	—	CE	C	CE	CE	CE	CE
10a	21	CE	C	CE	CE	CE	CE	CE	C	CE	CE	CE	CE
6	20	C	—	CE	CE	CE	—	CE	CE	CE	CE	CE	CE
10b	18	CE	C	CE	CE	CE	CE	CE	C	CE	CE	CE	CE
4	15	—	C	CE	CE	CE	—	CE	C	CE	CE	E	E
8a	12	CE	C	CE	CE	CE	CE	CE	C	CE	CE	CE	CE
10c	12	CE	C	CE	CE	CE	CE	CE	C	CE	CE	CE	CE
5a	11	—	C	CE	CE	CE	CE	CE	CE	CE	CE	E	E
7	10	—	C	CE	CE	CE	—	CE	CE	CE	CE	E	E
5b	9	—	C	CE	CE	CE	CE	CE	C	CE	CE	E	E
8b	8	CE	C	CE	CE	CE	CE	CE	C	CE	CE	CE	CE

Interlocutors (relations to the speaker):
1 = Grandparent, male 2 = Grandparent, female 3 = Parent, male 4 = Parent, female 5 = Brother 6 = Sister 7 = Grandparent generation, male 8 = Grandparent generation, female 9 = Parent generation, male 10 = Parent generation, female 11 = Child generation, male 12 = Child generation, female
The small letter after the number indicates the order of the child in the family, e.g. 10a is the first child of Family 10, 10b the second and 10c the third.

and English with male, non-family members of the grandparent generation (interlocutor 7), while 11 speakers use only Chinese with female, non-family members of the grandparent generation (interlocutor 8). The remaining five (speakers 6b, 10, 2a, 7b and 2b) use both Chinese and English with these interlocutors. Both Chinese and English are used also with parents and non-family members of the parent generation (interlocutors 3, 4, 9 and 10), and with siblings, male and female (interlocutors 5 and 6). Ten speakers use both Chinese and English with non-family members of their own generation (interlocutors 11 and 12), and six (speakers 7a, 8, 10, 7b, 5 and 4) use only English with these interlocutors.

The language choice patterns of female speakers of the child generation are broadly similar to those of their male counterparts, as shown in Table 4.6. The total number of these female children in the sample is 11. Five of them from two families (speakers 10a, 10b, 10c, 8a and 8b) use both Chinese and English with their grandfathers (interlocutor 1) and one (speaker 6) uses Chinese only (the rest do not have grandfathers in the family). Three out of ten (speakers 6, 5a and 7) use both Chinese and English with female members of the grandparent generation outside the family (interlocutor 8), and four (speakers 4, 5a, 7 and 5b) use English exclusively with non-family members of the child generation, both male and female (interlocutors 11 and 12).

Summary

The six matrices reveal that all but nine speakers (two male and seven female) vary their language choices according to interlocutor types. Most speakers use both Chinese and English with a range of interlocutors, except when the interlocutors are female grandparents within the family to whom all speakers use Chinese only. However, the most striking variations in language choice patterns these matrix demonstrate are the differences which exist *between* speakers both across and within the three generations. We can see, for example, that all female grandparents speak only Chinese in all situations, while two out of four male grandparents speak both Chinese and English with some interlocutors. In the parent generation, six speakers (four males and two females) use both Chinese and English with members of their own generation outside the family, whereas the other 14 parents speak Chinese only with the same types of interlocutor. In both the parent and grandparent generations, women seem to be more Chinese-oriented than men in terms of their language choice. Moreover, ten out of 27 speakers of the child generation speak only English with their non-family peers, while the rest speak both Chinese and English. Clearly, further analysis is needed to explain inter-speaker variation of the kind we see here.

Language Choice and Speaker Variables

On the basis of the analysis in the last section, I have generalised four patterns of language choice for communication with family members and seven for communication with non-family members. These generalised patterns are shown in Tables 4.7 and 4.8.

In theory, the number of possible distinct language choice patterns is $3^6 = 729$. However, the within-family choice patterns recorded for each of the 58 speakers all conform to one of four distinct types, while the outside-family patterns of the 58 individuals conform to one of seven types, as listed in the tables. In Table 4.7, Pattern 1 indicates the use of Chinese only in all situations. Pattern 2 is a clearly Chinese-dominant pattern. Patterns 3 and 4 can be described as slightly differently balanced bilingual patterns. The same four patterns can also be found in interactions with non-family members (Table 4.8), but in addition Pattern 5 can be distinguished, which suggests the use of both

Table 4.7 Generalised patterns of language choice with family members

	Interlocutors						
	1	*2*	*3*	*4*	*5*	*6*	*No. of speakers*
Pattern 1	C	C	C	C	C	C	9
Pattern 2	C	C	C	C	CE	CE	12
Pattern 3	C	C	CE	CE	CE	CE	26
Pattern 4	C	CE	CE	CE	CE	CE	11

1 = Female grandparent 2 = Male grandparent 3 = Male parent 4 = Female parent 5 = Male child 6 = Female child

Table 4.8 Generalised patterns of language choice with non-family members

	Interlocutors						
	1	*2*	*3*	*4*	*5*	*6*	*No. of Speakers*
Pattern 1	C	C	C	C	C	C	9
Pattern 2	C	C	C	C	CE	CE	14
Pattern 3	C	C	CE	CE	CE	CE	4
Pattern 4	C	CE	CE	CE	CE	CE	18
Pattern 5	CE	CE	CE	CE	CE	CE	3
Pattern 6	C	CE	CE	CE	E	E	5
Pattern 7	CE	CE	CE	CE	E	E	5

1 = Female grandparent generation 2 = Male grandparent generation 3 = Male parent generation 4 = Female parent generation 5 = Male child generation 6 = Female child generation

Chinese and English with all interlocutor types. Patterns 6 and 7 indicate the use of English only with the child generation and either Chinese only or both Chinese and English with female interlocutors of the grandparent generation who are non-family members. These last two patterns can be described as English-dominant bilingual patterns.

Following Edwards' (1986) example, I shall now attempt to establish whether speakers who make the same choices also share similar social characteristics. Notice that the analysis here differs from that in the previous section in that we are now trying to differentiate speakers according to the linguistic behaviours they display, rather than to identify language choice patterns in terms of predefined social grouping. The social characteristics of the speaker which I have examined include age, sex, and duration of residence in Britain. I shall now look at them in turn.

Age

In order to discover the relation between age and language choice patterns of speakers, I have used an Analysis of Variance (ANOVA) procedure. ANOVA is a powerful and versatile statistical technique which can be applied in a number of ways in different research designs. Detailed discussions of this procedure with special references to linguistic research can be found in Butler (1985) and Woods, Fletcher & Hughes (1986). The main objective of the current analysis is to test the extent to which speakers with the same language choice patterns belong to the same age group. This can be achieved by first grouping the speakers according to the language choice patterns they display and calculate the mean age of each group separately. Then the mean ages of different groups are compared with one another to see if they are sufficiently different for us to conclude that speakers who display different language choice patterns in fact represent different age groups. ANOVA would allow us to investigate possible differences between the mean age of several groups, each referring to a different language choice pattern. A statistic known as the F-ratio is produced which takes into account not only the mean age of individual speakers but also the sise of the group and the relative homogeneity of the group, that is the manner in which age of individuals within the group is distributed or varies around the mean. An F-ratio of 5.50, for example, would mean that the differences between groups are 5.5 times greater than the differences within groups. But to find out whether a given F-ratio is significant, an F-distribution table needs to be consulted which gives the significance level associated with that particular F-ratio. 'Significant' here is a technical term meaning that a particular level of F is not the result of chance. It is conventionally accepted that the figure of one in twenty ($p < 0.05$) is the minimum level of probability (that the difference between means could have occurred by chance). All the statistical tests in the present study, including ANOVA, have been carried out on Minitab, an easily learnt, flexible data manipulation software package (Ryan et al, 1985). Table 4.9 below gives the mean age of speakers with different language choice patterns. Results of ANOVA show significant differences in age between speakers who display different language choice patterns ($F = 25.39$ $p < 0.02$ (with family members); $F = 40.60$ $p < 0.02$ (non-family-member interlocutors)). A closer examination of the mean age of each group reveals that greater differences lie between speakers of the first two

Table 4.9 Mean age of speakers of different language choice patterns

	No. of speaker	Group mean age
With family members:		
Pattern 1	9	66.11
Pattern 2	12	43.50
Pattern 3	26	24.08
Pattern 4	11	25.09
With non-family members:		
Pattern 1	9	66.11
Pattern 2	14	44.14
Pattern 3	4	52.50
Pattern 4	18	23.00
Pattern 5	3	15.67
Pattern 6	5	13.80
Pattern 7	5	13.20

patterns and those of Patterns 3 and 4 for family communication, and between speakers of Patterns 1–3 and those of Patterns 4–7 for communication with non-family members. In fact, there is no significant difference in age between speakers of Pattern 3 and Pattern 4 for family communication, or between those of Patterns 5, 6 and 7 for communication with non-family members. On the whole, Chinese-dominant language choice patterns (those listed towards the top of scales in Tables 4.7 and 4.8) are used by older speakers, and the bilingual and English-dominant patterns (the ones listed at the lower parts of the scales) are adopted by younger speakers. There is, however, one interesting variation in the choice patterns with non-family members. As we can see in Table 4.9, speakers of Pattern 3 for communication with non-family-member interlocutors are much older (on average) than Pattern 2 speakers. To account further for this particular variation, other social characteristics of the speakers have been examined.

Sex

Table 4.10 shows the numbers of male and female speakers who make the same language choices with family and non-family members. We can see here that considerably more male speakers than female speakers fall into Pattern 3 for communication with family members and Pattern 4 for non-family communication with non-family members, while the percentage of women who fall into Pattern 1 is considerably higher than that of men. These figures suggest that

Table 4.10 Distribution of male and female speakers of different language choice patterns

	Male		Female		Total
With family members:					
Pattern 1	2	(6.7)	7	(25.0)	9
Pattern 2	6	(20.0)	6	(21.4)	12
Pattern 3	18	(60.0)	8	(28.6)	26
Pattern 4	4	(13.3)	7	(25.0)	11
With non-family members:					
Pattern 1	2	(6.7)	7	(25.0)	9
Pattern 2	6	(20.0)	8	(28.6)	14
Pattern 3	2	(6.7)	2	(7.1)	4
Pattern 4	12	(40.0)	6	(21.4)	18
Pattern 5	2	(6.7)	1	(3.6)	3
Pattern 6	3	(10.0)	2	(7.1)	5
Pattern 7	3	(10.0)	2	(7.1)	5

Total: 30 males and 28 females; percentage in brackets

male speakers tend more than female speakers to adopt the bilingual language choice patterns, while more female speakers have remained largely Chinese monolingual. However, Patterns 5, 6, and 7 which relate to communication with non-family members show that there is little difference in the number of male and female speakers who adopt the English-dominant patterns.

At this point, I will consider the interaction between the two variables of age and sex in relation to language choices of the speakers.

Age and sex

Table 4.11 gives the mean age of male and female speakers of different language choice patterns.

A series of t-tests were carried out in order to compare the mean ages of male and female speakers of each language choice pattern. Significant differences are found only for Pattern 3 and Pattern 4 speakers for communication with non-family member interlocutors ($t = 13.2$ $p < 0.0057$ (Pattern 3); $t = 2.69$ $p < 0.017$ (Pattern 4)), and in both cases men are older than women. Notice that the mean age of male Pattern 3 speakers for non-family communication is much higher than that of Pattern 2 speakers, while their female counterparts who fall into Pattern 3 are younger than those who fall into Pattern 2. This finding helps to

Table 4.11 Mean age of male and female speakers of different language choice patterns

	Males		Females	
	No. of speakers	*Group mean age*	*No.of speakers*	*Group mean age*
With family members:				
Pattern 1	2	69.5	7	65.1
Pattern 2	6	44.8	6	42.2
Pattern 3	18	25.6	8	20.8
Pattern 4	4	30.0	7	22.3
With non-family members:				
Pattern 1	2	69.5	7	65.1
Pattern 2	6	46.3	8	42.5
Pattern 3	2	66.5	2	38.5
Pattern 4	12	26.8	6	15.5
Pattern 5	2	13.5	1	20.0
Pattern 6	3	15.0	2	14.7
Pattern 7	3	15.0	2	10.5

clarify one aspect of Table 4.9 where the mean age of Pattern 3 speakers is much higher than that of Pattern 2 speakers. Analysis of the interaction between age and sex shows that the main reason for this variation is that some older male speakers have adopted a bilingual language choice pattern, whereas women of similar age use only or mainly Chinese patterns.

Duration of residence in the UK

Apart from age and sex, duration of residence in Britain of the speakers was examined to see whether differences in patterns of language choice were associated with differences in the length of stay in an English-dominant environment. Table 4.12 gives the average number of years of residence in Britain by speakers of different language choice patterns.

Statistical tests show no significant difference in duration of stay between speakers of the four language choice patterns for communication with family members. But the difference between speakers of the seven language choice patterns for communication with non-family members in terms of length of residence in Britain is significant ($F = 6.99$ $p < 0.02$), with Pattern 3 speakers having had a much longer stay (on average) than the other speakers.

Table 4.12 Average years of residence in Britain by speakers of different language choice patterns

	No. of speakers	*Average years of stay*
With family members:		
Pattern 1	9	15.22
Pattern 2	12	22.00
Pattern 3	26	17.78
Pattern 4	11	18.27
With non-family members:		
Pattern 1	9	15.22
Pattern 2	14	22.71
Pattern 3	4	33.00
Pattern 4	18	18.17
Pattern 5	3	15.67
Pattern 6	5	13.80
Pattern 7	5	13.20

Remarkably, the average years of residence in Britain of speakers of Patterns 6 and 7 — the English-dominant patterns — are the shortest of all speakers, while speakers with the longest duration of stay are those who use Patterns 2 and 3 — the Chinese-dominant bilingual patterns.

However, these figures obscure one important fact that speakers came to Britain at different ages; some were much older than others. Futhermore, there are 27 speakers in the sample who are British-born. It is therefore important to examine the interaction between duration of residence, age and sex of the speaker in relation to language choice patterns.

Duration of residence, age and sex

For this part of the analysis, speakers of various language choice patterns are examined in terms of their age at which they arrived in Britain (current age minus years of stay). Table 4.13 gives the mean age at arrival in Britain of male and female speakers of different language choice patterns.

Table 4.13 shows that those who have remained Chinese monolingual (Pattern 1) or have maintained the Chinese-dominant language choice patterns arrived in Britain at a much older age than speakers of bilingual and English-dominant patterns, suggesting once again that age is a more important variable. Sex differentiation is not statistically significant, as investigated by *t*-test, except

Table 4.13 Mean age at arrival in Britain of male and female speakers of different language choice patterns

	Males		Female	
	No. of speakers	Group mean age	No. of speakers	Group mean age
With family members:				
Pattern 1	2	58.50	7	48.23
Pattern 2	6	22.17	6	20.83
Pattern 3	18	7.11	8	5.13
Pattern 4	4	8.25	7	6.00
With non-family members:				
Pattern 1	2	59.50	7	48.43
Pattern 2	6	21.50	8	21.38
Pattern 3	2	39.00	2	18.50
Pattern 4	12	7.25	6	0.00
Pattern 5	2	0.00	1	0.00
Pattern 6	32	0.00	2	0.00
Pattern 7	3	0.00	2	0.00

($F = 12.76$ $p < 0.02$ (Male; with family members) $F = 20.93$ $p < 0.02$ (Male; with non-family members) $F = 36.14$ $p < 0.02$ (Female; with family members) $F = 60.28$ $p < 0.02$ (Female; with non-family members))

for speakers of Patterns 3 and 4 (with non-family members) who tend to be males rather than females.

In sum, variations in language choice pattern are found to be associated primarily with age, with older speakers using either Chinese only or the Chinese-dominant language choice patterns, and the younger adopting either bilingual or English-dominant patterns. Generally speaking, sex and length of stay in Britain do not appear to affect significantly language choice of the speaker, except that more older male speakers than female speakers have adopted bilingual patterns and that those who remained Chinese monolingual or Chinese dominant were much older when they came to Britain. The findings as a whole suggest that a language shift from Chinese monolingualism to English-dominant bilingualism is taking place in the Tyneside Chinese community within the span of three generations.

To explore further this apparent language shift, individual speakers' abilities to use Chinese and/or English for various communicative purposes were investigated. The basic assumption here is that a bilingual's language use depends to a large extent upon his or her language ability; as Spolsky (1988) suggests, speakers normally prefer to use the language they know better for a particular communicative task. While language ability does not offer a complete explanation of language choice, it can illuminate the pattern of language shift that is taking place in the Tyneside Chinese community. This variable will be discussed in detail in the following section.

Variation and Change in Language Ability Across Generations

Assessing language ability of bilingual speakers has long been an active area of debate among psychologists, applied linguists, and sociolinguists. Generally speaking, psychologists are concerned not with the actual use of languages but with the psychological state of the individuals who have access to more than one linguistic code, which Hamers & Blanc (1989) refer to as *bilinguality* rather than bilingualism (see also Mackey, 1962). A number of experimental tests to assess bilinguality are available, including, for example, reaction or latency-time tests, completion and word-detection tests, verbal association tests.[1] Although these psychometric measures have produced many interesting findings, their general applicability is questionable. Special difficulties arise when the test subjects are speakers from ethnic minority communities, since many ethnic minority children follow curricula in the language of the majority and may not have reached the level of language development required for the experimental measures to be valid by the time that the tests are administered. Moreover, cultural differences between social groups may also affect test results. If, for example, one wants to discover the knowledge of vocabulary of a linguistic minority child but presents him or her with pictures of objects familiar in the majority culture, as in the Peabody Picture Vocabularly Test (Dunn, 1959), but which are unfamiliar in the child's own culture, his or her lack of response offers no assessment value. Indeed, Fishman (1968) regards many of the experimental tests devised by language psychologists as ethnocentric and quite inappropriate for assessing the actual language ability of bilinguals (for comments on the psychological assessments of bilinguality see Baetens Beardsmore, 1986).

Applied linguists, on the other hand, are concerned with language acquisition and development of bilingual speakers within the context of education. Formal testing plays a very important role. Speakers are measured according to unilingual norms rather than the specificity of bilingual behaviour (Rivera, 1983; Baetens Beardsmore, 1986). While standard testing practices now in place in schools may be a useful means of reporting on learner status (e.g. by providing norm-referenced information on learner ranking), they often provide inaccurate information about speakers' skills of language use in social interaction.

Here, the distinction drawn by Wald (1981) between *language proficiency* and *language ability* is of particular relevance. Language proficiency normally refers to the mastery of the language code (verbal or non-verbal), and thus concerns mainly such features as lexical items and rules of sentence formation, pronunciation, and literal meaning. It may also include the use of cohesion devices to relate utterance forms (e.g. pronouns, transition words, and parallel structures) and coherence rules to organise meanings (e.g. repetition, progression, consistency, and relevance of ideas). Language proficiency can usually be gained through formal learning and can be measured by standardised tests. Language ability, on the other hand, is 'the actual knowledge a speaker has of a language which is made use of in a variety of situations' (Wald, 1981: 2). It is usually acquired through socialisation, and cannot properly be assessed out of context. As Wald argues, formal, standardised assessment procedures which focus on language proficiency tend to underestimate ability, particularly of speakers from socially underprivileged backgrounds, because they generally cannot discriminate between non-standard, stigmatised vernacular form and under-developed forms (see also Lavandera, 1978; Martin-Jones & Romaine, 1985; L. Milroy, 1985).

Since the beginning of the 1980s, there has been a growing awareness among applied linguists of the potential applications of sociolinguistic methods and principles to the task of bilingual assessment (see, for example, Rivera, 1983). The main attraction of a sociolinguistic orientation is its emphasis on the overall skill in *using* language for natural purposes in realistic situations and the way(s) in which the investigator/assesser collects and interprets/assesses data. Rather than setting out standards in advance and testing how near the subjects are to these standards, sociolinguists typically define communicative norms on the basis of detailed observation of social interaction and take into account both stylistic (or intra-speaker) and social (inter-speaker) variations (see further Preston, 1989).

In the present study, I have adopted the sociolinguistic principles of assessing language ability of the speaker in use and have tried to examine whether or not individual speakers can use Chinese and/or English to perform a range of practical, communicative tasks. On the basis of extensive participant observation, I have designed four six-point scales, going from zero to five, to measure individual speakers' ability to use spoken Chinese, written Chinese, spoken English, and written English respectively. Each scale consists of five conditions and every speaker is assigned one point for each condition he or she satisfies. The resulting scores are used to construct language ability indices in which speakers are rated from zero (fulfilling none of the five conditions) to five (fulfilling all conditions). The five conditions according to which the speaker's spoken and written language ability is assessed are as follows:

Spoken language (for both Chinese and English):
1. Can understand routine greetings, simple questions and statements (e.g. questions and statements about weather, health, prices of goods in shops, etc.).
2. Can answer such simple questions and make simple statements.
3. Can partake in casual conversation (usually about domestic topics among friends).
4. Can understand radio and television programmes, films (including videos), and (where applicable) speeches at formal or festive gatherings (e.g. Chinese New Year receptions).
5. Can communicate effectively and with general ease in a range of social contexts.

Written language (for both Chinese and English):
1. Can read simple signs and notices (e.g. in streets and shops).
2. Can write own name and a few simple words.
3. Can fill in simple forms and write informal letters.
4. Can read books, newspapers, magazines, and formal business documents.
5. Can effectively fulfil a range of tasks which requires the use of written language.

Conditions 1 and 2 (for both spoken and written languages) are chosen to indicate that the speaker has the ability to comprehend and to use the language for basic communicative tasks. Anyone who cannot fulfil these conditions (zero score) would be considered as having no ability to use the language. Condition 3 is used as an indicator for average language ability, and Conditions 4 and 5 for above average and near native ability. It must be emphasised here that these conditions are not designed as indicators of speakers' linguistic competence (Chomsky, 1965). They are not used to examine the mental disposition of the bilingual speaker or the complexity or well-formedness of the linguistic structures he or she produces. Rather, they are intended to reflect particular uses of the language for different communicative purposes and are empirically defined measures which are commonly used by members of the community themselves in judging others' as well as their own language ability. During my fieldwork, I found that people often made comments such as 'She speaks good English' and 'His Chinese isn't very good'. When asked about their criteria for such judgements they would say 'She talks to English people'; 'She reads English newspapers'; or 'He can only write his name in Chinese'; 'He doesn't understand Chinese films'. Given the fact that many of the speakers have not received any formal education either in Chinese or in English or both, it would be quite unreasonable to subject them to standardised language tests.

Nevertheless, these measures do reflect, to some extent, the speaker's sociolinguistic knowledge. As far as spoken language is concerned, the measures are designed to reflect the mastery of conversational rules by individual speakers. For example, a speaker who fulfils condition 5 for spoken English must be aware of the paired structure of conversational interaction and of the preferred versus dispreferred second pair parts, pre and embedded sequences, etc., whereas a speaker who fulfils condition 2 would not have such knowledge, except that he or she is aware of the basic turn-taking routine. The question of spoken language ability cannot fully be discussed without reference to specific conversational data, and I shall do this in Chapter 6 when I examine in detail speakers' code-switching strategies. For the moment, we shall look at language ability in fairly general terms, using the measures described above.

One other point to be made before we look at individual speakers' scores is that in the existing literature on language choice and language shift in linguistic minority communities, bilingual speakers' ability to use written language(s) has not been subjected to the same vigorous and systematic examinations as their ability to use spoken language(s). Yet bilinguals, especially young bilinguals, can very often speak two languages with similar degree of fluency while being literate in only one — usually the language they learn in school. More importantly perhaps, members of bilingual communities do seem to regard the ability to read and write as an indicator of a speaker's communicative competence. Taylor (1987) points out that in communities such as the Chinese where written language becomes a symbol of traditional culture (see also Martin-Jones, 1984), a reduction or loss of ability to read and write their ethnic language may take on particular social significance for the members of those communities. As the Linguistic Minorities Project (1985) argues, the speaker's bi-literacy level ought to be examined as part of an overall assessment of bilinguals' language ability (see also Williams & Snipper, 1990). Thus, I have included the use of written languages (Chinese and English) in my observation and assessment in the present study.

Detailed scores of individual speakers on the four language ability scales can be seen in Appendix II. Tables 4.14 and 4.15 present the four language ability indices for male and female speakers.

To investigate the relationships between the four sets of indexes and to establish whether differences in the language ability scores are related to differences in speakers' social characteristics such as age, sex and duration of stay in Britain, a series of Spearman's rank order correlation tests were carried out.[2] The hypotheses here are that:

- speakers who score higher for Chinese (both spoken and written) would score lower for English and vice versa, thus confirming the language shift which is believed to be taking place in the community

Table 4.14 Language ability indices for male speakers

Speaker no.	A	B	C	SC	WC	SE	WE
25	73	GF	12	5	2	0	0
51	68	GF	25	5	4	3	3
1	66	GF	8	5	3	0	0
37	65	GF	30	5	5	3	3
26	56	F	31	5	4	2	2
45	53	F	27	5	4	3	3
32	49	F	23	5	5	3	3
10	47	F	39	5	4	2	2
39	44	F	30	5	4	3	3
53	44	F	25	5	4	3	3
5	41	F	20	5	5	3	3
15	40	F	16	5	5	4	4
20	37	F	17	5	5	3	3
2	35	F	12	5	5	3	3
47	24	S	24	3	1	5	5
28	22	S	22	4	2	5	5
48	22	S	22	4	2	5	5
12	21	S	21	4	2	5	5
13	19	S	19	3	1	5	5
34	18	S	18	3	1	5	5
49	18	S	18	3	1	5	5
29	17	S	17	4	1	5	5
43	16	O	16	3	1	5	5
55	16	S	16	2	1	5	5
7	15	S	15	3	1	5	5
35	15	S	15	2	1	5	5
22	14	S	14	2	1	5	5
8	12	S	12	3	1	5	5
17	11	S	11	3	1	5	5
4	10	S	10	3	1	5	5

Total number of speakers: 30
A = Age B = Generation (GF = Grandfather, F = Father, S = Son, O = Other relative) C = Years of residence in Britain
SC = Spoken Chinese WC = Written Chinese SE = Spoken English WE = Written English

Table 4.15 Language ability indices for female speakers

Speaker no.	A	B	C	SC	WC	SE	WE
44	72	GM	18	5	0	0	0
9	70	GM	12	5	0	0	0
31	67	GM	6	5	0	0	0
14	65	GM	18	5	2	0	0
52	63	GM	23	5	2	0	0
38	61	GM	30	5	2	0	0
19	58	GM	10	5	4	0	0
27	52	M	31	5	4	2	2
46	60	M	27	5	4	2	2
11	46	M	26	5	4	2	2
54	45	M	21	5	4	2	2
33	42	M	20	5	5	2	2
40	40	M	22	5	4	2	2
6	38	M	17	5	5	2	2
16	37	M	18	5	5	4	3
21	35	M	15	5	5	2	2
3	32	M	12	5	5	3	3
50	22	O	22	4	1	5	5
56	21	D	21	4	4	5	5
30	20	D	20	4	1	5	5
57	18	D	18	4	1	5	5
18	15	D	15	4	2	5	5
41	12	D	12	3	1	5	5
58	12	D	12	2	1	5	5
23	11	D	11	3	1	5	5
36	10	D	10	2	1	5	5
24	9	D	9	2	1	5	5
42	8	D	8	3	1	5	5

Total number of speakers: 28
A = Age B = Generation (GM = Grandmother, M = Mother, D = Daughter, O = Other relative) C = Years of residence in Britain
SC = Spoken Chinese WC = Written Chinese SE = Spoken English WE = Written English

- older speakers would score higher on the scales for Chinese (spoken and written), while younger speakers score higher on the scales for English (spoken and written)
- variations in language ability scores are in some way related to differences in gender and duration of residence in Britain of the speakers.

Correlations between different language ability scores

The correlation tests for the current study were carried out on Minitab. They show highly significant but negative correlation between speakers' language ability scores for spoken Chinese and for spoken English ($r = -0.885$ $p < 0.005$ (males); $r = -0.861$ $p < 0.005$ (females)), which indicates a sharp contrast between speakers' ability to use the two languages for various communicative tasks. More specifically, speakers who can normally use Chinese with general ease and fluency in a wide range of social contexts appear to have moderate or low command of English, whereas those whose use of Chinese is rather limited compensate with a better command of English. But correlation between the scores for written Chinese and written English is found to be significant for male speakers ($r = -0.784$ $p < 0.005$) only. This is because many women are either illiterate in both languages or have only moderate ability to use the written language.

Correlations between language ability and speaker age

To further examine the relationships between language ability and social characteristics of individual speakers, correlation tests were carried out between age and ability scores. It was found that the age of male speakers correlates positively with language ability scores on the scales for Chinese (spoken: $r = 0.879$ $p < 0.005$; written: $r = 0.772$ $p < 0.005$) and negatively with scores for English (spoken: $r = -0.882$ $p < 0.005$; written: $r = -0.882$ $p < 0.005$). This suggests that older males tend to score high on the Chinese scales, while younger male speakers score high on the English scales.

Similar correlations are found between age and language ability scores of female speakers for spoken Chinese ($r = 0.869$ $p < 0.005$), spoken English ($r = -0.946$ $p < 0.005$) and written English ($r = -0.947$ $p < 0.005$). But there is no significant correlation between age and language scores of female speakers for written Chinese. This is because both the oldest and youngest female speakers scored very low on the scale. In fact three out of seven female speakers of the grandparent generation are illiterate in Chinese, and only two speakers from the child generation scored more than one point on the scale (see Table 4.15).

Table 4.16 gives further details of the mean age of speakers of different language ability scores.

Table 4.16 Mean age of speakers of different scores on the language ability indices

Score	Male		Female		Total	
	No. of speakers	Mean age	No. of speakers	Mean age	No. of speakers	Mean age
Spoken Chinese:						
5	14	51.3	17	51.4	31	51.3
4	4	20.5	5	21.6	9	19.8
3	9	15.9	3	10.3	12	14.5
2	3	15.0	3	10.3	6	12.7
1	0	—	0	—	0	—
0	0	—	0	—	0	—
Written Chinese:						
5	6	44.5	5	36.8	11	41.0
4	6	52.0	7	44.6	13	48.0
3	1	66.0	0	—	1	66.0
2	4	34.5	4	51.0	8	42.8
1	13	15.8	9	13.6	22	14.9
0	0	—	3	69.7	3	69.7
Spoken English:						
5	16	16.9	11	14.4	27	15.9
4	1	40.0	1	37.0	2	38.5
3	9	48.4	1	32.0	10	46.9
2	2	51.5	8	43.5	10	45.1
1	0	—	0	—	0	—
0	2	69.0	7	65.1	9	66.1
Written English:						
5	16	16.9	11	14.4	27	15.9
4	1	40.0	0	—	1	40.0
3	9	48.4	2	34.5	11	45.9
2	2	51.5	8	43.5	10	45.1
1	0	—	0	—	0	—
0	2	69.0	7	65.1	9	66.1

Total numbers of speakers: 58 (30 Males and 28 females)

These findings provide further evidence of the ongoing language shift within the Tyneside Chinese community, which is closely related to speaker age.

Correlations between language ability and sex

A series of t-tests on the mean age of male and female speakers confirms that there is no significant sex-based differences in language ability scores; that is, both older male and older female speakers score higher on the Chinese scales and both younger males and younger females score higher on the English scales. However, there are three older women who score nil for written Chinese (i.e. illiterate), whereas their male counterparts all appear to have some ability to read and write.

Correlations between language ability and duration of residence in Britain

Further tests were carried out to investigate relationships between individual speakers' language ability and their duration of residence in Britain. Only moderate correlations are found between language ability scores for spoken and written Chinese and duration of stay (spoken: $r = 0.445$ $p < 0.025$ (males); $r = 0.453$ $p < 0.025$ (females); written: $r = 0.445$ $p < 0.025$ (males); $r = 0.389$ $p < 0.025$ (females)). There is no significant correlation between the ability to use English (either spoken or written) and length of residence, which seems to form a corollary to our previous findings of the relationship between language choice patterns and duration of stay in Britain (see above). The average years of stay in Britain by speakers of different language ability scores are presented in Table 4.17.

At this point, it seems reasonable to suggest that there is a connection between language ability and language choice patterns identified in earlier. To examine the relation between the two aspects of the speaker's language behaviour, further correlation tests were undertaken.

Language ability and language choice

Since the language ability indices give every speaker a numerical score for his or her use of spoken Chinese, written Chinese, spoken English and written English, we can now rank all the speakers according their scores. In the meantime, we can use the language choice patterns which we have already identified (four for communication with family members and seven for non-family member interlocutors) as another set of ranks, from Pattern 1 indicating Chinese monolingualism to Pattern 7 English-dominant bilingualism. Rank order correlations between language ability scores and language choice patterns can give some indication of whether speakers who use Chinese with more interlocutor types also use the language for wider communicative purposes and whether those who speak more English have a more flexible command of the language.

Table 4.17 Average number of years of residence in Britain by speakers of differing language ability scores

	Male		Female		Total	
Score	No. of speakers	Average year	No. of speakers	Average year	No. of speakers	Average year
Spoken Chinese:						
5	14	21.8	17	19.2	31	20.4
4	4	20.5	5	21.6	9	19.8
3	9	15.9	3	10.3	12	14.5
2	3	15.0	3	10.3	6	12.7
1	0	—	0	—	0	—
0	0	—	0	—	0	—
Written Chinese:						
5	6	19.7	5	16.4	11	18.2
4	6	27.8	7	22.6	13	25.0
3	1	8.0	0	—	1	8.0
2	4	19.3	4	21.5	8	20.4
1	13	15.8	9	13.6	22	14.9
0	0	—	3	12.0	3	12.0
Spoken English:						
5	16	16.9	11	14.4	27	15.9
4	1	16.0	1	18.0	2	17.0
3	9	23.2	1	12.0	10	22.1
2	2	30.0	8	22.4	10	23.9
1	0	—	0	—	0	—
0	2	10.0	7	16.7	9	15.2
Written English:						
5	16	16.9	11	14.4	27	15.9
4	1	16.0	0	—	1	16.0
3	9	23.2	2	15.0	11	21.7
2	2	30.0	8	22.4	10	23.9
1	0	—	0	—	0	—
0	2	10.0	7	16.7	9	15.2

Table 4.18 Correlations between language choice patterns and language ability scores

	Males		Females	
	r	*p*	*r*	*p*
With family members:				
Spoken Chinese	−0.481	< 0.005	−0.636	< 0.005
Written Chinese	−0.386	< 0.025	n.s.	
Spoken English	0.591	< 0.005	0.810	< 0.005
Written English	0.591	< 0.005	0.808	< 0.005
With non-family members:				
Spoken Chinese	−0.823	< 0.005	−0.857	< 0.005
Written Chinese	−0.668	< 0.005	n.s.	
Spoken English	0.827	< 0.005	0.960	< 0.005
Written English	0.827	< 0.005	0.959	< 0.005

Results of the correlation tests are presented in Table 4,18. Positive correlations indicate higher language ability scores and higher (English-dominant) language choice patterns, and negative correlations indicate higher language ability scores but lower (Chinese-dominant) language choice patterns. As we can see, speakers who score higher on the Chinese scales (both spoken and written) do indeed use Chinese only or Chinese-dominant language choice patterns (both with family members and with non-family member interlocutors), while those who score higher on the scales for English use the English-dominant patterns, except for women whose scores for written Chinese do not seem to correlate with their language choice patterns.

Summary

In this chapter, I have examined in some detail the language choice patterns of a sample of 58 speakers in the Tyneside Chinese community, using a number of statistical procedures. Results suggest that a rapid inter-generational language shift from Chinese monolingualism to English-dominant bilingualism is currently taking place. This shift is exemplified not only in a change of habitual language choice with different interlocutor types, but also variations in the ability to use the two languages in both speech and writing. A number of extra-linguistic factors have been examined and it has been found that age is the most significant factor associated with this change in language choice and language ability, with older speakers using only or mainly Chinese in a wide range of situational contexts and younger speakers using both Chinese and English or predominantly English for different communicative purposes.

However, age alone tells us little about the social mechanisms underlying the language shift process; indeed, it may misleadingly imply that variations in language choice and language ability reflect life-cycle changes rather than changes over time. A simplified example of a life-cycle change in language choice might be that of a speaker who has been speaking only Chinese since childhood and starts to speak a mixture of Chinese and English upon reaching 20 years old. We have no evidence that such is the case in the Tyneside Chinese community. What we have seen here is synchronic variations which exist both within and across generations. For example, while in general the grandparents have remained Chinese monolingual, two of the male grandparents in the sample have not only acquired some English but also use it with a range of interlocutors; and while the majority of the child generation use both Chinese and English, some members of that generation have begun to use only English for peer-group interaction. Furthermore, there are particular types of interlocutors with whom speakers use only Chinese (e.g. female grandparents), whereas with others both Chinese and English or English only may be used. To explain variations such as these, we need to look for factors other than speaker age which can account for the underlying processes whereby speakers make their choices. In the following chapter, I shall explore the social mechanism underlying the ongoing language shift, making use of the concept of social networks.

Notes

1. Examples and discussion of these tests can be found in Lambert (1955, 1964, 1969).
2. Spearman's test calculates the extent to which the rank order of scores for each individual on one measurement is similar to the rank order of scores on another measurement. Fasold gives a non-linguistic illustration of the principles of this test:

> Imagine we had height and weight measurements for a group of 100 children between the ages of 5 and 15. We would expect that the taller children would weigh more and the shorter youngsters would weigh less. If we were to list all the children in order by height, they would automatically be very nearly also in order by weight. This would be an example of *positive* correlation; a youngster with greater height would also probably have greater weight, and vice versa. If we were to take the same children and compare two different characteristics, this time age and the amount of time it takes a child to run 50 metres, we would expect a *negative* correlation. By and large, older children should be able to run 50 metres in *less* time than younger children. In neither case would the correlation necessarily be perfect. There would probably be some shorter youngsters who happen to weight more than a taller child, and also a few older children who took more time to run 50 meters than some younger children. Correlation gives a measure of how much one characteristic varies with another. If the two vary together perfectly in a *positive* direction, then we would obtain a coefficient of correlation of +1.00. If they varied in the exact opposite direction from each other, the *correlation coefficient* would be −1.00. If

they were not related to each other at all, the coefficient of correlation would be 0.00. Thus, coefficients of correlation vary in value between −1.00 and +1.00. A coefficient of correlation of 0.83, for example, would represent a very strong positive correlation. A value of −0.53 would be a moderate negative correlation. (Fasold, 1984: 102–3, original italics)

Although generally speaking the closer the correlation coefficient, r, comes to 1.0, the closer the relationship between the two sets of figures, the value of r is influenced by the number of individuals in a sample tested, and it is important to know how much reliance can be placed on this value; that is, whether or not it can be said that there is a relationship at a given level of r. Standard statistics textbooks normally list the critical values of the Spearman rank correlation coefficient, p (see, for example, Butler, 1985).

5 Social Networks and Variations in Language Choice

As outlined in Chapter 1, social networks involve not only the speaker but also people with whom the speaker interacts, and social network analysis essentially measures an individual's degree of integration into informally constituted social groups. This degree of integration can act as a *norm enforcement mechanism* so that members of particular networks display similar social behaviours (including linguistic behaviour) which systematically differ from those of non-members (Bott, 1957). Gal's (1979) study, for example, reveals that there are regularly patterned relations between a speaker's language choice and the characteristics of his or her social networks. Those with strong peasant ties in Oberwart, Austria, adopt a Hungarian-dominant language choice pattern, while those with urban networks (of different ages) have shifted towards the use of German. Gal further argues that it is through such association between language choice and particular groups of speakers that different linguistic systems acquire different social symbolism. I shall in this chapter explore the relationships between social networks and language behaviour within the Tyneside Chinese community building upon the model developed by Gal (1979) (and of course by L. Milroy (1987a) and Bortoni-Ricardo (1985) as well).

The chapter is organised into six sections. In the first I outline, different types of social networks which affect speakers' linguistic behaviour, and in the second I discuss methods for collecting social network data. In the third section I attempts to identify social network patterns of the 58 sample speakers in terms of three generations, and in the fourth and fifth sections I analyse the relations between individuals' social network patterns and their language choices and language abilities. I conclude with a discussion of the effect of social networks upon intra-speaker variation in language choice, that is, the same speakers' choices of language(s) with different interlocutors. Throughout the chapter, I refer to the language choice patterns and language ability indices which I identified and examined in Chapter 4.

Network Types

Network analysts sometimes find information about individuals' social contacts difficult to obtain not only because it tends to be personal (though not necessarily private), but also because a given individual may possess a range of ties which can be manipulated for particular purposes at different times. It is therefore important to specify which types of networks one wants to study before data is collected and analysis begins.

Personal network types can be identified either in terms of shape and pattern of the ties which Mitchell (1969) calls the 'morphological' aspects of networks, or of the content of the relationships — the 'interactional' aspects of ties. As was mentioned in Chapter 1, investigators from several disciplines who are interested in developing formal methods of analysing social networks have tended to concentrate on *morphological* or *structural* features such as density of the ties, while social anthropologists who want to account for the observable behaviour of individuals tend to give equal, if not more, weighting to the *interactional* properties or *content* of the relationships (see also Mitchell, 1986). The main structural and interactional characteristics of networks are discussed in detail by Mitchell (1969: 10–29). Some would argue that the two types of features are interrelated and both are important in any analysis of the role of social networks in the day-to-day living of individuals (Surra, 1988; Cochran, 1990).

In principle, social networks are boundless. They link people to one another throughout the whole society however remotely. It would be impractical and unnecessary in most research, however, to identify all the network members of a particular individual or a family. Empirical evidence suggests that for practical reasons social networks are generally 'anchored' to individuals. This principle of 'anchorage' effectively limits the first-order network to, normally, something between 30 and 50 individuals (Mitchell, 1986: 74; see also L. Milroy, 1987b). First-order networks are those with whom the anchor person (or ego) is in direct and regular contact. If we consider second or higher-order contacts, the number would increase to a pragmatically infinite limit.

Within the first-order range, it is possible to distinguish between exchange and interactive networks (Milardo, 1988: 26–36). Exchange networks are collectives of people with whom the probability of rewarding exchanges (and unrewarding exchanges in cases of conflict-habituated relationships; see Barrera, 1981) is high. In other words, these are the people with whom the ego not only interacts routinely, but also exchanges direct aid, advice, criticism, support and interference. Traditionally, kins and close friends form an essential part of an individual's exchange network. Interactive networks, on the other hand, consist of people with whom ego interacts frequently and perhaps over prolonged periods of time, but crucially, the probability of rewarding exchange is low, that is, the ego does not rely on these contacts for personal favours and other material or symbolic resources. An example of interactive ties would be a shop owner and his or her customers.

Typically, exchange networks are 'strong ties', in terms of both structural and interactional features, while interactive networks tend to be loosely structured 'weak ties' (Granovetter, 1973; Milardo, 1988). Some individuals have more exchange networks than interactive ones or vice versa within their first-order network range, therefore their network types could be characterised as relatively dense and multiplex or loose and uniplex (see also Chapter 1).

In addition to the exchange and interactive ties, there is a subset of personal networks which comprise 'passive ties'. These 'passive ties' are marked by an absence of regular contact, but are equally considered important by ego who depends on such relationships for sentimental and moral support or influence. Many people, for example, would have relatives or friends who for various reasons are physically distant from them, but who are still regarded as important relations. Such relations are particularly relevant to migrants who tend to cling psychologically to their traditional ties, despite the passing of time. 'Passive ties' fall somewhere between first-order and second-order or higher-order networks. Unlike first-order contacts they do not involve regular interaction with the ego, yet their affective impact on ego is strong in contrast with second-order networks.

Collecting Social Network Data

The diversity and fluidity of individuals' social network contacts present a challenge to potential investigators. Milardo (1988) discusses a number of field procedures for collecting information for network analyses, including name-elicitation, self-report, and observation of sample social interaction. Name-elicitation and self-reports are perhaps the most frequently used methods for collecting information on personal networks and they make it possible to gather large amounts of comparable data in a relatively short time. A potential problem, however, concerns the criteria according to which informants are invited to nominate their network constituency. Variations in interpretation of terms such as 'friend' and 'significant other' can be expected across age, gender and social group. This problem may be overcome (at least partially) by tactful interview questions. As Fischer (1982) suggests, for example, the interviewer may in formulating the questions present the interviewee with a set of social settings (e.g. household, work, school) in addition to several categories of individuals defined specifically in terms of the probability of rewarding exchanges. He gives an example of how such questions may be framed:

'Some people never talk with anyone, either on or off the job, about how to do their work. Other people do discuss things like decisions they have to make, work problems they have to solve, and ways to do their work better. Is there anyone you talk with about how to do your work? [If yes] Who do you talk with about your work?' (Fischer, 1982: 324)

It is obvious that questions like this cannot be asked within a highly structured schedule. Instead, ethnographic interview procedures where informal conversation replaces the question–answer exchanges are preferred (see also Chapter 3). Ethnographic interviews can be supplemented with participant observation, which, in addition to revealing ego-centred ties, allows the investigator to examine a set of networks as a whole (Mitchell, 1986).

In the present study, I have employed a combination of participant observation and ethnographic interview to collect information on individuals' network ties. It was felt that all three types of networks — exchange, interactive and 'passive' — should be examined, because they exert different degrees and kinds of influence upon speakers' language behaviour. As discussed earlier, exchange networks comprise people with whom an individual makes friends and upon whom he or she depends for material and moral support. Their impact upon ego tends to be strong. Differences in two individuals' (or two groups of individuals') exchange networks may result in quite different social behavioural norms, as anthropologists have shown (e.g. Cochran, 1990). Interactive networks, on the other hand, refer to the people with whom individuals have frequent contacts but without material and moral attachment. Their effect upon the individuals' behaviour may be less direct and systematic, but nevertheless significant. In comparison, 'passive' ties are the people with whom ego cannot interact on a regular basis, but are still considered as important relations. They reflect individuals' psychological orientation and social attitudes.

For the present study, the exchange networks of the 58 speakers in the sample were identified in two stages. First, participant observation elicited an initial list of around 30 contacts with whom the speaker interacted regularly and exchanged goods and information. Then the list was presented to the speaker who was asked whether those on the list were indeed regarded by himself or herself as important relations. The list was amended accordingly and a resulting 20 non-kin contacts were used as the basis for analysing the speaker's exchange networks. The number 20 was selected, following Mitchell (1986), as a reasonable basis for quantitative analysis.

It should be explained here that the reason to exclude kin from the exchange network is because I found that differences in family sise often resulted in some speakers having a large number of family members with whom they interacted regularly and upon whom they depended materially and morally, while some others had none. For examples, speakers from a family of seven people may (but not necessarily of course) have six kin out of the listed 20 exchange ties, whereas those from a family of four can at most have three (see Appendix I for information on family sise). More significantly, perhaps, such differences in the proportion of kin within the exchange network are not always the result of the speakers' own choosing. Some people interact and exchange goods and services with their relatives on a regular basis simply as part of routine family life. It was therefore felt necessary to focus on non-family ties to allow more meaningful comparisons between speakers.

The term 'regularly' also needs some explanation. When I first began to collect information on individual speaker's network ties, I focused on people with whom the speakers interacted on a daily basis. It soon became apparent that many of the people with whom the speakers exchanged direct support, material goods, advice and criticism, that is 'exchange' networks, met only once or twice a week, although they might communicate with each other more often via telephone. In a few cases, the intervals in between two meetings with friends were even longer, due to the overall slower pace of life that the speakers led. Thus, 'regularly' here may refer to daily, weekly or even monthly (but no longer than monthly), depending on individual circumstances. The most important point is that the contacts were regarded as 'regular' by the speakers themselves.

In order to examine individuals' degree of social integration, I have constructed two network indices: an 'ethnic' index — which is calculated in terms of the number of Chinese versus non-Chinese ties out of the 20 exchange network ties listed for each speaker — and 'peer' index — reflecting the number of people belonging to the same generation as the speaker as opposed to those of other generations (either older or younger). For example, Speaker 51, who is a grandparent, has of his listed 20 exchange ties 16 which are Chinese (ethnic index) and eight which are of the grandparent generation (peer index). We can compare his networks with those of Speaker 43, who is a child, and of his 20 listed exchange networks only two are Chinese and seven are of the child generation. Speaker 51 would thus rank higher than Speaker 7 on the 'ethnic' index, but lower on the 'peer' index. There are two basic hypotheses here:

- Speakers whose exchange networks consist of a relatively large number of ethnic (Chinese) ties would display more 'traditional' social behaviours such as using the Chinese-dominant language choice patterns, while those with fewer ethnic ties within their exchange networks would have moved away from such tradition and have adopted an English-oriented behaviour.

- Speakers whose exchange networks consist of a relatively large number of 'peer' ties would display behaviours which conform to the overall pattern of the generation to which they belong.

Notice here that the indicators used in measuring personal networks are different from those used by Gal (1979), Milroy (1987a), and Bortoni-Ricardo (1985). Milroy (1987a: 141) comments on the principles in selecting the appropriate network indicators and designing network measures. They must first of all reflect the conditions which have repeatedly been found important in a wide range of network studies in predicting the extent to which normative presures are applied by the local community, and they must be recoverable from data collected in the field and easily verifiable. The 'ethnic' and 'peer' indices for the current analysis were constructed with these principles in mind.

Similar 'ethnic' and 'peer' indices are constructed for interactive networks which are intended to reflect the overall opportunities available to individual speakers to interact with Chinese and non-Chinese or peer and non-peer group members. However, whereas the numbers for the exchange networks indicate specific individuals, those for the interactive networks represent proportions. Each speaker is observed in terms of with how many people he or she interacts routinely but without exchange of material or moral support, and the total numbers of interactive ties would obviously vary between individual speakers, due partly to their employment and education (see later). The percentages of these contacts who are Chinese and who belong to the same generation are calculated and used to construct 'ethnic' and 'peer' indices.

In addition to the exchange and interactive networks, I have examined 'passive' ties — those with whom the speakers cannot interact regularly because of physical distance, but whom the speakers regard as important relations and from whom material and moral support would be forthcoming when needed. Each speaker is invited to nominate ten such ties and the numbers of Chinese versus non-Chinese among these ties are used to construct an ethnic index. This index is intended to reflect speakers' psychological orientation towards Chinese and non-Chinese relationships.

Although the current analysis does not specifically measure the structural properties (e.g. density or reachability) of the networks, it is assumed that exchange networks are usually dense and multiplex ties and interactive networks are relatively loose and uniplex ties (see further Milardo, 1988). Details of the network indices are listed in Appendix III. I shall now examine the distribution of the three types of networks — exchange, interactive, and 'passive' — in terms of three generations — grandparents, parents and children. The relationship between network ties and language behaviour will be discussed after an overall picture of generational contrasts in social network patterns has emerged.

Table 5.1 Average number of Chinese ties in exchange networks by generation and sex

	Males		Females	
Generation	No. of speakers	Average Chinese ties	No. of speakers	Average Chinese ties
Grandparents	4	15.0	7	20.0
Parents	10	14.0	10	17.0
Children	16	1.0	11	1.2

Total: 20 ties per speaker

Generational Differences in Social Network Patterns

Exchange networks

Table 5.1 gives a summary of Chinese ties in the exchange networks of male and female speakers from three generations.

As Table 5.1 shows, over three-quarters of the listed exchange network of the grandparents and parents comprise Chinese contacts, and the seven female grandparents have no non-Chinese exchange contact at all. The children, on the other hand, have on average only a little more than one Chinese tie out of a total of 20. These figures suggest that as far as exchange networks are concerned, the grandparent and parent generations have on the whole remained strongly ethnic-oriented. They have established few close friendship ties with individuals outside the Chinese community, a point also made by Watson (1977) and the Home Affairs Committee (HAC, 1985a) (see further Chapter 2). The British-born children, however, seem to have moved away from such community-based networks and have made friends mainly with non-Chinese. Although female speakers of three generations have contracted more Chinese ties than their male counterparts, the difference is not statistically significant as investigated by a series of t-tests.

In comparison with the inter-generational differences in ethnic ties within the exchange networks, the numbers of 'peer' ties which both male and female speakers of the three generations contract do not seem to differ so sharply. Table 5.2 gives the average numbers of contacts within the exchange network who belong to the same generation as the speaker.

The exchange network ties of most adult speakers appear to be roughly evenly divided between those who belong to their own generation and those who do

Table 5.2 Average number of peer ties in exchange networks by generation and sex

	Males		Females	
Generation	No. of speakers	Average peer ties	No. of speakers	Average peer ties
Grandparents	4	9.8	7	11.3
Parents	10	9.6	10	11.7
Children	16	13.9	11	14.1

Total: 20 ties per speaker

not. Some children seem to have contracted more peer-group ties than adults, although the difference as investigated by ANOVA is not statistically significant. These figures suggest that speakers, young or old, tend to make friends mainly with people of their own generation. The implications which such network patterns may have on their language behaviour will be discussed later in this chapter.

Next examined are the interactive networks of the three generations.

Interactive networks

Table 5.3 presents ethnic contacts which male and female speakers of three generations have in daily social interaction. The figures in this table, and those in Table 5.4, represent percentages, rather than actual numbers, of Chinese contacts within the interactive networks.

As the table reveals, the proportion of Chinese people with whom the speakers are in routine contact decreases progressively in younger generations. More than 78% of the interactive contacts of male grandparents are Chinese, and the seven female grandparents have no non-Chinese interactive contacts at all. In contrast, less than half of the interactive networks of the parent generation are Chinese, and the overwhelming majority of the interactive networks of the children are non-Chinese.

These differences need to be considered in the light of the employment and education situation of different generations. Since eight out of a total of eleven grandparents are not employed (see Appendix I for details), their chances of interacting with non-Chinese on a regular basis are fewer. All of the parent generation, on the other hand, are working in either Chinese restaurants, takeaways and shops, or local companies and factories, and there are plenty of

Table 5.3 Percentage of Chinese ties in interactive network by generation and sex

	Males		Females	
Generation	No. of speakers	Average Chinese ties %	No. of speakers	Average Chinese ties %
Grandparents	4	78.25	7	100.00
Parents	10	31.20	10	41.90
Children	16	4.06	11	14.00

Table 5.4 Percentage of peer ties in interactive networks by generation and sex

	Males		Females	
Generation	No. of speakers	Average peer ties %	No. of speakers	Average peer ties %
Grandparents	4	58.25	7	58.29
Parents	10	54.90	10	55.40
Children	16	99.19	11	99.18

opportunities for these Chinese employees to interact with non-Chinese people. What is particularly interesting, however, is that despite the opportunities available to them, members of the parent generation do not seem to have made friends with many non-Chinese people. This is clear if we compare Table 5.3 with Table 5.1.

The child generation, in contrast, spends most day-time hours outside the family where there are normally very few other Chinese children around (see also Chapter 2). In the evenings, they tend to get together with their schoolmates who are mostly non-Chinese, while their parents work in the restaurants or take-aways. The opportunities for them to interact with other Chinese beyond the immediate family are rare. This pattern can account both for the very small proportion of Chinese contacts this generation possesses as part of their interactive networks, and the very few Chinese friends which they have made, as illustrated in Table 5.1.

Table 5.5 Average number of Chinese ties in 'passive' networks by generation and sex

	Males		Females	
Generation	No. of speakers	Average Chinese ties %	No. of speakers	Average Chinese ties %
Grandparents	4	10.0	7	10.0
Parents	10	10.0	10	10.0
Children	16	5.6	11	5.5

Total: 10 ties per speaker

Table 5.4 provides further information of the type of people with whom members of the three generations routinely interact.

As Table 5.4 shows, around half of the interactive contacts of the grandparents and parents (male and female) are members of their own generation and the other half are of other generations, older or younger. This seems to correspond to the pattern shown in Table 5.2, in which the exchange networks of the grandparent and parent generations are more or less evenly divided between peers and non-peers. All of the daily contacts of the children however, are with members of their own generation. The differing patterns of employment and education associated with different generations may be used to explain the different proportions of peer-group contacts as well. The grandparents and parents have more opportunities to meet with people from a range of different groups through their profession or community-based activities (even though their ties may be ethnic-oriented — (i.e. with Chinese people only), while the children spend most of their time with other children of similar age at school.

Lastly, we look at the 'passive' ties of the three generations. These represent persons whom the speakers regard as important, but who are physically distant from them.

'Passive' networks

As Table 5.5 shows, all the 'passive' ties of the grandparents and parents (male and female) are Chinese, whereas about half of the 'passive' ties of the children are Chinese and the other half non-Chinese. The figures are all the more meaningful when we remember that they have been nominated by the speakers themselves as important relations. It shows that despite their many

Table 5.6 Correlations between individual network ties and age:

	Males		Females	
	r	p	r	p
Ethnic ties:				
Exchange networks and age	0.839	< 0.005	0.875	< 0.005
Interactive networks and age	0.879	< 0.005	0.830	< 0.005
'Passive' networks and age	0.898	< 0.005	0.871	< 0.005
Peer-group ties:				
Exchange networks and age	–0.689	< 0.005	–0.571	< 0.005
Interactive networks and age	–0.816	< 0.005	–0.672	< 0.005

years of residence in Britain and the opportunities they have had to interact with non-Chinese people, grandparents and parents have remained psychologically bounded to traditional, ethnic ties. The children, on the other hand, have begun to move away from these ties both physically and psychologically and have integrated a considerable number of affectively significant non-Chinese contacts into their social networks.

A further comment to be made here is that the 'passive' ties nominated by the grandparents and parents are invariably with persons in the Far East, their original homes, while those nominated by the children are very often friends who used to live in the Tyneside region and are now in other parts of Britain or elsewhere. These findings support Watson's (1977) proposal that many Chinese emigrants still regard China and Hong Kong as home, which is no longer the case for the British-born children (see also Redding, 1990).

Network scores and speaker age

Since the network indices assign to every speaker numerical scores to represent each kind of his or her network ties, we can examine differences in individual speaker's personal network structure in addition to generational distributions. The 58 speakers were therefore ranked according to their relative numbers of Chinese and peer-group ties in the three types of networks. The ranks were then correlated with speaker age, using Spearman's rank order correlation test. Results of the tests are presented in Table 5.6.

As Table 5.6 shows, the ethnic indices of the three types of networks correlate with speaker age positively, which suggests that the older the speakers are the more Chinese ties they contract (or the younger the fewer Chinese ties).

Table 5.7 Rank order correlations between different types of networks for male and female speakers

	1	2	3	4
Males ($p < 0.005$)				
2	−0.746			
3	0.799	−0.714		
4	−0.795	0.773	−0.734	
5	0.861	−0.786	0.762	−0.874
Females ($p < 0.005$)				
2	−0.647			
3	0.837	−0.546		
4	−0.728	0.476	−0.653	
5	0.881	−0.679	0.735	−0.855

1 = Exchange (Chinese) 2 = Exchange (peer) 3 = Interactive (Chinese) 4 = Interactive (peer) 5 = Passive
Total number of speaker: 30 males and 28 females

The correlation between age and peer-group ties is significant (though not as good as that with ethnic ties) but negative. This correlation reflects the fact that younger speakers have relatively more peer-group members than older speakers as part of their exchange and interactive networks.

Interactions between different types of networks

Rank order correlation tests were also carried out to investigate the relations between the three types of social networks. As Table 5.7 shows, significant and positive correlations are found between the three sets of ethnic indices, which indicate that speakers who have more Chinese ties as part of their exchange networks tend also to have more Chinese ties in their interactive and 'passive' networks, while those who have more non-Chinese ties as part of their exchange networks tend also to have more non-Chinese ties in interactive and 'passive' networks. At the same time, speakers who have more members of their own generation (peers) as part of their exchange networks also seem to have more peer-group ties in their interactive networks. However, the correlations between the ethnic indices and peer indices are significant at a lower level, and negative. This suggests that speakers who have more Chinese ties do not necessarily have as many peer-group contacts. As shown in Table 5.6, younger speakers who have fewer Chinese ties tend to build relationships mainly with peers.

In sum, the analyses of social distributions of the three types of network ties show a general pattern of change from predominantly Chinese ties to predominantly non-Chinese, peer-group ties across three generations. This change is generally related to speaker age, with older speakers having more ethnic ties, even though they may have plenty of opportunities to interact with people outside their own ethnic community, and younger speakers having more non-Chinese ties of their own generation. We may surmise that there is a parallel relationship between this pattern of change in social networks and the language shift from monolingual Chinese to English-dominant bilingualism described in Chapter 4. I shall now examine this relationship more systematically, first of all by comparing the differences in social network patterns of speakers who make different language choices.

Social Networks and Language Choice Patterns

The analytic procedure employed in this section is similar to that in Chapter 4: I begin by grouping the 58 speakers in the sample according to their language choice patterns (four for family communication and seven for communication with non-family member interlocutors) and calculate mean network scores of each group separately in terms of 'ethnic' and 'peer' ties of three types of networks — exchange, interactive and passive; then the mean scores of different speaker groups are compared with each other to see whether or not they are significantly different. The procedure of Analysis of Variance (ANOVA) is employed to investigate differences in mean network scores of speakers with different language choice patterns. In this section, I shall first look at the relationships between exchange networks and language choice patterns; moving then on to interactive networks. For both types of network, speakers' scores on the ethnic indices (Chinese ties) will be considered before scores on the peer-group indices. Lastly, I will discuss, the relationship between 'passive' networks and language choice patterns of speakers.

Exchange networks and language choice patterns

Table 5.8 gives the mean scores of speakers of four different language choice patterns with family members (see further Chapter 4) on the ethnic index of exchange networks.

As may be suspected, there is a sharp contrast in the number of ethnic ties of Patterns 1 and 2 speakers and Patterns 3 and 4 speakers. Those who use the Chinese monolingual and Chinese-dominant language choice patterns (Patterns 1 and 2) contract all or most of their exchange networks with Chinese people, while speakers of the English-dominant bilingual patterns contract only one-third or less of their ties with other Chinese. There are no significant differences

Table 5.8 Mean scores of speakers with four language choice patterns with family members on the ethnic index of exchange networks

	Males		Females	
	No. of speakers	Mean network score	No. of speakers	Mean Network score
Pattern 1	2	20.0	7	20.0
Pattern 2	6	16.2	6	18.8
Pattern 3	18	3.3	8	3.4
Pattern 4	4	7.3	7	6.1

$F = 14.01 \; p < 0.02$ (Males) $F = 21.20 \; p < 0.02$ (Females)
Total: 20 ties per speaker

between male and female speakers of the same language choice patterns in the number of ethnic ties contracted.

Table 5.9 reveals similar contrasts for language choice patterns with non-family-member interlocutors. Those who have adopted the Chinese monolingual or Chinese-dominant patterns (Patterns 1–3) have contracted significantly more Chinese ties, while those who adopt the bilingual and English-dominant patterns (Patterns 4–7) have few or no Chinese ties in their exchange networks (see Table 5.9). Again, differences between male and female speakers of the same patterns are not statistically significant.

While the contrast in the number of ethnic ties of speakers of different language choice patterns is very clearly shown in Tables 5.8 and 5.9, the numbers of peer ties (i.e. members of the same generation as the speaker) within the exchange network show no significant difference between speakers with various language choice patterns. Tables 5.10 and 5.11 present the mean scores of speakers of different language choice patterns on the peer index for exchange networks.

As the tables show, speakers on the whole divide their exchange networks fairly evenly between those who belong to their own generation and those who do not. Speakers of Patterns 5 and 6 (communication with non-family members) have contracted rather more peer-group ties, although they are not statistically significant compared with the rest of the sample. These results are particularly interesting when they are related to age differences of the speakers of various language choice patterns discussed in some detail earlier; that is, older speakers have generally maintained Chinese-dominant patterns while younger speakers have shifted towards English-dominant bilingual patterns. Analysis of the rela-

Table 5.9 Mean scores of speakers with seven language choice patterns with non-family members on the ethnic index of exchange networks

	Males		Females	
	No. of speakers	Mean network score	No. of speakers	Mean network score
Pattern 1	2	20.0	7	20.0
Pattern 2	6	16.0	8	18.3
Pattern 3	2	15.0	2	12.0
Pattern 4	12	4.8	6	1.5
Pattern 5	2	0	1	1.0
Pattern 6	3	0.3	2	0.5
Pattern 7	3	0.7	2	1.0

$F = 14.08$ (males) $p < 0.02$ $F = 79.79$ (females) $p < 0.02$ (Female Pattern 5 speakers omitted from F-test)
Total: 20 ties per speaker

Table 5.10 Mean scores of speakers with four language choice patterns for family communication on the peer index of exchange networks

	Males		Females	
	No. of speakers	Mean network score	No. of speakers	Mean network score
Pattern 1	2	10.5	7	11.3
Pattern 2	6	9.5	6	12.2
Pattern 3	18	12.7	8	13.5
Pattern 4	4	12.5	7	13.0

$F = $ n.s. (males and females)
Total: 20 ties per speaker

tionship between network and language choice suggests that Chinese and Chinese-dominant language choice patterns are the norm for peer-group communication among older speakers, while bilingual and English-dominant patterns are the norm for peer-group communication among younger speakers. I shall return to this point in later.

Table 5.11 Mean scores of speakers with seven language choice patterns for communication with non-family members on the peer index of exchange networks

	Males		*Females*	
	No. of speakers	*Mean network score*	*No. of speakers*	*Mean network score*
Pattern 1	2	10.5	7	11.3
Pattern 2	6	9.7	8	12.0
Pattern 3	2	9.0	2	10.5
Pattern 4	12	12.2	6	13.5
Pattern 5	2	14.0	1	15.0
Pattern 6	3	15.7	2	16.0
Pattern 7	3	13.0	2	13.5

F = n.s. (males and females)
Total: 20 ties per speaker

Let us now turn to consider the relationship between interactive networks of speakers and language choice patterns.

Interactive networks and language choice patterns

Table 5.12 presents the average percentage of Chinese (as opposed to non-Chinese) contacts within the interactive networks of speakers with four language choice patterns for family communication.

Table 5.12 shows that Pattern 1 speakers, male and female, have no regular contact with non-Chinese at all. Speakers of other language choice patterns, on the other hand, have plenty of opportunities to interact with non-Chinese people, even though some of them may not have established friendship ties with them (cf. Table 5.8). An important point emerges here concerning the relationship between language choice and social networks. We may suggest that the nine Pattern 1 speakers have not been able to use English because they have no social contacts with non-Chinese people. Equally, it could be argued that because the nine speakers have no ability to use English, they have not been able to contract any ties outside their own ethnic community. This dialectic relationship between language use and personal network ties is crucial to understanding the interactional process through which social structures form and transform themselves (see further Chapter 1). Note here that speaker age does not seem to have the same kind of relationship with language choice as network structures do. While we may sug-

Table 5.12 Average percentages of Chinese contacts of interactive networks for speakers with four language choice patterns for family communication

	Males		Females	
	No. of speakers	Average Chinese ties %	No. of speakers	Average Chinese ties %
Pattern 1	2	100.00	7	100.00
Pattern 2	6	37.00	6	50.83
Pattern 3	18	13.28	8	17.25
Pattern 4	4	9.75	7	18.57

$F = 14.24$ $p < 0.02$ (males) $F = 29.28$ $p < 0.02$ (females)

gest that some speakers display certain linguistic behaviour because they are old (or young), we cannot say that speakers are old (or young) because of their language choice. Thus, while social networks are clearly related to speaker age, they offer a better explanation of the social mechanisms underlying language choice.

Table 5.13 shows patterns of ethnic contacts similar to those shown in Table 5.12 within the interactive networks of speakers with seven language choice patterns (communication with non-family members).

As seen in Table 5.13, the main contrast lies in between speakers of Pattern 1 and those of other patterns. There is no significant difference between male and female speakers of the same language choice patterns in terms of the percentage of Chinese contacts of their interactive networks.

Next examined is the proportion of peer-group ties within the interactive networks. Table 5.14 presents this information for speakers with four language choice patterns (communication with family members).

We can see that speakers of Patterns 3 and 4 — the English-dominant bilingual patterns — interact more with members of their own generations. If we relate these findings to the age differences between speakers, that is younger speakers have more peer ties, we may argue that exclusive use of English is the norm for peer group interaction among the young.

This argument is further supported by the differing proportions of peer-group contacts within the interactive network of speakers with seven language choice patterns for communication with non-family member interlocutors, which are presented in Table 5.15.

Table 5.13 Average percentages with Chinese contacts of interactive networks for speakers of seven language choice patterns for communication with non-family members

	Males		Females	
	No. of speakers	Average Chinese ties %	No. of speakers	Average Chinese ties %
Pattern 1	2	100.00	7	100.00
Pattern 2	6	35.33	8	44.75
Pattern 3	2	56.50	2	26.50
Pattern 4	12	11.67	6	21.17
Pattern 5	2	4.50	1	12.00
Pattern 6	3	0.00	2	3.00
Pattern 7	3	5.33	2	4.50

$F = 16.51$ $p < 0.02$ (males) $F = 16.55$ $p < 0.02$ (females) (Female Pattern 5 speakers omitted from F-test)

Table 5.14 Average percentages of peer-group contacts of interactive networks for speakers with four language choice patterns for family communication:

	Males		Females	
	No. of speakers	Average Chinese ties %	No. of speakers	Average Chinese ties %
Pattern 1	2	65.50	7	58.29
Pattern 2	6	51.00	6	51.17
Pattern 3	18	90.78	8	92.75
Pattern 4	4	74.50	7	85.14

$F = 7.64$ $p < 0.02$ (males) $F = 11.43$ $p < 0.02$ (females)

As Table 5.15 shows, speakers of bilingual and English-dominant language choice patterns interact with members of their own generations exclusively (with respect to their interactive networks), whereas those adopting the monolingual

Table 5.15 Average percentages of peer-group contacts of interactive networks for speakers with seven language choice patterns for communication with non-family members:

	Males		Females	
	No. of speakers	Average Chinese ties %	No. of speakers	Average Chinese ties %
Pattern 1	2	65.50	7	58.29
Pattern 2	6	51.00	8	50.87
Pattern 3	2	51.00	2	73.50
Pattern 4	12	85.83	6	98.50
Pattern 5	2	100.00	1	100.00
Pattern 6	3	100.00	2	100.00
Pattern 7	3	100.00	2	100.00

$F = 7.35$ p < 0.02 (males) $F = 33.90$ $p < 0.02$ (females) (Female Pattern 5 speakers omitted from F-test)

Chinese and Chinese-dominant patterns interact with peers as well as others. This finding allows us to make a further prediction that cross-generational interaction initiated by adults would normally be Chinese monolingual, or at least Chinese dominant. Such a claim is supported by data on habitual language choice patterns of the parent and grandparent generations, discussed in Chapter 4, which show that these speakers generally use Chinese as their primary language for communication.

Lastly, 'passive' ties of speakers with different language choice patterns were examined.

'Passive' networks and language choice patterns

Table 5.16 gives the number of Chinese relations which the speakers with four language choice patterns (family communication) regard as significant, although they cannot interact with them in person on a regular basis.

As Table 5.16 shows, speakers of the Chinese monolingual and Chinese-dominant patterns regard only Chinese relations as important, while those of Patterns 3 and 4 have some non-Chinese relations as well as Chinese ones as part of their 'passive' networks.

Table 5.16 Average number of Chinese relations within the 'passive' networks of speakers with four language choice patterns for family communication

	Males		Females	
	No. of speakers	Average Chinese ties %	No. of speakers	Average Chinese ties %
Pattern 1	2	10.00	7	10.00
Pattern 2	6	10.00	6	10.00
Pattern 3	18	6.72	8	6.50
Pattern 4	4	7.25	7	6.86

$F = 4.07$ $p < 0.02$ (males) $F = 7.17$ $p < 0.02$ (females)
Total: 10 ties per speaker

Table 5.17 Average number of Chinese relations within the 'passive' networks of speakers with seven language choice patterns for communication with non-family members

	Males		Females	
	No. of Speakers	Average Chinese ties %	No. of Speakers	Average Chinese ties %
Pattern 1	2	10.00	7	10.00
Pattern 2	6	10.00	8	10.00
Pattern 3	2	10.00	2	10.00
Pattern 4	12	7.92	6	6.00
Pattern 5	2	4.50	1	5.00
Pattern 6	3	5.00	2	4.50
Pattern 7	3	3.67	2	4.00

$F = 12.57$ $p < 0.02$ (males) $F = 37.34$ $p < 0.02$ (females) (Female Pattern 5 speakers omitted from F-test)
Total: 10 ties per speaker

Similar patterns emerge in Table 5.17, which presents the average number of Chinese relations within the 'passive' networks of speakers with seven different language choice patterns (communication with non-family members).

As has been argued earlier, 'passive' ties reflect the speakers' psychological orientation and social attitude. Their impact on language behaviour may be indirect but nevertheless significant.

Summary

The various analyses reported in this section show quite clearly that the differences in language choice patterns are closely related to speakers' network ties. Those who adopt monolingual Chinese or Chinese-dominant language choice patterns have a strong Chinese-based network; they interact only or mainly with other Chinese; and they remain psychologically attached to their geographically distant Chinese relations. Those who adopt bilingual or English-dominant patterns, on the other hand, seem to have contracted more non-Chinese ties, with some having a majority of non-Chinese contacts. They interact more frequently with non-Chinese people and value such relations. Regarding the peer-group ties which speakers of different language choice patterns contract, we see that speakers who use both Chinese and English or English-dominant patterns interact more with members of the their own generation and make more friends within their peer group, while those who use Chinese only and Chinese-dominant patterns interact both with peers and non-peers. Furthermore, there is a clear difference between children and adults in terms of both their social network ties and language choice patterns. While the children who adopt the English-dominant language choice patterns have developed extensive ties with non-Chinese peers, the network contacts of the Chinese monolingual and Chinese-dominant adults are strongly ethnic-oriented and not confined to peers. One implication of such generational differences would be that adults prefer to speak and to be spoken to in Chinese, whereas the British-born children prefer English as their primary language of communication. I shall discuss this point further with reference to inter-generational code-switching patterns in Chapter 6.

I shall now turn to the relationship between network ties and language ability of individual speakers.

Social Networks and Language Ability

As described in Chapter 4, the shift in language choice pattern from Chinese monolingualism to English-dominant bilingualism in the Tyneside Chinese community is accompanied by inter-generational variation in the ability to use the two languages for different communicative tasks. The general pattern is that older speakers have acquired only limited command of English, while

Table 5.18 Correlations between language ability indices and ethnic index of exchange networks

	Males		Females	
	r	*p*	*r*	*p*
Spoken Chinese	0.840	< 0.005	0.852	< 0.005
Written Chinese	0.759	< 0.005	n.s.	
Spoken English	−0.906	< 0.005	−0.920	< 0.005
Written English	−0.906	< 0.005	−0.918	< 0.005

Total number of speakers: 30 males + 28 females = 58

younger speakers have almost lost their ability to use written Chinese. What I intend to find out in this section is whether differences in the speaker's language ability co-vary with his or her social network pattern; more specifically, whether speakers with strong Chinese-based networks have a better command of Chinese which they use for different communicative purposes, and those with strong non-Chinese-based networks have a better command of English which they use in various situational contexts.

Since each speaker has been assessed on a six-point scale for spoken Chinese, written Chinese, spoken English and written English respectively (see further Chapter 4), their scores can be ranked and correlated with network indices (see Appendices II and III for details), following the procedure adopted to examine the relationship between network ties and speaker age (see earlier in this chapter). I shall now discuss the relationships between language ability and three types of networks — exchange, interactive, and 'passive' — in turn. For each network type, 'ethnic' index (Chinese ties) will be considered before 'peer' index.

Exchange networks and language ability

Table 5.18 presents rank order correlations between language ability scores and ethnic ties of the exchange networks of the speakers.

As the figures reveal, there are significant and positive correlations between the ethnic index of the exchange network and the language ability indices for spoken Chinese and written Chinese of male speakers. That is to say that male speakers who have more Chinese ties as part of their exchange networks score higher on the scales for Chinese, both spoken and written; and those who have fewer Chinese ties score lower on the Chinese scales. For female speakers, on

Table 5.19 Correlations between language ability indices and peer index of exchange networks

	Males		*Females*	
	r	p	r	p
Spoken Chinese	−0.745	< 0.005	−0.602	< 0.005
Written Chinese	−0.804	< 0.005	−0.394	< 0.025
Spoken English	0.771	< 0.005	0.619	< 0.005
Written English	0.771	< 0.005	0.624	< 0.005

Total number of speakers: 30 males + 28 females = 58

the other hand, a significant and positive correlation is found between the ethnic index of their exchange networks and spoken Chinese ability scores, but not with the scores for written Chinese. This is because female speakers at both ends of the age scale — the oldest and the youngest — have shown little or no ability to use written Chinese, in contrast with male speakers of whom only the youngest cannot use written Chinese.

In comparison, the correlations between the ethnic index of the exchange networks of the speakers and their language ability indices on the English scales (for both spoken and written language) are significant but negative. This means that speakers, male and female, who have more Chinese ties as part of their exchange networks have only a limited command of English, while those who have fewer Chinese ties can use English for a wider range of communicative tasks.

Next, we look at the relationship between peer-group ties within the exchange networks and language ability.

As Table 5.19 shows, the correlations between the numbers of peer-group members within the exchange networks of male speakers and their Chinese ability scores are significant but negative. As has been revealed above, while the differences in the number of peer-group members of the three generations are not statistically significant, younger speakers seem to contract rather more exchange network ties with members of their own generation than the older speakers do. Rank order correlations between peer-group index and age confirm this pattern ($r = -0.689$ $p < 0.005$ (males); $r = −0.571$ $p < 0.005$ (females)). It was shown in Chapter 4 that speakers who score lower on the Chinese scale are generally younger in age than those who score higher. Thus, we see here that speakers who have relatively more peer-group ties (younger speakers) rank

Table 5.20 Correlations between language ability indices and ethnic index of interactive networks

	Males		Females	
	r	p	r	p
Spoken Chinese	0.800	< 0.005	0.674	< 0.005
Written Chinese	0.721	< 0.005	n.s.	
Spoken English	−0.875	< 0.005	−0.823	< 0.005
Written English	−0.875	< 0.005	−0.818	< 0.005

Total number of speakers: 30 males + 28 females = 58

lower on the Chinese ability indices (spoken and written), resulting in the negative correlations.

For the same reason, the correlation between female speakers peer-group ties in the exchange networks and their spoken Chinese ability scores is also negative. There is, however, no significant correlation between female speakers' peer ties and their written Chinese scores, the reason being that both the youngest and the oldest female speakers are illiterate in Chinese.

Correlations between the language ability scores for English, both spoken and written, and the peer-group ties of the exchange networks of both male and female speakers are found to be significant and positive. They suggest that speakers with more peer-group ties tend to score higher on the English scales, and from the analysis of network and age we know these are younger speakers (see below). We are therefore able to confirm that English is used more among the younger generations as the language for peer-group interaction.

I now turn to interactive networks and their relationships with language ability of the speakers.

Interactive networks and language ability

Table 5.20 gives the rank order correlations between the ethnic index of interactive networks and the language ability indices.

Interestingly, the correlations are not as good as those between the ethnic index of the exchange networks and the speakers' language ability scores, which suggests that interactive networks have relatively less influence upon language ability than exchange networks. Nevertheless all but female speakers' written Chinese scores correlate significantly with the ethnic index of interactive net-

Table 5.21 Correlations between language ability indices and peer index of interactive networks

	Males		Females	
	r	p	r	p
Spoken Chinese	−0.875	< 0.005	−0.845	< 0.005
Written Chinese	−0.893	< 0.005	−0.549	< 0.005
Spoken English	0.817	< 0.005	0.707	< 0.005
Written English	0.817	< 0.005	0.702	< 0.005

Total number of speakers: 30 males + 28 females = 58

works. The correlations with Chinese language scores are positive, indicating that speakers with more Chinese contacts in the interactive networks use Chinese for a wider range of purposes, while those with fewer Chinese interactive contacts have a limited command of Chinese. The correlations with English language scores, on the other hand, are negative, which suggests that speakers with more Chinese contacts score lower on the English scales and the speakers with fewer Chinese contacts score higher on them. Again, we may argue that there is a dialectic relationship between social network and language ability; that is, social networks of the speaker facilitate the acquisition and development of appropriate language ability and the speaker's command of the relevant language enables him or her to contract certain types of network (either with Chinese or with non-Chinese) for social interaction.

Table 5.21 gives the results of correlation tests between peer index of the interactive networks and language ability scores.

As we can see, the peer index of the interactive networks correlates negatively with Chinese ability scores, suggesting that speakers with more members of their own generations in their interactive networks have only limited command of Chinese. The correlations with English scores are, however, positive, which indicates that speakers who interact more with peer-group members have a better command of English which they can use for a variety of communicative tasks.

Lastly, the ethnic index of 'passive' networks is correlated with language ability scores of the speakers.

'Passive' networks and language ability

Table 5.22 shows that the ethnic index of the 'passive' networks correlates positively with language ability scores on the Chinese scales. That means that

Table 5.22 Correlations between language ability indices and ethnic index of 'passive' networks

	Males		Females	
	r	p	r	p
Spoken Chinese	0.941	< 0.005	0.970	< 0.005
Written Chinese	0.887	< 0.005	0.508	< 0.005
Spoken English	−0.872	< 0.005	−0.858	< 0.005
Written English	−0.872	< 0.005	−0.858	< 0.005

Total number of speakers: 30 males + 28 females = 58

speakers who have more Chinese relations in their 'passive' networks score higher on the Chinese scales, both for spoken and written. The correlations with English scores are negative, reflecting once again a converse relationship between ethnic ties and the ability to use English.

Summary

We have seen in this section that ethnic indices of the three network types (exchange, interactive and 'passive') correlate with Chinese language ability scores positively and with English scores negatively. This suggests that speakers with more Chinese ties generally have a better command of Chinese which they use for a wide range of communicative purposes, but that the same speakers tend to have rather restricted ability to use English. Conversely, speakers with more non-Chinese ties are generally able to use English in different kinds of situational context, but have only a limited command of Chinese.

The peer indices also correlate with Chinese negatively and English positively. That is to say that the ability to use Chinese by speakers with relatively more members of their own generations in their networks tends to be limited, and from the analysis of age differentiation we know that these are younger speakers. Conversely, the ability to use Chinese by speakers with relatively fewer peer-group contacts is better, and they tend to be older speakers.

These findings become more interesting when we recall that not all speakers of the same generations score the same on either the network indices or the language ability indices. For example, two of the male grandparents scored three points on the spoken English scale, suggesting that they have the ability to participate in casual conversations in English, while the other two male grandparents in the sample have acquired no English at all. Similarly, one of the female parents scored four for her spoken English, indicating a fairly good command of the language, but the others of the same generation score only two points. Variations such as these cannot be explained by reference to the age factor; on the contrary, one of the male grandparents who scores three on the spoken English scale is aged 68 — the second oldest of the sample of 30 male speakers. An examination of the network indices of these 'anomalous' speakers reveals that they all have relatively fewer ethnic ties — one of the English-speaking male grandparents has 14 Chinese ties in his exchange network and the other has 16, compared to the two monolingual Chinese male grandparents who both have 20 Chinese ties (i.e. no non-Chinese ties at all). The female parent who scores four for her spoken English has only six Chinese ties in her exchange network. We may therefore conclude with some confidence that social network is a better explanatory variable in accounting for both inter-generational (or group) differences and intra-generation (or individual) variation.

As we argued in Chapter 1, the concept of social network does more than differentiate speakers, either in groups or individually. It provides deeper insight into the social mechanisms underlying linguistic variation which exists on both the social (inter-speaker) dimension and stylistic (intra-speaker) dimension. We have already noted the dialectic relationship between social networks and language choice in that speakers belonging to different network groups behave linguistically in different ways. Those whose networks are strongly ethnic-orientated tend to use the Chinese monolingual or Chinese-dominant language choice patterns, whereas those who have a less ethnically based, peer-group network tend to adopt the bilingual or English-dominant patterns. According to Bell (1984), variations between speakers also affect the speech of a single speaker in different situations (see further Chapter 1) in that individual speakers adapt their language behaviour to resemble linguistically members of the same social group and to accommodate their audience. In the remainder of this chapter, I want to look more closely at this connection between inter-speaker variation and intra-speaker linguistic variation in language choice. I shall also discuss the question of the social symbolism of Chinese and English in the Tyneside Chinese community.

Interactions Between Inter-speaker and Intra-speaker Variations in Language Choice

In Chapter 1, I described Gal's (1979) model of language choice which employs the implicational scale technique to examine both the social and stylistic dimensions of linguistic variation. Implicational scaling was first introduced into linguistics by Creole researchers as a means of organizing variable data (DeCamp, 1971; Rickford, 1987; for a critique see Romaine, 1982). It was used by Gal (1979) rather innovatively to conceptualise and display observed language choices by individual speakers. The basic idea was to rank both the speakers (social dimension) and interlocutors (style dimension) according to the choices speakers made so that we could differentiate fairly clearly not only speakers who made the same choices but also the same speaker's varying choices with different interlocutors. Following Gal's example, I have constructed two implicational scales for the present study presenting language choices by male and female speakers separately (see Tables 5.23 and 5.24). In these scales, speakers are ranked on the vertical axis and interlocutors on the horizontal axis. Those who are listed towards the top of the scale are speakers who use Chinese (C) on more occasions (i.e. with more (types of) interlocutors), with those who use more English (E) towards the bottom. Interlocutors are also ranked according to the language choices of the speakers. Those who are spoken to in Chinese by more speakers are listed towards the left, and those spoken to more in English towards the right. Thus, the use of C with any particular interlocutor implies that C will be used with all interlocutors to the left of the scale, while if E is used with any interlocutor, it will be used with all interlocutors to the right. The use of both C and E to the same interlocutor will appear between the use of only C and the use of only E, and these are the situations where code-switching may (but does not necessarily) occur. Any choice that does not fit this pattern will be considered 'unscalable' (marked by *). The language choice pattern of any individual speaker can thus be read across each row. At the same time, the kinds of differences that exist between speakers regarding their language choices with any particular interlocutor can be revealed by reading down each column. In order to see the relationship between social networks and these language choice patterns, the ethnic indices of the three types of network ties (exchange; interactive; 'passive') are also given in the scales, together with speaker age and generation cohorts.

Looking at the ranking of the interlocutors on the horizontal axis, we see that the ones listed at the far left end of the scale are grandparents and at the far right end are children, indicating that generally grandparents invite more use of Chinese and children invite more use of English. This ranking largely corresponds with that of the speakers on the vertical axis, where those who are listed towards the top of the scales are grandparents and children are listed towards the bottom. We may therefore suggest in a general way that only Chinese is used by grandparents and to grandparents; while English is used by children and to children; and both Chinese and English may be used by parents and to parents. As Gal (1979) argues, it is through this kind of association between choices of language(s) and particular types of interlocutors that languages acquire their social symbolism. We may say, for example, that in the Tyneside Chinese community Chinese is associated primarily with the grandparents, thus it is the 'we code' for that generation and older speakers generally; and English is associated chiefly with British-born children who may regard it as their 'we code'. Note that even this rather tentative generalisation seems more complicated than Gumperz's (e.g. 1982) proposal that the ethnic language of the community would be the 'we code' and the language of the majority 'they code'. Gumperz's distinction would not be able to account for the change that takes place across generations in the same community.

A closer examination of the implicational scales reveals that the interaction between the social and stylistic dimensions of language choice is in fact much more complex than has been suggested. First of all, not all speakers of the same generation share the same language choice patterns. There are a few cases where speakers are ranked either higher or lower than other members of their generation on the horizontal scale. For instance, speakers 51 and 37 in Table 5.23 (aged 68 and 65 respectively) are ranked much lower than the other male grandparents and even some of the parents, suggesting that they use relatively more English; meanwhile, those who are listed at the very bottom of the scales are not the youngest speakers of the child generation in the sample. It seems that these speakers have adopted language choice patterns other than those of their own generation at large. As I have argued, such variations in language choice patterns cannot be accounted for by the age factor. Here, the significance of social networks comes to the fore. Compared with the rest of the grandparent generation, speakers 51 and 37 have fewer ethnic ties in their networks; and compared with the other children, those listed at the bottom of the scales have even fewer Chinese contacts. It seems that these speakers have moved away from the networks of the generation to which they might be said to belong and consequently have developed behavioural patterns which are different from other members of their generation.

Such inter-speaker variations are closely associated with interlocutor types in that speakers with different network patterns adopt different language choice patterns with various interlocutors. We can see, for example, that speakers of the parent generation who have relatively more Chinese ties in their networks (those listed towards the top of the scales) use Chinese only for communication between spouses, whereas those with relatively fewer Chinese ties may use both Chinese and English with the same type of interlocutors; while all children use Chinese only with grandparents (especially female grandparents) and both Chinese and English with parents, some use only English with their peers. Thus, the suggestion that we may characterise the choice between Chinese and English by identifying the generations with which they are associated and subsequently infer the social symbolism of the two languages may be too simplistic. What the implicational scales have revealed here is that particular languages are associated with particular groups of speakers who are members of the same social networks, and social networks may vary on an individual basis, regardless of age

Table 5.23 Implicational scale for observed langauge choices by male speakers. (Scalability 98.2%)

A	B	C	a	b	c						Interlocutors						
						1	2	3	4	5	6	7	8	9	10	11	12
25	6GP	73	20	100	10	—	C	C		C	C	C	C	C	C	C	C
1	1GP	66	20	100	10	—	C	C		C	C	C	C	—	C	C	C
45	9P	53	15	42	10	C	C	C		—	C	C	C	—	CE	CE	CE
10	3P	47	18	52	10	C	C	C		—	C	C	C	—	CE	CE	CE
5	2P	41	16	22	10	—	C	C		—	C	C	C	—	CE	CE	CE
26	6P	56	17	59	10	—	C	C	C	—	C	C	C	—	CE	CE	CE
20	5P	37	17	19	10	C	C	C		—	C	C	C	CE	CE	CE	CE
53	10P	44	15	18	10	C	C	CE*	C	—	CE*	C	CE	CE	CE	CE	CE
2	1P	35	16	18	10	—	C	C	C	—	C	CE	CE	—	CE	CE	CE
32	7P	49	12	49	10	C	C	C		CE	CE	CE	CE	CE	CE	CE	CE
51	10GP	68	16	63	10	C	C	C		CE	CE	CE	CE	CE	CE	CE	CE
37	8GP	65	14	50	10	C	C	C		—	CE	CE	CE	CE	CE	CE	CE
39	8P	44	14	11	10	C	C	C	CE	—	CE	CE	CE	CE	CE	CE	CE
15	4P	40	2	22	10	C	C	CE		—	CE	CE	CE	CE	CE	CE	CE
28	6C	22	1	32	6	—	C	CE	C*	CE	CE	CE	CE	CE	CE	CE	CE

A	B	C	a	b	c									
47	9C	24	2	8	7	C	CE	—	CE	CE	—	CE	CE	CE
48	9C	22	3	0	9	C	CE	—	CE	CE	—	CE	CE	CE
12	3C	21	5	0	8	C	CE	—	CE	CE	—	CE	CE	CE
13	3C	19	0	0	8	C	CE	—	CE	CE	—	CE	CE	CE
49	9C	18	0	0	6	C	CE	—	CE	CE	—	CE	CE	CE
7	2C	15	2	0	6	C	CE	—	CE	CE	—	CE	CE	CE
8	2C	12	0	0	5	C	CE	—	CE	CE	—	CE	CE	CE
29	6C	17	0	9	5	CE	CE	C*	CE	CE	CE	CE	CE	CE
4	1C	10	0	0	4	CE	CE	C*	CE	CE	—	—	CE	CE
34	7C	18	0	0	5	C	CE	—	CE	CE	CE	CE	E	E
17	4C	11	1	0	6	C	CE	—	CE	CE	CE	—	E	E
43	8C	16	0	0	4	C	CE	CE	CE	CE	CE	—	E	E
55	10C	16	0	10	5	CE	CE	CE	CE	CE	CE	—	E	E
35	7C	15	0	0	3	CE	CE	—	CE	CE	CE	CE	E	E
22	5C	14	2	6	3	CE	CE	—	CE	CE	CE	—	E	E

A = speaker number B = family membership (GP = Grandparent; P = Parent; C = Child; the numbers denote Families 1–10) C = age a = ethnic index of exchange network (Total: 20 ties per speaker) b = ethnic index of interactive networks (percentage) c = ethnic index of 'passive' networks (Total: 10 ties per speaker) 1 = grandparent, female 2 = grandparent, female 3 = grandparent generation, female male 4 = grandparent, male 5 = parent, male 6 = parent, female 7 = parent, female 8 = parent generation, male 8 = parent generation, female 9 = child, female 10 = child, male 11 = child generation, male 12 = child generation, female

Table 5.24 Implicational scale for observed language choices by female speakers. (Scalability 99.6%)

A	B	C	*a*	*b*	*c*	*1*	*2*	*3*	*4*	*5*	*6*	*7*	*8*	*9*	*10*	*11*	*12*
44	9GP	72	20	100	10	—	C	C	C	C	C	—	C	—	C	C	C
9	3GP	70	20	100	10	—	C	C	C	C	C	—	C	—	C	C	C
31	7GP	67	20	100	10	—	C	C	C	C	C	—	C	C	C	C	C
14	4GP	65	20	100	10	—	C	C	C	C	C	—	C	C	C	C	C
52	10GP	63	20	100	10	—	C	C	C	C	C	—	C	C	C	C	C
38	8GP	61	20	100	10	—	C	C	C	C	C	C	C	C	C	C	C
19	5GP	58	20	100	10	—	C	C	C	C	C	C	C	C	C	C	C
46	9P	50	18	41	10	C	C	C	C	C	C	—	C	—	CE	CE	CE
11	3P	46	20	54	10	C	C	C	—	C	C	—	C	—	CE	CE	CE
6	2P	38	20	20	10	—	C	C	—	C	C	—	C	—	CE	CE	CE
21	5P	35	20	65	10	C	C	C	—	C	C	—	C	CE	CE	CE	CE
3	1P	32	18	67	10	—	C	C	—	C	C	—	C	—	CE	CE	CE
27	6P	52	17	58	10	—	C	C	—	C	C	C	C	CE	CE	CE	CE
33	7P	42	15	50	10	C	C	C	—	C	C	C	CE	CE	CE	CE	CE
54	10P	45	18	11	10	C	C	C	—	C	C	CE	CE	CE	CE	CE	CE

Interlocutors

A	B	C	a	b	c	1	2	3	4	5	6	7	8	9	10	11	12
16	4P	37	6	3	10	C	C	C	—	—	—	CE	—	CE	CE	CE	CE
40	8P	40	18	50	10	C	C	C	—	—	CE	CE	—	CE	CE	CE	CE
50	9C	22	2	58	8	C	C	CE	CE	CE	CE	CE	—	—	CE	CE	CE
56	10C	21	3	57	8	C	C	CE	CE	CE	CE	CE	CE	CE	CE	CE	CE
57	10C	18	2	0	5	C	C	CE	CE	CE	CE	CE	CE	CE	CE	CE	CE
41	8C	12	1	4	6	C	C	CE	CE	CE	CE	CE	CE	CE	CE	CE	CE
58	10C	12	1	8	4	C	C	CE	CE	CE	CE	CE	CE	CE	CE	CE	CE
42	8C	8	0	0	4	C	C	CE	CE	CE	CE	CE	C*	CE	CE	CE	CE
30	6C	20	1	12	7	—	CE	CE	CE	CE	CE	CE	—	—	CE	E	E
18	4C	15	0	0	5	C	C	CE	CE	CE	CE	CE	—	CE	C	E	E
24	5C	9	1	6	4	C	C	CE	CE	CE	CE	CE	—	CE	C	E	E
23	5C	11	0	0	3	C	CE	CE	CE	CE	CE	CE	—	CE	CE	E	E
36	7C	10	2	9	5	C	CE	CE	CE	CE	CE	CE	—	—	CE	E	E

A = speaker number B = family membership (GP = Grandparent; P = Parent; C = Child; the numbers denote Families 1–10) C = age a = ethnic index of exchange network (Total: 20 ties per speaker) b = ethnic index of interactive networks (percentage) c = ethnic index of 'passive' networks (Total: 10 ties per speaker) 1 = grandparent, female 2 = grandparent, female 3 = grandparent generation, male 4 = parent, female 5 = parent generation, female 6 = parent generation, male 7 = grandparent, male 8 = parent, male 9 = child, female 10 = child, male 11 = child generation, male 12 = child generation, female
Scalability is calculated as the percentage of cells that fit the scale model, and 85 per cent scalability is normally considered to be a sufficient approximation of perfect scaling (Guttman, 1944; Gal, 1979; Fasold, 1990).

and generation. Therefore, language choice and the social symbolisms of languages may vary depending on the identity of the speaker as well as of the interlocutor and their inter-personal relationship.

Summary

In this chapter, I have considered in some detail the relationship between social networks and language behaviour of the speaker. It has been suggested that there is a shift from strong ethnic-oriented networks to predominantly non-Chinese, peer-group networks across the generations. This shift is closely related to the language shift process described in Chapter 4, in that speakers with more ethnic ties adopt the Chinese only or Chinese-dominant language choice patterns and have a rather restricted command of English, whereas those with fewer ethnic ties use the bilingual and English-dominant patterns and generally have a better command of English. Peer-group ties, on the other hand, are capable of reinforcing generation-specific behavioural norms — in particular, the British-born children, who contract most of their exchange ties with non-Chinese peers and interact more readily than their parents and grandparents with other children, using English as the primary language for in-group interaction.

The relationship between social networks and language use forms the basis for the complex symbolisms that Chinese and English represent in the community, that is, both languages are in use in the community as a whole but each with particular groups of speakers and interlocutors. Thus, the two languages may be regarded as 'we code' or 'they code', depending on the social networks to which particular language users belong.

The implicational scales of language choice which we have seen not only help to clarify the interaction between inter-speaker and intra-speaker linguistic variations but also locate specifically the contexts in which conversational code-switching is likely to occur. Such situations are indicated by the letters C(hinese) and E(nglish) appearing together. It seems a rational next step to investigate more systematically the discourse strategies whereby speakers use the two languages in conversational interaction (NB. CE in the implicational scales does not offer any information about the quantity of or the way in which the two languages are used in conversation). I shall examine these strategies in the next chapter.

6 Conversational Code-Switching

It is a mistake to assume that code-switching occurs in all bilingual communities on all occasions. In language shift situations at least, code-switching occurs only between certain speakers in certain contexts. The analysis presented in the last two chapters reveals, for example, that nine speakers in our sample of the grandparent generation (seven females and two males) are Chinese monolingual, and are therefore not capable of code-switching at all. Even among those who have the ability to use both languages (though at very different levels), there are addressee-related variations in language preferences: none of the speakers speak English to the monolingual grandparents, ten British-born children use only English with their peers, and the majority of parents speak only Chinese with members of their own generation, especially outside the family setting. Thus, in the Tyneside Chinese community code-switching is speaker and context-specific. It is *not* a community-wide phenomena. In fact, code-switching makes up no more than 50 minutes of the total 23 hours of tape-recorded data — a very small proportion of the corpus.

Since the general preference is therefore for monolingualism, code-switching in conversation is always purposeful, if sometimes unconscious. In other words, speakers generally know what the preferred language is for an ongoing interaction, and they choose a different language in order to draw the attention of addressees to some specific discourse structure, so that that part of the conversation could be interpreted differently from the rest of the interaction.

In this chapter, I shall examine in detail how Tyneside Chinese/English bilingual speakers make use of code-switching as a linguistic resource for specific communicative purposes. First, I shall outline the analytic framework used in the current analysis. I shall then present a detailed, turn-by-turn analsyis of Chinese/English code-switching. Lastly, a number of general code-switching patterns will be discussed in relation to language choice preferences at the community level.

A Sequential Approach to Code-Switching

The analytic approach which I shall adopt in examining conversational code-switching will be sequential as opposed to classificatory. The former is

Table 6.1 Levels of code-switching

					Code-switching	
Speaker 1	*Language* A					
Speaker 2	*Language* A				−	
Speaker 1	*Language* A					
Speaker 2	*Language* B					
Speaker 1	Sentence 1	*Language* B			+	Level A
	Sentence 2	*Language* A			+	Level B
	Sentence 3	Constituent 1	*Language* A			
		Constituent 2	*Language* B		+	Level C

characterised by its emphasis on the embedding of language choice in the turn-by-turn organisation of interaction, while the latter tends to categorise in various ways the grammatical structures or discourse functions of code-switching. The choice of this particular approach is by no means arbitrary. It is determined by both its strengths over other analytic models, which were discussed in Chapter 1, and the nature of the data corpus under examination.

It is possible to distinguish code-switching at three different discourse levels (see Table 6.1). In a given piece of conversation, we may find two speakers using different languages in consecutive turns (Level A). Within a turn, a single speaker may switch code at sentence boundaries (Level B). This is what Poplack (1980) referred to as 'inter-sentential code-switching'. Level A and Level B are closely linked in that the end of a sentence is potentially a turn transition point (see below). The third level of code-switching refers to different constitutents within a sentence being coded in different languages.

The following are some Chinese/English examples of the different levels of code-switching.

Example — Level A:
Mother: You want some, John?
Child: *Ngaw m yiu.*
               (I don't want.)
Mother: M yiu a?
               (Don't want?)

Example — Level B:
Mother: Nay sik mut-ye a?
               (What do you want to eat?)
Child: (1.0) Just apples.

Mother: Just [n] just apples? *Dimgai m sik yoghurt a*?
                 (Why not have some yoghurt?)
Child: (2.0) No yoghurt.

Examples — Level C:
(a) so it means *kueidei gong dodi yingmen lo.*
          (they speak more English)
(b) danhai *at least* ngaw meng kuei gogo ji dim.
    (but)   (I understand what he says)
(c) ngaw wei *solve* di *problem.*
    (I will)   (that/those)

It is clear from the existing literature that different bilingual communities or groups within a community may adopt quite different code-switching strategies. For example, intra-sentential code-switching (Level C) is found most prominently in the more stable bilingual communities with an established history of language contact, while contrastive choices of language by two different speakers at turn boundaries, i.e. Level A code-switching, are often found in conversational interactions involving participants of differing language abilities and attitudes (e.g. Poplack, 1980, 1988; Scotton, 1976, 1983). In the current data corpus, code-switching is overwhelmingly at Levels A and B, i.e. at turn and sentence boundaries, which may in itself be a result of the different generational language choice preferences. The structural models, such as the one proposed by Poplack (e.g. 1980; Sankoff and Poplack, 1981) (and indeed the more recent models proposed by DiSciullo, Muysken & Singh 1986, and Myers-Scotton, 1990), focus on intra-sentential code-switching, whereas a sequential approach takes into account all three different levels of code-switching and interpret them in conversational contexts.

A sequential analysis of code-switching requires an analytic model which seeks to discover by detailed examination of recurrent patterns in naturally occuring data what people actually do with two different languages in day-to-day conversational exchanges. Such a model, as Auer argues, is provided by Conversation Analysis (CA). The principles of CA are clearly explained by, for example, Heritage (1989), Atkinson & Heritage (1984) and Levinson (1983).[1] Here I want to consider briefly two of the main findings of CA regarding the organisation and management of conversation, namely, turn-taking and adjacency pair, as they have considerable implications for the subsequent analysis of Chinese/English conversational code-switching.

Turn-taking

One of the basic observations made by conversation analysts is that conversation interaction is characterised by an orderly sharing of speakership. In order to achieve smooth and frequent transitions from one speaker to another, conversational participants employ a 'local management system' — a set of rules with ordered options which operates on a turn-by-turn basis. Sacks, Schegloff & Jefferson (1974) argue that this local management system requires the assumption that turns are constructed of minimal units. These 'turn-constructional units' may include sentential, clausal, phrasal and lexical constructions. The end of such a unit is a transition relevance place (TRP) — a point at which speakership may (but does not always) change.

Sacks, Schegloff & Jefferson (1974) have largely left open the question of how interactants project the imminent approach of TRP so that turn exchange can be prompt and smooth. They seem to assume that conversation participants normally possess some discourse and syntactic knowledge which they may use in anticipating the end of a particular turn (e.g. grammatical completion of a sentence; routine exchange of telephone calls, hospital visits and shopping). Some investigators have suggested that while the ends of some turns can be roughly projected by the hearer who draws upon such knowledge, speakers constantly and actively give out complex signals to indicate that they are about to finish. The psychologist Starkey Duncan (1969, 1972, 1973), for example, identifies the following behaviours as being implicated by the speaker in marking the end of a turn - he calls them 'turn-yielding cues' (see also Ellis & Beattie, 1986: Ch. 10; Graddol, Cheshire & Swann, 1987: 154–5):

(1) Intonation: the use of any rising or falling intonation contour;
(2) Drawl on the final syllable, or on the stressed syllable of terminal clause;
(3) Sociocentric sequences: the use of one of the several stereotyped expressions, typically following a substantive statement, e.g. 'or something', 'you know', 'but ah', etc.;
(4) Pitch/loudness: a drop in pitch and/or loudness;
(5) Syntax: grammatical completion of a clause;
(6) Gaze: a speaker's head turning towards the listener is associated with a substantial increase in the probability of the listener taking a turn;
(7) Gesture: many kinds of gesture are synchronised with speech and completion of a body movement often coincides with turn completion. (Duncan, 1972)

Duncan (1972) argues that it is cues like these sent out by the speaker, together with the listener's discourse and syntactic knowledge, that help participants to synchronise turn exchanges with precision. A number of investigators have studied 'turn-yielding cues' specifically. Goodwin (1981), for example, has analysed the way in which conversation participants use gaze direction, bodily orientation and posture in relation to turn construction units and turn-taking (see also Kendon, 1977, who has studied gaze direction from a primarily psychological perspective). Schegloff (1984) has studied the relationship between gestures and turns at talk. Local (1986) has identified various phonetic features which are used by the speaker to indicate turn-endings in Tyneside English (see also Local, 1992). All these features are described by Gumperz as 'contextualisation cues', which I have discussed in Chapter 1 (see Gumperz, 1982, 1992).

In addition to psychologists and linguists, the search for various kinds of turn-yielding cues has been carried out by researchers from a range of disciplines with different focuses. Some of their findings are clearly more relevant than others to the study of bilingual code-switching. For example, ethnographers' research on speakership transition strategies in different communities and social groups highlights the cultural variability of the turn-taking system. In a study of the organisation of conversation in Thai, Moerman (1988) argues that while turn-taking occurs in any conversation, the ways in which speaker transition are accomplished may differ from one culture to another, primarily due to the different cues participants use. We shall see shortly that bilingual speakers have the additional resource of code-switching which they may use to co-ordinate turn-taking.

Adjacency pair

One important implication of turn-taking is that conversation is organised into a sequence of exchanges, with one speaker's turn leading to that of another speaker. Schegloff & Sacks (1973) have further explored the sequential organisation of conversation by invoking the notion of 'adjacency pairs' — paired utterances which are sequentially constrained in that the occurrence of a first part creates a slot for the appropriate second pair part. Prototypical types of adjacency pairs include question–answer, greeting–greeting, offer-acceptance, and apology–minimisation. Critical to the concept of 'adjacency pairs' is that a first pair part sets up a conditional relevance and expectation which the second speaker fulfils. Failure to fulfil conditionally relevant expectations by producing appropriate second pair parts results therefore in a 'noticeable absence'.

A great deal of research in CA has been done on the second parts of adjacency pairs in terms of what has become known as 'preference organisation' (e.g. Levinson, 1983; Pomerantz, 1984; Atkinson & Drew, 1979). Preference organisation in its simplest form refers to the ranking of alternative second pair parts, such as acceptance or refusal of an offer, or agreement or disagreement with an assessment. It has been argued that alternative second pair parts are not generally of equal status, rather, some second turns are 'preferred' while others are 'dispreferred'. Preferred seconds tend to be structurally simpler and to follow the first parts smoothly, whereas dispreferred seconds are usually accompanied by various kinds of structural complexity and are typically delivered:

(a) after some significant delay
(b) with some preface marking their dispreferred status, often the particle 'well'
(c) with some account of why the preferred second cannot be performed.

In other words, dispreferred second pair parts are linguisticly marked (see further Levinson, 1983: 307).

Preference organisation extends far beyond the ranking of second parts of adjacency pairs. It can operate to structure turns subsequent as well as prior to a given turn. The example below, taken from Levinson (1983: 335), shows that a dispreferred second is delayed by a 'next turn repair initiator', which gives the next turn speaker an opportunity to *repair* the prior turn in the following turn, and the dispreferred 'second' turn only occurs when Ch fails to do the repair in the way acceptable to M, and thereby becomes displaced into the fourth turn.

Ch: I wan my ow:n tea .hh my*self*
M: (You) want what? =
Ch: = My tea my*se:lf*
M: No:w? We are all having tea together

Schegloff, Jefferson & Sacks (1977) have studied in some detail various strategies used by speakers to repair their contributions in conversation. They make two important distinctions: first, self-initiated versus other-initiated repair, which refers to repair by a speaker respectively with or without prompting; second, self-repair versus other-repair, the former being carried out by the speaker of the repairable item and the latter by another party. The fact that other-initiated repairs (either self-repair or other-repair) are often delayed, by various means, is a manifestation of the tendency of dispreferred seconds generally to be marked by structural complexity (Levinson, 1983: 334).

The existence of repairs, especially other-initiated ones, has significant implications for the sequential organisation of conversation. As Levinson's example shows, in the slot reserved for an answer to Ch's question, M asks 'Want what?', to which Ch replies 'My tea myself'. This exchange between M and Ch is embedded within the exchange initiated originally by Ch, and can be schematised as follows:

Ch: Q(uestion) 1
M: Q 2
Ch: A(nswer) 2
M: (Q 3) A 1

Schegloff (1972) describes a structure such as Q2–A2 as an 'insertion sequence'. Insertion sequences occupy the place of a second pair part and are in effect independent structures embedded between the two halves of a pair. To account for such structures, Levinson (1983) argues that strict adjacency is too strong a requirement for naturally occurring conversational exchange, and quotes a series of examples of insertion sequences which involve numerous levels of embedding.

While insertion sequences defy a strict adjacency pairs analysis of structure, they seem to support conversation analysts' claims about preference organisation in that these sequences can be seen as components of delay by which speakers mark dispreferred seconds (Levinson, 1983: 334).

It should be pointed out here that CA has been developed primarily on the basis of English, monolingual data. Although the underlying structures of conversation may be universal in the sense that any conversation has to allow participants to express agreement as well as disagreement, or as we have seen earlier to take turns, the strategies which participants use to contextualise conversational organisations may be culture specific (Duranti, 1988).

I shall now examine the manner in which Chinese/English bilingual speakers in Tyneside use code-switching as a contextualisation cue to signal turn completion, to mark dispreference and insertion sequences, and to repair problem spots in conversational interaction, following a CA-style analytic procedure.

Code-switching as a Contextualisation cue in Chinese/English Conversation

The examples presented in this section are taken from tape-recordings of spontaneous conversation involving speakers of different generations in family settings (see Chapter 3 for a description of the data-collecting methods). While the focus of analysis is primarily on discourse structures, the ultimate goal is to relate interactional-level code-switching practices to community-level language choice and language shift patterns.

Contextualising turn-taking

Consider sequence (1):

(1) (Two male speakers in their mid-twenties.)
    A: ... He should be home now (.) I think
       (1.5)
    A: maybe ye (.) perhaps I (.) *koeige namba geido a*
                         (What's his number?)
    B: yibaatsaam (.) yichat (.) yichatchatluk
       (283)   (27)   (2776)

Immediately prior to this sequence, the speakers have been talking in English about borrowing a tent from a friend to go camping. A wants B to telephone him (the friend) right away, but B has said he would ring later. This brings us to the beginning of (1). Looking at his watch, A says to B 'He should be home now'. A very short pause precedes the tag 'I think', and we can locate a TRP at this point by virtue of grammatical completion. Although the current speaker, A, has not selected a specific next turn speaker, there is only one other person present. In dyadic situations such as this, B is normally expected to be the next speaker, although not necessarily at the first TRP (Sacks, Schegloff & Jefferson, 1974). B, however, passes up a second opportunity to speak (note the one-and-half-second gap) and A therefore continues. After two short, incomplete utterances ('maybe ye'; 'perhaps I'), A switches from English to Cantonese and asks for the telephone number of the friend, so that he can call the man himself. His code-switching, along with an interrogative structure, specifically marks the selection of B as the next turn speaker, and turn transition is subsequently accomplished when B gives A the telephone number in Cantonese. We can schematise the sequential pattern of language choice in this extract as follows:

A: English (initial turn construction unit)
B: No take up of right to turn
A: English (self-continuation)
  Cantonese (turn allocation)
B: Cantonese (first response)

Code-switching of this kind has frequently been said to function as a procedure for address specification, emphasis or reiteration (e.g. McClure, 1977; Williams, 1980; Zentella, 1981; Gumperz, 1982). While code-switching may indeed serve such functions in different conversational contexts, a more satisfying analysis will surely seek to offer a framework which reveals the underlying procedure whereby speakers achieve particular functional goals. I would argue that code-switching is used here primarily to signal turn handovers, in a manner parallel to prosodic and gestural cues in monolingual conversations. By comparing B's responses to A at the first TRP and after A switches from English to Cantonese, we can see that this does seem to be the interpretation by the participants themselves. Sebba & Wootton (1984) report similar patterns among London Jamaican conversationalists, who also tend to code-switch at turn-final positions to indicate turn completion and turn transition. Extracts (2) and (3) provide further examples of code-switching being used to contextualise turn-handovers:

(2) (A is male in his early thirties and B is female in her mid-twenties.)
  A: Where shall we go?
    (2.0)
  A: ... that's (.) there's an Italian (.) pizza, *ho ma*?
                    (Good?)

B: *Ho a. Pizza a?*
        (Good. Is it pizza?)

(3) (Two teenage girls.)
A: *lei*(.) *m yuen a* (.) *ho kan chejaam* (.) [y'haven't ...
        (to) (not far)   (very near bus-stop)
B: [mm
A: *Nay ji m ji* [*a?*
        (Do you know?)
B: [*ngaw m ji.*
                         (I don't know.)

In (2), B wants to get a snack of some kind. A asks her in English where to go, but B does not respond. Still speaking English, A then suggests (after a two-second pause) a nearby Italian restaurant where they can have pizza. But he switches to Cantonese to asks *'Ho ma?'* ('Good?' or 'Is it OK?'). In monolingual Cantonese conversation, this tag functions to invite comment on a suggestion or acceptance of an offer, but here, much as in (1) above, the language switch marks the end of the current speaker's turn and the selection of the next turn speaker. B accepts A's suggestion and turn transition is accomplished.

Considered from a structural perspective, (2) is an example of tag-switching, which is one of the commonest types of code-switching observed in the literature (e.g. Poplack, 1980). However, from a sequential (or CA) perspective, a tag-switch located at the end of a turn often marks a change of speakership.

In (3) A is describing to B the location of a shop. The first part of A's turn is in Cantonese, but she indicates the turn completion by selecting B as the next speaker. This is marked by a second person pronoun address form, accompanied by code-switching to English. But A's 'y'haven't' overlaps with B's back channel 'mm', and no speaker transition takes place. The subsequent behaviour of A is particularly interesting. She reiterates her turn handover component, this time as an interrogative which as the first part of a pair is a 'strong' procedure for accomplishing turn handover. This is contextualised by a switch back to Cantonese *'Nay ji m ji a?'* ('Do you know?'). The promptness of B's response is shown by the slight overlap, and turn transition is achieved.

These examples show that when considered from a sequential perspective, language choice becomes meaningful not with respect to some previously assigned values, for example as a 'we' or 'they' language. Rather, meaning is interpretable primarily with reference to the language used in preceding and following utterances (either a turn or part of a turn). Code-switching contextualises turn transition by building up a contrast, much as do changes in pitch or tempo or as the phonetic variations described by Local (1992).

While the above examples are all taken from dyadic conversations, the competitive nature of turn-taking where speakers deploy various resources to allocate, seise or retain the floor, is most visible in multi-party, peer conversation. Whereas in dyadic conversation the identity of a next turn speaker is usually clear (whether or not the turn has been specifically allocated), in multi-party conversation self-selection by one or another speaker takes place unless the next turn speaker is specified (see further Sacks, Scheggloff & Jefferson, 1974). Extract (4) suggests that code-switching is used also to contextualise such competitive self-selection in multi-party conversation.

(4)   (Four women in their late twenties and early thirties.)
      A: *mo* (.) *ngaw mo gin* (.) *jung mei gin gwoh Cheung saang*
               (haven't … I haven't met … never met Mr Cheung)
      B: [mm
      C: [*junglai mo* [*a*
               (Never?)
      D: [*Y'what?*
      C: *Koei mo gin gwoh Cheung saang.*
               (She hasn't met Mr Cheung.)
               (1.5)
      D: Maybe you are too busy.
      B: (Laugh) *M dak haan a.*
               (Not free.)
      C: Maybe both (.) either of you (.) *m dak haan a*
               (not free)
      A: No, no. I'm not busy. My sis (.) sister-in-law come Monday.

The notable feature of this sequence is perhaps the contrasting choices of code by different speakers in consecutive turns. All the participants self-select and after A's first turn their choices of language are different from the one in the preceding turn. This type of contrasting choice of code differs from the code-switching we have seen in the first three examples in that the code-switching in (1), (2) and (3) is carried out by the same speaker, whereas in (4) it is done by different speakers. Such contrastive choices of language by different speakers in consecutive turns are not always clearly distinguished in the existing literature from the changing of language by the same speaker in the same turn (either inter-sentential or intra-sentential). Such a distinction is nevertheless important, because both the discourse and socio-cultural meanings contextualised, and hence the inferences drawn by participants from the two types of code-switching may be very different. Code-switching by the same speaker, as exemplified in Extracts (1)–(3) above, demonstrates the speaker's willingness and ability to accommodate his or her interlocutor, while contrastive choices of language by different speakers in consecutive turns, as

shown in (4), indicate not only the preference and competence of the participants, but also possibly their role relationships. Thus for example some speakers may be able to understand Code A but to respond only in Code B, while
others might insist on maintaining a preferred Code A as a mark of the respect
due to them by virtue of their position in the community or family. We shall
see shortly further examples of contrastive choices of language in adult–child
(inter-generational) interaction (see below).

The availability of contrasting choice of language as a resource to be
deployed in turn-competition in multi-party conversation is particularly clear in
the case of violative interruptions. In Extract (5), B marks his attempt to seise
the floor in this way.

(5)   (A, the father, is speaking to a friend when B, the son cuts in.)
      A: *Nay dou [ji dousaai ...*
             (You know it already ...)
      B: [You seen my book?
      A: What book?

An interesting comparison is provided by (6), where we can see that following an interruption the same strategy of contrastive choice of language may be
used to regain the floor.

(6)   (A, a girl in her late teens, is relating a story about her boyfriend when B,
      her younger sister, interrupts.)
      A: He forgot where he left it, right, so I thought I'd [better ...
      B: [*Mutye beng a?*
                                                   (What illness?)

      A: You listen ...

Sometimes even when the overlap is accidental, as in (7), rather than violative, as in (6), choice of language may contextualise a participant's (successful)
claim to the floor.

(7)   (A, B, C are three teenage girls.)
      A: *... maai m do a.*
             (Can't buy it.)
      B: [*Ngaw seunggoh ...*
             (I last ...)
      C: [Did you (.) d'you go to Dillons?
      A: Dillons?
      C: Yeah. The new one.
             (1.0)
             Nay ji-m-ji a?
             (Do you know?)

> **B:** *Hai.*
>
> (Yes.)

In this extract, the girls are talking about a book which A wants to buy but has failed to find in the bookshop. She completes her turn without selecting the next speaker, and the turns of B and C accidentally overlap as they self-select. While B uses Cantonese to align with A's choice of language, C's choice involves a contrast. Although there may be more than one reason for B subsequently to give up her turn, this sequence suggests that C's choice of language has contributed to her success in attracting A's attention, since after a pause she switches back to Cantonese to address B.

One pattern that emerges from the last four examples is that English is repeatedly used to mark the 'last words' in a competitive conversational sequence. The capacity of code-switching to trigger implicatures by building up a structural contrast with preceding and subsequent turns does not rule out the possibility of speakers marking particular conversational structures with particular languages. Indeed it is arguable that through such a repeated association between language and conversation structure the various linguistic options within the community repertoire become socially symbolic (see also Gal, 1979; Scotton, 1988). For example, the data presented in this section suggest an interplay between on the one hand the perception by these Chinese/English bilinguals that English is in some sense the language of authority and on the other its frequent association with (successful) bids during turn-competitions. However, such a claim needs to be supported not only with evidence drawn from an extensive body of qualitatively analysed data, but with reference to the kind of inter-speaker variation which is usually handled by means of quantitative analysis. For example, group A speakers may tend to use language A while group B speakers use language B with respect to the same conversation structure. Given the differences in ability in and preference for different languages by speakers of various social backgrounds, as described in Chapters 4 and 5, considerations of inter-speaker variation patterns play a crucial role in determining the social meanings which are inferred from language choice. I shall discuss further the wider questions raised here in the concluding section.

So far I have looked at a range of issues raised by the use of a code-switching at turn transition points. As we have seen, when the current speaker issues a question, a request, or a command, the next turn speaker may respond in various ways — by remaining silent as in (1), by giving a positive or negative response as in (2), (3), and (4), or by asking another question as in (7). I turn now to examine how code-switching serves to contextualise the next turn speaker's responses in terms of preference organisation.

Contextualising preference organisation

Consider extract (8).

(8) (B, a 12-year-old boy, is playing with a computer in the living-room. A is his mother.)
    A: Finished homework?
    B: (2.0)
    A: Steven, *yiu mo wan sue?*
                 (want to review (your) lessons)
    B: (1.5) I've finished.

In this extract, B does not at first respond to his mother's question, and she switches from English to Cantonese to reiterate her question. This reiteration is apparently understood by B as an indirect request to review his lessons. A pause marks his response as dispreferred, and his language choice contrasts with that of his mother in the immediately preceding turn. Interestingly, however, B's utterance may be read also as an answer to A's first question in English, delivered after some delay. Thus, it comprises both a tying-back by same language usage to the original question, and a divergence from preceding language choice, where divergence choice signals dispreferred activity. Similar patterns of preference marking are evident also in the following sequences.

(9) (Dinner table talk between mother A and daughter B.)
    A: *Oy-m-oy faan a? Ah Ying a?*
           (Want some rice?)
           (2.0)
    A: Chaaufaan a. Oy-m-oy?
           (Fried rice. Want or not?)
           (2.0)
    B: I'll have some shrimps.
    A: *Mut-ye?* (.) *Chaaufaan a.*
           (What?)   (Fried rice.)
    B: *Hai a.*
           (OK.)

(10) (A, male in his late twenties; B, female, early forties; C, B's teenage daughter)
    A: *Sik gai a.*
           (Eat chicken.)
    B: mm.
           (5.0)
    A: Haven't seen Robert Ng for a long time.
           (2.0)

> **A:** Have you seen him recently?
> **B:** No.
> **A:** Have you seen Ah Ching?
> **B:** ... (2.0) (To C) *Ning ngaw doei haai lai.*
> (Bring my shoes.)
> (To A) *Koei hoei bindou a?*
> (Where was she going?)

In (9) mother A, speaking Cantonese throughout, offers her daughter rice. The initial offer, or in CA terms the first pair part, sets up conditional relevance and expectation which needs to be fulfilled by a second part. As has been mentioned earlier, failure to fulfil conditionally relevant expectations by producing appropriate second pair parts results in a 'noticeable silence' (see abov,. see further Levinson, 1983), which is exactly the case of this example when B delays her response. We can see the speakers' orientation to the paired structure in the mother's reaction to her daughter's silence — the offer is repeated in an emphatic form to elicit a response after the the first attempt failed. The child's response to the mother's repeated offer is a request for an alternative to rice, which the mother apparently understands as a refusal, as she requests a repair in the following turn which is followed with yet another offer of rice. Notice that B's indirect refusal is marked in two steps — first a two second delay, then the choice of English which contrasts the code choice in the immediately preceding turn by the mother. The child's final acceptance of the mother's offer of rice is in Cantonese, which corresponds to the language choice of the mother, but differs from the one she has used to mark her indirect refusal.

Extract (10) has already been described in Chapter 3. As in (8) and (9), the second pair part response in (10) is delivered after a period of silence and other delay components including insertion sequences. But what is remarkable here is that all the dispreferred seconds in the three examples are accompanied also by contrastive choices where the next turn speakers use a language different from that of the preceding turn speakers. This kind of code non-alignment is reported also by Auer (1984a) and Sebba & Wootton (1984) in German/Italian and London English/Jamaican creole bilingual communities respectively.

The different language choice patterns in respect of preferred versus dispreferred second parts are particularly clearly evident in (11), where A is the mother, B her nine-year-old daughter, and C, her 12-year-old son.

> (11) **A:** Who want some? [Crispy a.
> **B:**   [Yes.
> **A:** *Yiu me?*
> (Want some?)

B: *Hai a.*
         (Yes.)
         (A handing over some spring-rolls to B.)
A: (To C) Want some, John?
C: *Ngaw m yiu.*
         (I don't want.)
A: *M yiu a? Crispy la.*
         (Don't want?)
C: (Shaking head) mm

In this sequence, B twice accepts A's offer of spring-rolls, twice using the same language as A (Cantonese and English respectively) for this preferred response. However, when C declines A's offer, we find a pattern similar to the one which is evident in (8), (9) and (10) speakers, dispreferred responses are marked by contrasting language choices.

As noted above, dispreferred responses in monolingual, English conversation are often marked by various structural complexities including: pause before delivery; the use of 'prefaces' such as discourse markers like 'but' and 'well', token agreements, apologies, and qualifiers. Also common are the use of 'accounts' or explanations for why the preferred second part is not forthcoming (see Levinson, 1983: 334–5 for more details). From the examples we have seen so far, it seems reasonable to suggest that contrasting choices of language can be used to mark dispreference in bilingual conversation in much the same way as those markedness features in monolingual conversation. In fact, Auer (1991) argues that code-switching is the most significant discourse marker in bilingual conversations in the sense that apparently deviant (or marked) choices of language are more noticeable than other linguistic features. It is perhaps for this reason that while code-switching co-occurs with some dispreference markers such as pauses, it seems sometimes to substitute for particular language-specific markers. For example, in our data English dispreference markers such as 'well' and 'but' do not occur when contrastive language choices are used to mark dispreference. This raises the question of how far dispreference markers are universal and how far they are language specific, a question worth exploring in future research in cross-linguistic research.

One further point of interest which emerges from these examples is that code-switching marking dispreferred seconds is mostly found in inter-generational conversation and in the majority of cases it is children who use English to mark their dispreferred responses to the Chinese first pair parts uttered by their parents or grandparents. Code-switching is less frequently used to mark (dis)preference in conversations among speakers of the same generation and the language direction of the switch is less consistent in such a situation. This finding lends support to a point made earlier that the association between conversation structure and language varies according to (groups of) speakers. Thus, in order to understand the social meaning of code-switching, we need to relate specific interactional strategies to the more general patterns of language choice and language ability at the inter-speaker (or community) level described in Chapters 4 and 5. I shall return to this point later.

I conclude this discussion of bilingual preference organisation with a brief look at two further examples of code-switching which marks different kinds of dispreferred seconds — respectively a disagreement with an assessment and a refusal of an offer.

(12) (Two young women are looking at new dresses.)
    A: *Nau, ni goh.*
        (This one.)
    B: *Ho leng a.*
        (Very pretty.)
    A: *Leng me?* (1.5) Very expensive.
        (Pretty?)
    B: *Guai m gaui a?*
        (Expensive or not?)
    A: *Hao guai.*
        (Very expensive.)

(13) (A, a man in his early thirties is talking with B, who is a woman of a similar age.)
    A: Manhing drive you home.
    B: (1.0) *ngaw daap basi hoei.*
        (I'll take a bus.)
    A: *Yiga m ho hoei. Yan daw (.) ho naan daap basi a.*
        (Don't go now. So many people. Very difficult to get on a bus.)
    B: (Waits for A to call Manhing.)

In (12), B offers her assessment of A's new dress — *'Ho leng a.'* (Very pretty). A's response to this consists first of a 'reflective' question in Cantonese — *'Leng me?'* (Pretty?). This type of question is formed by partial repetition plus the question marker *'me'* and has discourse functions similar to English tags such as 'isn't it?' or 'really?'. Here, the subsequent interaction suggests that it functions as a 'hedge' heralding a further dispreferred assessment, and itself indicates only a qualified agreement with B's original assessment (see Pomerantz, 1984, for comments on responses to assessment). Notice that A switches to English for her second assessment. When B asks for confirmation in the following turn *'Guai m guai a?'* 'Expensive or not?', A's 'preferred' response is in Cantonese, the same language as B's question.

In (13), A is offering to ask Manhing, his son, to drive B home. B declines the offer by saying that she can take the bus. She marks her refusal first with a one-second pause — a common dispreference marker, and then by choosing Cantonese, which contrasts with A's choice of language. But A repeats his offer and gives a reason for not taking the bus at that particular time of the day. Notice that A's reformulation of his offer is accompanied by switching from English, the language he used for his original offer, to Cantonese, the language B has used for her dispreferred response.

As we noted above, preference organisation affects not only the second part speaker's contributions but also operates across a given speaker's turns, giving rise to 'repairs' of first parts of the pair in subsequent turns. In (13) A's reformulation of his original offer after a dispreferred response is one example of such a repair. I turn now to look more extensively at the language choices deployed in initiating and making repairs in Chinese/English bilingual conversation.

Contextualising repair

Consider extract (14).

(14) (A and B are both female speakers in their early forties.)
    A: ... *koei hai yisaang.*
        (He's a doctor.)
    B: Is he?
    A: *Yichin* (.) *hai Hong Kong.*
        (Before) (In Hong Kong.)

In this extract, A and B are talking about the occupation (as a doctor) of a Chinese who has recently settled in Newcastle. However, A here has not specified his period of employment as a doctor as past or present time; in Chinese, time reference is expressed not by alternative verb forms as in English but by adverbials (e.g. 'yesterday', 'next year'). B's question 'Is he?' (in CA terms a 'next turn repair initiator') offers A an opportunity to confirm or to reformulate her original assertion. In the event, A subsequently repairs her original statement by specifying both the time and place of the man's period of employment as a doctor. Notice that B relises her repair initiator in a language which contrasts with the language of A's turns.

A comparable example is (15) in which B's repair initiator is also marked out with a contrasting language choice.

(15) (A and B are both female; A is in her forties and B is in her mid-twenties.)
    A: *Da m do. Koeige telephone gonggan. Koei dang yatjan joi da.*
        (Can't get through. Her telephone is engaged. She'll ring again in a short while.)

B: She ring?
A: *Hai a, ngaw da.*
     (Yes, I'll ring.)

Here, A is trying to telephone a friend, but the line is engaged. Initiating a repair on A's first turn *'Koei dang yatjan joi da.'* ('She'll ring again in a short while.'), B chooses English to ask 'She ring?'. This is followed by A's repair *'Hai a, ngaw da'* ('Yes, I'll ring'). As in (14), we find that the language of the repair initiator token contrasts with the language of the preceding and following turns.

It should be pointed out that the fact that the two second speakers in both examples ask the first turn speakers to confirm or to reformulate their statements suggests that to them as participants there is a problem, although to non-participants what needs repair may not be transparent. Only through a sequential analysis which focuses on each move of the conversationalists themselves can we, as analysts, detect any repairable spots and infer meanings.

Now compare (14) and (15) with (16) below.

(16) (A is female in her late thirties and B is male in his late-twenties.)
     A: He's a /ku:/ ... (.) I don't know how to say (.) send message (.)
          Nay ji-m-ji a?
          (Do you know?)
     B: Oh, courier.
     A: Yes, courier.

In (16), A uses English to comment on a relative of hers who travels frequently between Britain and Hong Kong. As the subsequent interaction reveals, she is trying to locate and pronounce the lexical item 'courier'. The subsequent repair by B differs from those exemplified in (14) and (15) (other initiated self-repairs), in that it is a self-initiated other repair by A herself. Nevertheless, (16) is comparable to the two preceding sequences in that the language of the repair initiator contrasts with the language of the preceding and following turns.

Further examples show that code-switching can also contextualise self-initiated self-repairs, that is, repairs that are done by the speaker himself or herself within the same speaking turn without prompting from others. Consider, for example, (17):

(17) **A:** His sister (.) *koei-ge mooi* is my good friend.
          (his younger sister)

Here, the English word 'sister' is problematic; Chinese has two different kin terms which differentiate 'younger sister' from 'elder sister'. To accomplish a repair which clarifies the referent of 'sister', the speaker code-switches to Cantonese, switching back to English to continue with her talk.

Sometimes, speakers deploy other resources to mark a particular item within an utterance as problematic. Instead of replacing it with a contrasting-code item as in (17), an 'attention catcher' (or in Sacks & Schegloff's, 1979, terms 'try marker') may be inserted in a different language before the speaker repeats or clarifies the problematic item. In (18) below, for example, A inserts a code-switched tag, 'you know', to flag her subsequent repetition of the word *daji* (typist).

(18) **A:**   *Koei hai gongsi jo daji* you know *daji yuen.*
           (She works in a company as a typist (you know) typist.)

The code-switches in (17) and (18) have one feature in common — a predictable end at which point the speakers switch back to the original languages.

Patterns similar to those displayed here have been reported elsewhere in the code-switching literature. Researchers have frequently observed that code-switching can serve the functions of word-finding, self-editing (with or without discernible errors), repetition, emphasis, clarification, confirmation, and so forth. However, all these functions can be described within a more principled, intergrated framework as phenomena arising from repair, a very general conversation organisational procedure.

A general methodological point to be made here is that the sequential approach to conversational code-switching as presented here is intended to incorporate the existing models into an 'interpretative' framework which focuses on the participants' methods of using code-switching as a communicative strategy in bilingual interaction. This point is worth emphasising, because very often new analyses of code-switching are presented as if they contradict rather than complement each other, and without suggesting ways in which they might be integrated into a more coherent model.

From what we have seen so far, there seem to be three main ways in which code-switching can contextualise repair. First, a repair initiator may be issued in a contrasting language, the speaker of the repairable item then doing the repair himself or herself. Second, the repairable item(s) may be replaced with an equivalent in a different language; this can be done by the speaker without prompting from others (self-initiated self-repairs) or by different speakers (other-initiated other-repairs). The third is to insert an item in a different language to draw the listener's attention to the repairable. Certain English language expressions such as 'you know', 'right', 'see' seem often to be used for this purpose. Schiffrin (1987) examines the functions of such 'discourse markers' in monolingual conversation, but the existing CA literature has little to say about the marking of repairs in bilingual discourse. Further analysis along the lines suggested here may therefore contribute not only to our understanding of code-switching as a contextualisation cue but to conversation management more generally.

Conversation analysts have frequently pointed out that repair procedures reflect to a high degree the collaboration and co-operation among participants which is an essential aspect of orderly conversation, and which itself embodies a higher level of inter-subjective social consensus (for a recent and comprehensive discussion, see Schegloff, 1992). Failure to respond to repair initiators or to do required repairs can have undesirable communicative consequences, as is illustrated by the following sequence.

(19) (A, 18, son of B, female, early forties, is looking for the car keys to go out.)
    A: Where's the keys?
    B: *Mut-ye?*
        (What?)
        (2.5)
        Gaha lokyu a.
        (It's raining.)
    A: I won't be long.
    B: No.

In this extract, which requires a rather complex exposition, A's question about the location of the keys can be understood as a pre-request to use the car to go out. However, B does not reply directly but follows A's utterance with another question *'Mut-ye?'*, ('What?'). This may be seen as a candidate 'next turn repair initiator', which gives the first part speaker A an opportunity to re-formulate the prior turn in the next turn in order to avoid an imminent dispreferred response. Notice that although the question is contextualised by being realised in a language contrasting with the language of A's pre-request, A fails to make the apparently required repair. After a two-and-half second gap, B's comment on the weather may be seen (in light of the interactional outcome) to consitute a hedged refusal of A's pre-request, which she has evidently interpreted as a request to use the car. Again, B has chosen to use Cantonese for her turn, but A continues to indicate his wish to take the car and fails furthermore to align his choice with B's. His mother's ultimate non-compliant response follows without further delay.

While it is not possible to predict on an 'if only' basis possible alternative outcomes of requests, we can note that A's failure to achieve the desired compliant response from B is associated in (19) with his failure to read the contextualisation cue provided by A's language switch and to use appropriate procedures. Gumperz (1982: 133) discusses a comparable case, where a failure to read such a cue gives rise to a similarly unsatisfactory interactional outcome.

A clear example of failure to carry out repair leading to communication breakdown is provided in (20).

(20) (A, an eight-year-old girl, and C, a boy of about 15, are children of B, mother of mid-forties.)

A: Cut it out for me (.) please.
B: (2.5)
A: Cut it out for me, mum.
C: [Give us a look.
B: [*Mut-ye*?
  (What?)
A: Cut this out.
B: *Mut-ye*?
  (What?)
C: Give us a look.
  ... (2.0)
B: *Nay m ying wa lei*?
  (You don't answer me?)
A: (To C) Get me a pen.

Following a null response from B to A's request for help she repeats it, using a vocative on this occasion to specify her mother as the next turn speaker. B's subsequent next turn repair initiator '*Mut-ye*?' ('What?') overlaps with C's turn — he self-selects as next speaker. A then issues her request for the third time, but B repeats the same next turn repair initiator token. Again A fails to do the repair which B apparently expects, and the lack of alignment between the language choices of A and B is again noticeable, as in (19). A's three repeated requests are in English and show no sign of the change of form which would indicate a repair, while B's repair initiators are in Cantonese. It is instructive to compare this example with the alignment evident in the last two turns of (9), where the same repair initiator is followed both by a compliant response and a shift of language. At the end of (20), however, we find something close to a communicative breakdown, in the sense that B offers no response at all to A's repeated requests. After a two-and-half-second silence, B asks A why she does not respond to her. A then turns to C, abandoning the exchange between herself and B. Compare this with (19), where a response is ultimately provided, albeit a non-compliant one.

These extracts serve to highlight the role of code-switching as a central device for successful communication. Essentially, code-switching is a discourse strategy whereby bilingual speakers accommodate and collaborate with each other. By changing from one language to another, speakers indicate their awareness of potential trouble spots in the interactional process and repair those which have already arisen. Failure to do so in accordance with the matrix of contextualisation cues and conventions apparently accepted by co-interlocutors can, as we have seen, lead to the breakdown of an ongoing conversation.

The wider issue of how such discoursal meanings is related to the broader social significance of code-switching has been elaborated by various researchers. For example, Scotton (1988) argues that while the tendency is for speakers to use the language with which they feel more comfortable, they are generally aware of the set of rights and obligations involved in the ongoing exchange and would choose the form of their conversational contribution appropriate to that set, even though it may sometimes mean that speakers have to use a language which they know less well. Any move that is inappropriate to this matrix of mutual rights and obligations may be interpreted by the participants as deliberate and poses a potential threat to social interaction (see also Heller, 1982). I shall return to this point in the concluding section of this chapter.

Contextualising pre-sequences and insertion sequences

The role of code-switching in assisting collaboration and co-orperation among participants is evident also with respect to its place in these kinds of conversational sequences. Earlier we saw that when the next speaker fails to take up the turn at a TRP, the current speaker has the option of self-continuation. The subject matter of the self-continuation can be the same as in the speaker's preceding turns, as in examples (1)–(3). Sometimes, however, a new topic is introduced or the participant constellation is changed, and when this happens code-switching seems frequently to mark the introduction of new conversation topics and changes in participant constellation — a finding well documented in the code-switching literature. Consider extract (21) for example:

(21) (A, male, is talking with his cousin B, female, both in their twenties, about one of their friends who has been ill.)

    A: … *m hou gong koei tengji.*
            (Better not tell him yet.)
            (2.0)
            Did you see Kim yesterday?
    B: Yeah.
    A: *Mou* [*mat si...*
            (It's not serious ...)
    B: [*Yau di tautung je, Mou mat si ge.*
            ((She) only has a little head-ache. It's nothing serious.)
    A: *Ngaw jing yiu man nay.*
            (I was just about to ask you.)

The gap following A's first turn indicates turn completion, but B does not take up the following turn, and A continues. However, his utterance 'Did you see Kim yesterday?' is not an elaboration on his previous remark, but is material inserted into the main body of the discourse — a question checking the precondition for his subsequent enquiry about their friend's health, which constitutes a pre-sequence. Examples such as (21) from the Tyneside Chinese data suggest that pre-sequences are often marked by code-switching in bilingual conversation. Consider also (22):

(22) (Two teenage girls talking about their school-life.)
    A: … he's bor[ing
    B: [mm
    A: I don't know (.) don't like him
         (2.0)
    A: *ah ngaw jau yau di mafaan ge lak*
         (I'll have some trouble.)
    B: Dimgaai a?
         (Why?)
    A: Yesterday right …

In this extract, B responds to A's initial turn with a back channel, which indicates continued attention but does not constitute an attempt to take the floor. B does not respond at all her next turn, and at this point A switches from English to Cantonese. But rather than continuing on the same subject matter — somebody at school whom A does not like, she introduces a different topic. Notice that what exactly she intends to talk about is not made clear by this code-switched turn; rather it seems that A is bidding to attract B's attention before continuing, and indeed her code-switched utterance succeeds in eliciting a response from B. However, she switches back into English for her subsequent narration.

Extract (23) is an example of code-switching marking out insertion sequences.

(23) (A is in her early thirties and B in her mid-twenties.)
    A: … you go (.) you got another one?
    B: *Yatgo dou mou a?*
         (There isn't even one (that satisfies you)?)
    A: (2.0) *mou a* (.) they [look …
            (haven't)
    B: [For who? *Waiman a?*
                        (Is it Waiman?)
    A: *Hai a.*
         (Yes.)
    B: *Nigo le?*
         (What about this one?)
    A: (Looking at the one B gives her.)

In (23), A is choosing a T-shirt for her son Waiman from a supply brought from Hong Kong. A's request for more T-shirts by B from which she could choose one '... you got another one?' constitutes a first part of a pair. But rather than complying by offering more T-shirts, B responds with a question *'Yatgo dou maou a?'* ('There isn't even one (that satisfies you)?'). After A confirms that she does not like any of them, B follows up with two further elliptical questions 'For who? *Waiman a?'* to which A answers *'Hai a.'* ('Yes.'). Only then does B offer another T-shirt to A. The second part is thus delayed, separated from its first part by the embedded exchanges. If we could concentrate on the relationship between language choice and conversational structure, we find the following schematised pattern:

A:	English	Request
B:	Chinese	Question 1
A:	Chinese–English	Answer 1 (+ Account)
B:	English–Chinese	Question 2
A:	Chinese	Answer 2
B:	Chinese	Offer

The embedded sequences are clearly marked out by a series of code-switches, while the final compliant offer aligns with the language of the previous turn.

Even more complex embeddings are evident in (24), but as in (23), insertion sequences are marked by code-switching, thus separating out inserted material from first and second pair parts.

(24) (A is elder brother to B (female), both in their teens. C is their mother. NB. The codes here are Mandarin Chinese (transcribed in pinyin) and English rather than Cantonese and English)

> **A:** *Qu na ge biezhen lai.*
> (Go and bring a pin.)
> **B:** Where's it?
> **A:** Ask mum.
> **B:** Ma.
> **C:** mm
> **B:** *Na you biezhen a?*
> (Where are the pins?)
> **C:** *Sh'ma?*
> (What?)
> **B:** *Biezhen zai nar?.*
> (Where are the pins.)
> **C:** *Kan kan zuobian chouti you mei you.*
> (Have a look in the left drawer.)
> **B:** Yes. (To A) How big?
> **A:** Anything.

Here, A is helping B repair her personal stereo. His request for a pin forms a first part, but B's response is a question which constitutes another first part and in turn creates a slot for a further second part. A's 'Ask mum' re-routes B's question. B's next turn is a summons, acknowledged by C and followed up with a question '*Na you biezhen a?*' ('Where are the pins?'). C responds to B's question with a request for clarification. B's answer '*Biezhen zai nar?*' ('Where are the pins?') repeats her question in a different form. C replies informatively, and B's 'Yes' acknowledges that she has found the pins. Finally, she returns to A and asks 'How big?' to which A replies 'Anything'.

Again if we leave out the content of the interaction for a moment and concentrate on the relationship between conversational structure and language choice, we can construct a schematised pattern which reveals that the different levels of embedding are quite clearly marked by code-switching:

A:	Chinese	Request
B:	English	Question
A:	English	Answer (Re-route)
B:	Chinese	Summon
C:	Chinese	Answer
B:	Chinese	Question
C:	Chinese	Request for clarification
B:	Chinese	Repetition of question
C:	Chinese	Answer
B:	English	Acknowledgement
		Question
A:	English	Answer

The first instance of code-switching occurs when B inserts a question in the position of second pair part. He has chosen English for the question, which contrasts with the language of A's first part. A's response to B's inserted question is also in English, forming a paired sequence. A then turns to a different interlocutor, a change of participant constellation marked by B's second code-switch from English to Chinese. The subsequent exchanges between B and C are all in Chinese until B finds the pins and turns back to A, and the third code-switch marks another change of participant constellation. The final question and answer pair is in English. The sequence as a whole clearly demonstrates the orientation of participants to the local organisational patterns of conversation, and their active use of code-switching as a strategic device to contextualise and so help each other keep track of these patterns as they proceed.

The general point here seems to be that code-switching contextualises inserted material in these conversations, parallel to the way in which various kinds of prosodic and phonetic marking described by Local (1992), in his account of turn-continuation and restarting, contextualises such material in monolingual conversations. Thus, code-switching also constitutes a resource available to participants (especially bilinguals) to 'indicate the status of parts of their talk' (Local, 1992: 220). In this case we find indications that participants deploy this resource to indicate inserted material which is to be understood as separated from the main topical focus of the talk. Thus, a code-switching strategy can help the speaker to re-start a conversation at the end of an interactive episode, or to change conversational direction. It also helps the participants keep track of the main 'drift' of the interaction by mapping out complexly nested structural patterns in the conversation.

I have tried to demonstrate in this section that bilingual speakers switch languages to draw attention to details of the projected course of conversation and to check each other's understanding. Code-switching can be deployed by the same speaker to mark turn allocation, self-repairs (including the marking of repair indicators), and some pre-sequences and embedded sequences. It can be deployed by different speakers in consecutive turns to contextualise self-selection as next turn speaker, interruption, dispreferred second pair parts, other-repairs (including repair initiators) and insertion sequences. Both types of code-switching generate meaning by building a contrast in language choice for two stretches of conversation, and constitute a resource available to accomplish the same kinds of interactional work as, for example, changes in pitch, gaze, and gestural activity.

It is important to emphasise that code-switching is only one of many linguistic resources available to bilingual speakers, and they may (and indeed do) select alternative cues in the sequential contexts which we have studied (recall that code-switching makes up only 50 minutes of a total 23 hours of tape-recording). It is equally important to bear in mind that in actual conversation a given utterance may simultaneously perform a number of discourse functions. For example, an utterance serving as a turn-allocation component may also function as a repair initiator, and a dispreferred second part may also be an insertion sequence. Accordingly, code-switching as a contextualisation cue is multi-functional, and this is one reason why traditional classificatory approach which attempts to enumerate *ad hoc* functional categories to which instances of code-switching may be subsumed are unsatisfactory (see also Auer, 1984a, 1990, 1991).

At various points of the analysis, I have alluded to the link between conversation structures and language choice. This relationship, however, is variable in so far as certain (groups of) speakers tend to use one language for a particular conversation structure, while others use a different language for the same interactional purpose. For example, while parents and grandparents sometimes use English to contextualise turn-allocation when they talk to the British-born children (e.g. extract (11)), this particular interactional task may be contextualised in

Chinese in peer-group interaction among the British-born Chinese speakers (e.g. extracts (1) and (2)). This is because the base language for the two types of interaction (inter-generational and intra-generational respectively) is very different — parents and grandparents normally speak Chinese and only switch to English for certain communicative effect in inter-generational talk; in contrast, the British-born generation normally use English for peer-group interaction and switch to Chinese for special purposes. Clearly, generational variations in code-switching strategies cannot be fully explained without reference to the more general patterns of language choice and language shift which was discussed in detail in Chapters 4 and 5. I shall now comment on the relationship between interactional-level code-switching and community-level language choice.

Code-switching and Community Choice Norms

Scotton (1983) argues that all bilingual speakers possess, as part of their communicative competence, a 'markedness metric', an innate, internalised model which enables them to recognise which language in the community repertoire is marked and which is unmarked in a specific interactional context and that choice of one language rather than another carries social import. What this means is that on the one hand bilingual speakers are creative, rational social actors and they exploit the available choices (linguistic or otherwise) for specific communicative purposes; on the other, they act within a normative framework — a set of rights and obligations — which is determined by the community to which they belong. With regard to the Tyneside Chinese community, the generation-specific and network-specific language choice preferences described in Chapters 4 and 5 provide such a frame and the various code-switching practices discussed in this chapter must be interpreted within this frame.

For example, it is clear from both long-term participant observation and detailed analysis of tape-recorded conversational data that English is the preferred language of the British-born children. The implication of this general language choice pattern is that the base language of a conversational exchange initiated by these speakers will highly likely be English. Thus, in order to build a contrast in code choice in an ongoing conversation, they switch to Chinese. This is indeed the case when they switch from English to Chinese to contextualise turn-handovers and insertion sequences in peer-group interaction (e.g. extracts (1), (2), and (22)). In contrast, the preferred language of parents and grandparents is Chinese. They do not normally switch language when talking with members of their own generations, except perhaps for a few cases of self-repair in English (most often taking the form of temporary lexical borrowing).

Speakers' awareness of the community norm and of the interactional, as well as social, effect of language choice is most evident in the marking of preference organisation. While there is a strong likelihood that the British-born children will use English to contextualise dispreferred seconds in inter-generational conversation, they normally switch to Chinese after the adults involved issue them repair initiators (e.g. extract (9)). The adults (parents or grandparents), for their part, normally insist on using Chinese when their first pair parts have been responded to by the children either in English or in silence, giving rise to contrastive language choices.

An interesting example of the speakers' ability to exploit the generational language choice norm is extract (8), in which the mother asks her 12-year-old son in English, rather than Chinese, whether he has finished his homework. She clearly knows that in choosing the preferred language of the child instead of her own preferred language, she is turning a simple question into an indirect request for the child to do his homework before playing with the computer, an implicature evidently understood by the child. Had the child not interpreted the meaning of this particular choice correctly, one assumes he could have been ordered by the mother to pack up his computer games and do his homework.

This example further illustrates that there is no simple, one-to-one relationship between code-switching structure and community-level language preference. The latter does not constrain individual instances of code-switching, rather it offers a frame of reference for participants — and analysts too for that matter — to interpret the meaning of language choice in conversation. While some instances of code-switching seem to serve primarily discourse functions (e.g. either Chinese or English may be used to contextualise turn competition where contrasting code choice is more significant than the use of a particular language) and are not easily related to language preference of the speaker, the very fact that speakers change from one language to another in conversation calls for special interpretation.

In sum, the various code-switching practices discussed in this chapter can be described as interactional reflexes of the generation-specific and network-specific language choice preferences of the Tyneside Chinese/English bilingual speakers. Through experience, they develop a sense of 'script' or 'schema' for which language is used to whom and when, and exploit the linguistic resources available to them to achieve special communicative effects.

Note

1. CA originated in the work of a group of American sociologists often known as 'ethnomethodologists', the most prominent of whom include Garfinkel (e.g. 1967) and Sacks (e.g. Sacks, Schegloff & Jefferson1974). However, CA differs from ethnomethodology proper in that the former is 'more firmly oriented toward the organisation of talk, or interaction, as an activity', whereas the latter 'has a more cognitive outlook, with an emphasis upon the analysis of the grounds upon which everyday activities are carried out' (Kendon, 1990: 46).

7   Summary and Conclusion

As described in the Introduction, the study presented in this book has two related objectives: (1) to offer detailed information on the sociolinguistic patterns of the Chinese communities in Britain, especially on bilingual language choice patterns of the Chinese in Tyneside in the northeast of England; (2) to work towards a coherent *social* model which can account for the relationship between community-level language choice and interactional-level code-switching, and for the relation of both to the broader social, economic and political context.

The study has developed in two stages. First, a detailed description of the language choice patterns of 58 speakers from ten Tyneside Chinese families was presented, in terms of both intra-speaker (choices according to interlocutor types) and inter-speaker variations. For the latter, a number of variables were examined, including speaker age, sex, and duration of residence in Britain. It was found that an age-related language shift from Chinese monolingualism to English-dominant bilingualism, through various degrees of bilingualism, was taking place within the Tyneside Chinese community. However, age alone could not fully explain the process of language shift; in particular, a number of speakers seemed to have adopted language choice patterns more characteristic of other generations than their own. It was in this context that the concept of social networks was introduced.

Three different types of social networks were analysed, namely, exchange (i.e. persons with whom ego not only interacts routinely but also exchanges direct aid, advice, criticism and support), interactive (persons with whom ego interacts frequently and perhaps over prolonged periods of time, but on whom ego does not rely for personal favours and other material or symbolic resources), and 'passive' (i.e. persons who are valued by ego as a source of influence and moral support, but are typically absent of regular direct contact), with regard to ethnic (i.e. Chinese versus non-Chinese) and peer-group composition. It was revealed that those who maintained a Chinese-dominant language choice pattern and who had the least knowledge of English forged strong exchange ties with other Chinese in the community, even though they had plenty of opportunities to interact with non-Chinese people; and their 'passive' networks were entirely Chinese. Speakers who adopted the English-dominant language choice patterns and who had a better command of English, on the other hand, developed non-Chinese, peer-group-based ties (both exchange and interactive networks); and even some of their 'passive' networks were non-Chinese. This correlation between language use/language ability and social network structure was consistent at both group (generation) and individual levels; that is, members of the grandparent generation had generally the strongest ethnic-based ties and used Chinese most often, while those of the parent generation contracted some non-Chinese ties and acquired limited English. The British-born child generation, in contrast, developed their network ties mainly with non-Chinese peers and used English much more often and with greater ease than their parents and grandparents. However, some individuals have developed social network patterns which resemble those of generations other than their own and their linguistic behaviours also differ from other speakers within the same generations. Two male grandparents who adopted a bilingual rather than a Chinese monolingual language choice pattern, for example, had more non-Chinese ties than the rest of the grandparents in the sample; and ten children who used only English with other British-born Chinese children were the ones who have few or no Chinese ties in their social networks. These younger speakers also contracted a larger number of peer-group ties than the parents and grandparents.

One particularly important point emerging from the analysis is that social networks affect and are affected by their members' language behaviour. On the one hand, social networks of individual speakers constrain their opportunities to learn and use particular languages or language varieties; on the other, use of certain language or language variety can contribute to the development of network contacts of individual speakers. Other speaker variables such as age and sex apparently do not have similar dialectic relationships with language, although they are associated in various ways with speakers' language choice and language ability.

The second stage of the study followed the first and focused on the various code-switching practices of individual speakers at the interactional (or conversational) level. A detailed, sequential analysis of tape-recorded conversational data revealed that speakers of the parent and grandparent generations tended to use Chinese most of the time and only switched occasionally to English to contextualise turn-allocation and repair initiators in inter-generational interaction (i.e. conversations with children). Members of the child generation behaved quite differently in that they tended to use English to contextualise dispreferred responses in conversations with parents and grandparents, and they used English almost exclusively with interlocutors of their own generation, switching to Chinese to mark insertion sequences occasionally. While such generational variations in code-switching practices can sometimes be related to practical constraints arising from linguistic competence of individual speakers, many examples discussed in Chapter 6 cannot, and are better interpreted as network-specific strategies of a socially symbolic kind.

On the basis of these findings, it is possible to construct a typology of bilingualism which covers the range of language patterns observed in the Tyneside Chinese community. Although it is phrased primarily with reference to the Chinese in Tyneside, this typology should be applicable, in principle, to other immigrant communities in western, industrialised countries.

Type 1. The monolingual community language speaker

Persons of this category rarely venture outside their family and ethnic community. Their social networks are entirely kin- and ethnic-based, which do not oblige them to learn another language. Thus, they remain monolingual in their ethnic community language no matter how many years they spend in the host country. In the Tyneside Chinese community, many women and elderly whom I have described as sponsored emigrants (i.e. they came to Britain either as immediate kin of the first generation immigrants or had personal contacts with people already established here) belong to this category. Obviously, this group of speakers are not engaged in bilingual code-switching at all.

Type 2. The functionally monolingual community language speaker

Such speakers use their ethnic community language in all key social contexts. They may, however, possess a limited capacity to understand or even speak the 'host' language; but their primary interaction is with members of their own ethnic community and they have few, if any, opportunities to use the 'host' language. Some of them may in fact try to avoid contact with those who speak languages other than theirs. Some parents (especially mothers) in the Tyneside Chinese community fall into this category. Their exchange and 'passive' ties are entirely Chinese, and they interact predominantly with Chinese speakers. Normally, these speakers do not code-switch. They may, on rare occasions, use one or two words and phrases in English for specific reasons.

Type 3. The functionally bilingual speaker

The first language of such persons is the ethnic language of the community, which they use in many key social contexts, but they also use the 'host' language in some other contexts on a regular basis. For example, they may use the community language at home and with members of their own ethnic group, but use the 'host' language at work. The term 'functional' is used here to imply that people of this category are competent in the 'host' language only to the extent that they can use it to fulfil specific tasks in specific contexts. Usually, such speakers keep the two languages separate and use only one of them at a time. They do, however, have the ability to code-switch in the course of conversation if the context requires them to do so (e.g. change of interlocutor).

With regard to the social network structure of such persons, they often contract two different sets of network ties simultaneously — one within the community and one outside — and the two sets do not normally overlap or interact with each other.

The economically active, first-generation Chinese emigrants in Tyneside and some sponsored emigrants who are involved in the food trade are examples of the functionally bilingual speaker. Chinese remains the stronger language in their linguistic repertoire, but for practical reasons, such as running the catering business, they have acquired some English and use it regularly in selected contexts. While ethnic ties constitute the larger proportion of their social networks, they do not avoid contact with outsiders; in fact some have made friends (as expressed in their 'exchange' networks) with English speakers. These people often serve as a bridge between the monolingual and functionally monolingual community language speakers on one hand and the wider world on the other where the use of English is necessary. People with special roles in the community, such as leaders of religious and community organisations and community school teachers, usually fall into this category.

Type 4. The 'mixed' bilingual speaker

Such persons are typically enmeshed in networks in which all speakers code-switch frequently between the community and 'host' language. Although they can keep the two languages separate if the context requires them to do so (e.g. in monolingual context), the mixed-code utterances they produce, with all kinds of structural complexities, constitute a distinctive linguistic mode.

There are very few people in the Tyneside Chinese community who could be categorised as 'mixed' bilinguals, as the community language choice norm is very much oriented towards monolingualism. Pong (1991), however, reports that some British-born Chinese youth who belong to the True Jesus Church in Newcastle do have a much higher level of competence in Chinese than their non-church-going peers and mix English and Chinese more frequently. Yet, these speakers normally confine their mixed-code discourse to one specific context, namely, interaction with other Church members of similar age. Li Wei (1988) and McGregor & Li Wei (1991) described code-switching and code-mixing practices of the Chinese students and professionals in Newcastle, who are not included in the current study. Like the True Jesus Chruch youth, they use the mixed code only in peer-group interaction.

Type 5. The functionally bilingual 'host' language speaker

Such persons grew up learning the community language which they still use regularly in the family and the community. But over the years, they have developed a high level of competence in the 'host' language through education and employment and they use it in a range of other key social contexts. They sometimes even use the 'host' language in contexts which have been normally or previously reserved for the community language, if such usage is not thought to cause any threat to the social relationships between the participants.

One important difference between this group of speakers and those of Type 4 is that their social networks comprise two generally unrelated and monolingual sets, although, unlike Type 3 speakers, their ties with the 'host' language-speaking set are stronger and more numerous than the ones within their own ethnic community.

Many of the British-born generation in the Tyneside Chinese community belong to this category. English is clearly their preferred language which they use most of the time, especially outside the family and the Chinese community. Their social networks are mainly non-Chinese, although they interact with Chinese speakers also.

Type 6. The functionally monolingual 'host' language speaker

Although the mother tongue of such persons is the ethnic community language, they maintain only a minimum and often passive knowledge of it (e.g. they can understand the community language but cannot speak it fluently). Their fluency in the 'host' language surpasses that of the community and they use the 'host' language as their primary language for communication in all key social contexts. Such speakers normally keep only a minimum contact with speakers of the community language (e.g. immediate family members) and the vast majority of their exchange social network ties are outside their own ethnic community.

In the Tyneside Chinese community, some British-born children fall into this category. Both their exchange and interactive networks comprise mainly non-Chinese peers; many of their 'passive' ties are also non-Chinese. They have no ability to read or write Chinese and can only understand a minimum amount of spoken Chinese. They speak English most of the time, and virtually identify themselves with their English-speaking, non-Chinese, peers.

There are of course other types of bilinguals which are not included in this typology. Schooling (1990), for example, suggests a category of what he calls 'the forced bilingual speaker' who grew up outside the family, learnt the 'host' language as the first language, and had no contact with the ethnic community to which his or her parents belong. If, for some reason, such persons return to live in their parents' region of origin in adolescence or adulthood, they may find themselves forced to learn their parents' ethnic language in order to participate in the life of the community. As Schooling points out, there are generally few people of this category, and none has been found in the Tyneside Chinese community. In theory, however, the typology presented here could be expanded to cover different types of bilingualism in a range of language contact situations.

This typology is intended as a tool for categorising and comparing different language contact situations. There are two possible levels of application — at the community level, we can use this typology to identify similarities and differences in language choice patterns between speaker groups. At the same time, this typology offers a framework for comparative analysis of code-switching patterns of individual speakers and, more importantly perhaps, helps us understand the relationship between this interactional-level practice and the wider social norms of the community to which the speakers belong.

Key to the content of this typology is the different social network structures of speaker groups and their relationships with language choice. As discussed in Chapter 5, social networks exert pressures on their members to use language in certain ways in different contexts. Speakers with the same social network contacts would conform to certain norms of language use, while speakers with different network ties would differ in their linguistic behaviour. By analysing network structures, we are able to understand and explain the social mechanisms underlying both synchronic variation and diachronic change in language choice patterns within and across communities.

As well as relating community and interactional levels of analysis, personal network ties can relate to macro social, economic and political structures. The main point I want to make here is that the various network types discussed in this book do not constitute themselves in a socially arbitrary fashion. Particularly, the characteristic occupational preferences of the economically active Chinese largely determine the nature of the ties which they contract with others. Similarly, the mainly kin-oriented and ethnic-oriented ties which the economically dependent adults contract are a natural consequence of the Chinese family system. The British-born generation, for their part, by attending school and participating in life outside the community, will contract ties with non-Chinese peers.

A coherent model of language choice and code-switching needs to make explicit the relationship between community networks — 'frames' within which language choice takes place — and larger-scale social and economic structures. As Gal (1988) points out, the success, persistence and precise form of the 'opposition' to mainstream values symbolised by minority language maintenance depends not upon community-internal linguistic or interactional factors, but upon the relation of the group to the national economy and to like groups in other cities or states. The outcome in terms of language (or dialect) survival or shift in Belfast may be different from that in Paris or Copenhagen; in Catalonia different from Gascony. It will be constrained by local variations in political, economic and social structure.

What seems to be required is a social (as opposed to a sociolinguistic) theory which can associate these network patterns with specifiable sub-groups which in turn emerge from larger scale social, economic and political processes. One useful integrated analysis is proposed by Giddens (1984), but the life-mode theory of the Danish anthropologist Thomas Højrup (1983), which is grounded more firmly in systematic ethnographic work, is particularly helpful. Details of the life-mode theory and its implications for sociolinguistics research have been discussed by J. Milroy (1992) and Milroy & Milroy (1992) (see also Li Wei, Milroy & Pong, 1992).

Offering an analysis which is designed to be generally applicable to Western Europe but allows for local, historically contingent differences in social and economic systems, Højrup proposes a division of the population into sub-groups which are described in terms of three life-modes. These life-modes are seen as both social and cultural, as necessary and inevitable constituents of the social structure as a whole which spring from economic systems of production and consumption. Thus, like social network types, they are not socially or culturally arbitrary, but are the effect of 'fundamental societal structures which split the population into fundamentally different life-modes' (Højrup, 1983: 47). The precise way in which they split the population will, however, vary between nation-states, depending on local political and economic systems. Højrup's analysis focuses on the differing ideological orientation of the three sub-groups to work, leisure and family, and from the point view of Chinese community in Britain, the distinction between, on the one hand, Life-mode 1, the life-mode of the self-employed, and on the other, Life-mode 2, that of the ordinary wage-earner, is particularly important. The life-mode of a different kind of wage-earner, the high-powered Life-mode 3 executive, is quite different from either of these.

A close-knit family-centred network with a strong solidarity ideology and little distinction between work and leisure activities is characteristic of the self-employed. Conversely, ordinary wage-earners will be embedded in less kin-oriented and generally looser-knit networks. This analysis, to which I cannot do justice here, converges with my own presented in this book, in the sense that a more Chinese-oriented pattern of language choice by speakers who are embedded in close-knit networks can be predicted and such a personal network structure is characteristic of Life-mode 1. For example, two speakers in our sample are a married couple (speakers 15 and 16) who are both wage-earners, employed by a local computer company. They interact on a daily basis with English speakers, and their command of English is very much better than other economically active but self-employed (Life-mode 1) Chinese. They would be classified as belonging to Life-mode 2 in Højrup's model. Højrup does not see the life-mode of the self-employed as a relic of an earlier period but as highly efficient and competitive given its flexibility of operation and the commitment of the producers. He uses the Danish fishing industry as an example, but his description equally well applies to the Tyneside Chinese family catering businesses.

Although the study presented in this book is focused upon a specific Chinese community in Britain, the analysis offered here, especially the social network perspective developed in the analysis, may be of more general application. I have suggested that the concept of social network can form an important component in an integrated social model of language choice: it links with the interactional level in focusing on the everyday behaviour of social actors, and with the economic and sociopolitical level in that networks may be seen as forming in response to social and economic pressures. I have briefly discussed this latter link in terms of Højrup's life-mode analysis.

I have tried to demonstrate that while network interacts with a number of other variables, it is capable of accounting more generally for patterns of language choice and code-switching than the variables such as generation, sex of speaker, duration of stay and occupation with which it interacts. It can also deal in a principled way with differences within a single generational group. Future research should perhaps aim to develop more sophisticated and systematic procedures in analysing how speaker variables such as age, sex, class, generation cohort and social network interact in their effect on language choice and code-switching. At the moment, we are planning such an analysis, using a computer program called GLIM (General Linear Interactive Modelling).

However, research into the relations of network and other social variables or broader sociopolitical structures should not sacrifice detailed sociolinguistic analysis of actual language choice practices of the language user. Speakers' very ability to use code-switching as an interactional strategy has significant consequences for social relations and social organisation, and should be seen as constitutive of social reality. As Heller remarks:

> By accomplishing conversational tasks through code-switching, interlocutors accomplish social relationships. By using code-switching as a discourse device, interlocutors signal a shared understanding of the context which renders the discourse strategies effective and meaningful, and so signal assumed co-membership in a social community. Further, since they are members of social groups, the outcome of negotiations of interpersonal relationships has an impact (at least potentially) on the nature of intergroup relations, as well as on the nature of group-internal processes. Codeswitching therefore must be understood as part of historical processes, whether it contributes to stability or to change. (Heller, 1988: 267)

By examining in detail how bilingual speakers organise conversational interaction and make sense of each other's use of language, we can understand better speakers' ability to creatively exploit the linguistic and social resources available to them in the (re)construction of social context. We need to know much more than we do now about the ways in which social relations are defined and redefined by the use of different languages in bilingual communities. There is a more general point here which needs to be emphasised: rather than collecting ever more data which, while intrinsically interesting, cannot easily be compared, researchers need to devote some energy to develop a framework within which some comparative analysis and interpretation can take place. The present study of language choice in the Tyneside Chinese community is an attempt at a first step in that direction.

Appendix I. Information on the Speaker Sample

Table 1 Family size

No. of people per family	No. of families
4	2
5	2
6	3
7	2
8	1
Total 58 people	10 families

Table 2 Generation cohorts

	Male	Female
Grandparents	4	7
Parents	10	10
Children	16	11
Total no. of speakers	30	28
First-generation emigrants	10	5
Sponsored emigrants	4	12
British-born	16	11
Total no. of speakers	30	28

Table 3 Speaker age

	Male	Female
Mean age	32.9	36.8
Oldest	73	72
Youngest	10	8
Mean age by generation		
Grandparents	68.0	65.1
Parents	44.6	41.7
Children	16.9	14.4
First-generation emigrants	50.4	53.0
Sponsored emigrants	53.5	50.7
British-born	16.9	14.4

Table 4 Employment status

	Male	Female
Employed	16	14
Not employed	2	6
In full-time education	12	8
Total	30	28
Employment type		
Restaurant owner	7	6
Take-away owner	3	3
Shop owner	1	1
Shop assistant	1	0
Electrician	1	0
Factory worker	1	0
Trainee engineer	1	0
Office worker	0	1
Travel consultant	0	1
Secretary	0	1
Youth training scheme (YTS)	1	1

Table 5 Duration of residence in Britain (for people born outside the UK only)

	Male	Female
Mean years	21.8	19.2
Longest	31	31
Shortest	8	6
Mean years of residence by generation		
Grandparents	18.8	16.7
Parents	23	20.9
First-generation emigrants	25.7	24.8
Sponsored emigrants	12	16.8

Appendix II. Language Ability Scores

Table 6 Spoken Chinese
Male

A	B	C	D	E	1	2	3	4	5	Score	a	b
25	6GF	73	SE	12	+	+	+	+	+	5	1	1
51	10GF	68	FE	25	+	+	+	+	+	5	3	3
1	1GF	66	SE	8	+	+	+	+	+	5	1	1
37	8GF	65	FE	30	+	+	+	+	+	5	3	3
26	6F	56	FE	31	+	+	+	+	+	5	2	2
45	9F	53	FE	27	+	+	+	+	+	5	2	2
32	7F	49	FE	23	+	+	+	+	+	5	3	4
10	3F	47	FE	29	+	+	+	+	+	5	2	2
39	8F	44	FE	30	+	+	+	+	+	5	4	4
53	10F	44	FE	25	+	+	+	+	+	5	4	2
5	2F	41	FE	20	+	+	+	+	+	5	2	2
15	4F	40	SE	16	+	+	+	+	+	5	3	4
20	5F	37	FE	17	+	+	+	+	+	5	2	2
2	1F	35	SE	12	+	+	+	+	+	5	2	4
47	9S1	24	BB		+	+	+	−	−	3	3	4
28	6S1	22	BB		+	+	+	+	−	4	3	4
48	9S2	22	BB		+	+	+	+	−	4	3	4
12	3S1	21	BB		+	+	+	+	−	4	3	4
13	3S2	19	BB		+	+	−	+	−	3	3	4
34	7S1	18	BB		+	+	+	−	−	3	3	6
49	9S3	18	BB		+	+	+	−	−	3	3	4
29	6S2	17	BB		+	+	+	+	−	4	3	5
43	8O	16	BB		+	+	−	+	−	3	4	6
55	10S	16	BB		+	+	−	−	−	2	4	7
7	2S1	15	BB		+	+	+	−	−	3	3	4
35	7S2	15	BB		+	+	−	−	−	2	3	7
22	5S	14	BB		+	+	−	−	−	2	3	7
8	2S2	12	BB		+	+	+	−	−	3	3	4
17	4S	11	BB		+	+	+	−	−	3	3	6
4	1S	10	BB		+	+	+	−	−	3	3	5

A = Speaker number B = Membership of the family C = Age D = Emigration background E = Years of stay in the UK
GF = Grandfather F = Father S = Son O = Other relative
FE = First-generation emigrant SE = Sponsored emigrant BB = British-born
a = Language choice patterns with family members b = Language choice patterns with non-family members

Female

A	B	C	D	E	1	2	3	4	5	Score	a	b
44	9GM	72	SE	18	+	+	+	+	+	5	1	1
9	3GM	70	SE	12	+	+	+	+	+	5	1	1
31	7GM	67	SE	6	+	+	+	+	+	5	1	1
14	4GM	65	FE	18	+	+	+	+	+	5	1	1
52	10GM	63	SE	23	+	+	+	+	+	5	1	1
38	8GM	61	FE	30	+	+	+	+	+	5	1	1
19	5GM	58	SE	10	+	+	+	+	+	5	1	1
27	6M	52	FE	31	+	+	+	+	+	5	2	2
46	9M	50	FE	27	+	+	+	+	+	5	2	2
11	3M	46	SE	26	+	+	+	+	+	5	2	2
54	10M	45	SE	21	+	+	+	+	+	5	4	2
33	7M	42	SE	20	+	+	+	+	+	5	3	2
40	8M	40	SE	22	+	+	+	+	+	5	4	3
6	2M	38	SE	17	+	+	+	+	+	5	2	2
16	4M	37	FE	18	+	+	+	+	+	5	3	3
21	5M	35	SE	15	+	+	+	+	+	5	2	2
3	1M	32	SE	12	+	+	+	+	+	5	2	2
50	9O	22	BB		+	+	+	+	−	4	3	4
56	10D1	21	BB		+	+	+	+	−	4	4	4
30	6D	20	BB		+	+	+	+	−	4	3	5
57	10D2	18	BB		+	+	+	+	−	4	4	4
18	4D	15	BB		+	+	+	+	−	4	3	6
41	8D1	12	BB		+	+	+	−	−	3	4	4
58	10D3	12	BB		+	+	−	−	−	2	4	4
23	5D1	11	BB		+	+	+	−	−	3	3	7
36	7D	10	BB		+	+	−	−	−	2	3	7
24	5D2	9	BB		+	+	−	−	−	2	3	6
42	8D2	8	BB		+	+	+	−	−	3	4	4

A = Speaker number B = Membership of the family C = Age D = Emigration background
E = Years of stay in the U.K.
GM = Grandmother M = Mother D = Daughter O = Other relative
FE = First-generation emigrant SE = Sponsored emigrant BB = British-born
a = Language choice patterns with family members b = Language choice patterns with
non-family members

Table 7 Written Chinese
Male

A	B	C	D	E	1	2	3	4	5	Score	a	b
25	6GF	73	SE	12	+	+	−	−	−	2	1	1
51	10GF	68	FE	25	+	+	+	+	−	4	3	3
1	1GF	66	SE	8	+	+	+	−	−	3	1	1
37	8GF	65	FE	30	+	+	+	+	+	5	3	3
26	6F	56	FE	31	+	+	+	+	−	4	2	2
45	9F	53	FE	27	+	+	+	+	−	4	2	2
32	7F	49	FE	23	+	+	+	+	+	5	3	4
10	3F	47	FE	29	+	+	+	+	−	4	2	2
39	8F	44	FE	30	+	+	+	+	−	4	4	4
53	10F	44	FE	25	+	+	+	+	−	4	4	2
5	2F	41	FE	20	+	+	+	+	+	5	2	2
15	4F	40	SE	16	+	+	+	+	+	5	3	4
20	5F	37	FE	17	+	+	+	+	+	5	2	2
2	1F	35	SE	12	+	+	+	+	+	5	2	4
47	9S1	24	BB		+	−	−	−	−	1	3	4
28	6S1	22	BB		+	+	−	−	−	2	3	4
48	9S2	22	BB		+	+	−	−	−	2	3	4
12	3S1	21	BB		+	+	−	−	−	2	3	4
13	3S2	19	BB		+	−	−	−	−	1	3	4
34	7S1	18	BB		+	−	−	−	−	1	3	6
49	9S3	18	BB		+	−	−	−	−	1	3	4
29	6S2	17	BB		+	−	−	−	−	1	3	5
43	8O	16	BB		+	−	−	−	−	1	4	6
55	10S	16	BB		+	−	−	−	−	1	4	7
7	2S1	15	BB		+	−	−	−	−	1	3	4
35	7S2	15	BB		+	−	−	−	−	1	3	7
22	5S	14	BB		+	−	−	−	−	1	3	7
8	2S2	12	BB		+	−	−	−	−	1	3	4
17	4S	11	BB		+	−	−	−	−	1	3	6
4	1S	10	BB		+	−	−	−	−	1	3	5

A = Speaker number B = Membership of the family C = Age D = Emigration background
E = Years of stay in the UK
GF = Grandfather F = Father S = Son O = Other relative
FE = First-generation emigrant SE = Sponsored emigrant BB = British-born
a = Language choice patterns with family members b = Language choice patterns with
non-family members

Female

A	B	C	D	E	1	2	3	4	5	Score	a	b
44	9GM	72	SE	18	–	–	–	–	–	0	1	1
9	3GM	70	SE	12	–	–	–	–	–	0	1	1
31	7GM	67	SE	6	–	–	–	–	–	0	1	1
14	4GM	65	FE	18	+	+	–	–	–	2	1	1
52	10GM	63	SE	23	+	+	–	–	–	2	1	1
38	8GM	61	FE	30	+	+	–	–	–	2	1	1
19	5GM	58	SE	10	+	+	+	+	–	4	1	1
27	6M	52	FE	31	+	+	+	+	–	4	2	2
46	9M	50	FE	27	+	+	+	+	–	4	2	2
11	3M	46	SE	26	+	+	+	+	–	4	2	2
54	10M	45	SE	21	+	+	+	+	–	4	4	2
33	7M	42	SE	20	+	+	+	+	+	5	3	2
40	8M	40	SE	22	+	+	+	+	–	4	4	3
6	2M	38	SE	17	+	+	+	+	+	5	2	2
16	4M	37	FE	18	+	+	+	+	+	5	3	3
21	5M	35	SE	15	+	+	+	+	+	5	2	2
3	1M	32	SE	12	+	+	+	+	+	5	2	2
50	9O	22	BB		+	–	–	–	–	1	3	4
56	10D1	21	BB		+	+	+	+	–	4	4	4
30	6D	20	BB		+	–	–	–	–	1	3	5
57	10D2	18	BB		+	–	–	–	–	1	4	4
18	4D	15	BB		+	+	–	–	–	2	3	6
41	8D1	12	BB		+	–	–	–	–	1	4	4
58	10D3	12	BB		+	–	–	–	–	1	4	4
23	5D1	11	BB		+	–	–	–	–	1	3	7
36	7D	10	BB		+	–	–	–	–	1	3	7
24	5D2	9	BB		+	–	–	–	–	1	3	6
42	8D2	8	BB		+	–	–	–	–	1	4	4

A = Speaker number B = Membership of the family C = Age D = Emigration background
E = Years of stay in the UK
GM = Grandmother M = Mother D = Daughter O = Other relative
FE = First-generation emigrant SE = Sponsored emigrant BB = British-born
a = Language choice patterns with family members b = Language choice patterns with
non-family members

Table 8 Spoken English

Male

A	B	C	D	E	1	2	3	4	5	Score	a	b
25	6GF	73	SE	12	–	–	–	–	–	0	1	1
51	10GF	68	FE	25	+	+	+	–	–	3	3	3
1	1GF	66	SE	8	–	–	–	–	–	0	1	1
37	8GF	65	FE	30	+	+	+	–	–	3	3	3
26	6F	56	FE	31	+	+	–	–	–	2	2	2
45	9F	53	FE	27	+	+	+	–	–	3	2	2
32	7F	49	FE	23	+	+	+	–	–	3	3	4
10	3F	47	FE	29	+	+	–	–	–	2	2	2
39	8F	44	FE	30	+	+	+	–	–	3	4	4
53	10F	44	FE	25	+	+	+	–	–	3	4	2
5	2F	41	FE	20	+	+	+	–	–	3	2	2
15	4F	40	SE	16	+	+	+	+	–	4	3	4
20	5F	37	FE	17	+	+	+	–	–	3	2	2
2	1F	35	SE	12	+	+	+	–	–	3	2	4
47	9S1	24	BB		+	+	+	+	+	5	3	4
28	6S1	22	BB		+	+	+	+	+	5	3	4
48	9S2	22	BB		+	+	+	+	+	5	3	4
12	3S1	21	BB		+	+	+	+	+	5	3	4
13	3S2	19	BB		+	+	+	+	+	5	3	4
34	7S1	18	BB		+	+	+	+	+	5	3	6
49	9S3	18	BB		+	+	+	+	+	5	3	4
29	6S2	17	BB		+	+	+	+	+	5	3	5
43	8O	16	BB		+	+	+	+	+	5	4	6
55	10S	16	BB		+	+	+	+	+	5	4	7
7	2S1	15	BB		+	+	+	+	+	5	3	4
35	7S2	15	BB		+	+	+	+	+	5	3	7
22	5S	14	BB		+	+	+	+	+	5	3	7
8	2S2	12	BB		+	+	+	+	+	5	3	4
17	4S	11	BB		+	+	+	+	+	5	3	6
4	1S	10	BB		+	+	+	+	+	5	3	5

A = Speaker number B = Membership of the family C = Age D = Emigration background
E = Years of stay in the UK
GF = Grandfather F = Father S = Son O = Other relative
FE = First-generation emigrant SE = Sponsored emigrant BB = British-born
a = Language choice patterns with family members b = Language choice patterns with non-family members

Female

A	B	C	D	E	1	2	3	4	5	Score	a	b
44	9GM	72	SE	18	−	−	−	−	−	0	1	1
9	3GM	70	SE	12	−	−	−	−	−	0	1	1
31	7GM	67	SE	6	−	−	−	−	−	0	1	1
14	4GM	65	FE	18	−	−	−	−	−	0	1	1
52	10GM	63	SE	23	−	−	−	−	−	0	1	1
38	8GM	61	FE	30	−	−	−	−	−	0	1	1
19	5GM	58	SE	10	−	−	−	−	−	0	1	1
27	6M	52	FE	31	+	+	−	−	−	2	2	2
46	9M	50	FE	27	+	+	−	−	−	2	2	2
11	3M	46	SE	26	+	+	−	−	−	2	2	2
54	10M	45	SE	21	+	+	−	−	−	2	4	2
33	7M	42	SE	20	+	+	−	−	−	2	3	2
40	8M	40	SE	22	+	+	−	−	−	2	4	3
6	2M	38	SE	17	+	+	−	−	−	2	2	2
16	4M	37	FE	18	+	+	+	+	−	4	3	3
21	5M	35	SE	15	+	+	−	−	−	2	2	2
3	1M	32	SE	12	+	+	+	−	−	3	2	2
50	9O	22	BB		+	+	+	+	+	5	3	4
56	10D1	21	BB		+	+	+	+	+	5	4	4
30	6D	20	BB		+	+	+	+	+	5	3	5
57	10D2	18	BB		+	+	+	+	+	5	4	4
18	4D	15	BB		+	+	+	+	+	5	3	6
41	8D1	12	BB		+	+	+	+	+	5	4	4
58	10D3	12	BB		+	+	+	+	+	5	4	4
23	5D1	11	BB		+	+	+	+	+	5	3	7
36	7D	10	BB		+	+	+	+	+	5	3	7
24	5D2	9	BB		+	+	+	+	+	5	3	6
42	8D2	8	BB		+	+	+	+	+	5	4	4

A = Speaker number B = Membership of the family C = Age D = Emigration background
E = Years of stay in the UK
GM = Grandmother M = Mother D = Daugther O = Other relative
FE = First-generation emigrant SE = Sponsored emigrant BB = British-born
a = Language choice patterns with family members b = Language choice patterns with
non-family members

Table 9 Written English
Male

A	B	C	D	E	1	2	3	4	5	Score	a	b
25	6GF	73	SE	12	–	–	–	–	–	0	1	1
51	10GF	68	FE	25	+	+	+	–	–	3	3	3
1	1GF	66	SE	8	–	–	–	–	–	0	1	1
37	8GF	65	FE	30	+	+	+	–	–	3	3	3
26	6F	56	FE	31	+	+	–	–	–	2	2	2
45	9F	53	FE	27	+	+	+	–	–	3	2	2
32	7F	49	FE	23	+	+	+	–	–	3	3	4
10	3F	47	FE	29	+	+	–	–	–	2	2	2
39	8F	44	FE	30	+	+	+	–	–	3	4	4
53	10F	44	FE	25	+	+	+	–	–	3	4	2
5	2F	41	FE	20	+	+	+	–	–	3	2	2
15	4F	40	SE	16	+	+	+	+	–	4	3	4
20	5F	37	FE	17	+	+	+	–	–	3	2	2
2	1F	35	SE	12	+	+	+	–	–	3	2	4
47	9S1	24	BB		+	+	+	+	+	5	3	4
28	6S1	22	BB		+	+	+	+	+	5	3	4
48	9S2	22	BB		+	+	+	+	+	5	3	4
12	3S1	21	BB		+	+	+	+	+	5	3	4
13	3S2	19	BB		+	+	+	+	+	5	3	4
34	7S1	18	BB		+	+	+	+	+	5	3	6
49	9S3	18	BB		+	+	+	+	+	5	3	4
29	6S2	17	BB		+	+	+	+	+	5	3	5
43	8O	16	BB		+	+	+	+	+	5	4	6
55	10S	16	BB		+	+	+	+	+	5	4	7
7	2S1	15	BB		+	+	+	+	+	5	3	4
35	7S2	15	BB		+	+	+	+	+	5	3	7
22	5S	14	BB		+	+	+	+	+	5	3	7
8	2S2	12	BB		+	+	+	+	+	5	3	4
17	4S	11	BB		+	+	+	+	+	5	3	6
4	1S	10	BB		+	+	+	+	+	5	3	5

A = Speaker number B = Membership of the family C = Age D = Emigration background
E = Years of stay in the UK
GF = Grandfather F = Father S = Son O = Other relative
FE = First-generation emigrant SE = Sponsored emigrant BB = British-born
a = Language choice patterns with family members b = Language choice patterns with
non-family members

Female

A	B	C	D	E	1	2	3	4	5	Score	a	b
44	9GM	72	SE	18	–	–	–	–	–	0	1	1
9	3GM	70	SE	12	–	–	–	–	–	0	1	1
31	7GM	67	SE	6	–	–	–	–	–	0	1	1
14	4GM	65	FE	18	–	–	–	–	–	0	1	1
52	10GM	63	SE	23	–	–	–	–	–	0	1	1
38	8GM	61	FE	30	–	–	–	–	–	0	1	1
19	5GM	58	SE	10	–	–	–	–	–	0	1	1
27	6M	52	FE	31	+	+	–	–	–	2	2	2
46	9M	50	FE	27	+	+	–	–	–	2	2	2
11	3M	46	SE	26	+	+	–	–	–	2	2	2
54	10M	45	SE	21	+	+	–	–	–	2	4	2
33	7M	42	SE	20	+	+	–	–	–	2	3	2
40	8M	40	SE	22	+	+	–	–	–	2	4	3
6	2M	38	SE	17	+	+	–	–	–	2	2	2
16	4M	37	FE	18	+	+	+	–	–	3	3	3
21	5M	35	SE	15	+	+	–	–	–	2	2	2
3	1M	32	SE	12	+	+	+	–	–	3	2	2
50	9O	22	BB		+	+	+	+	+	5	3	4
56	10D1	21	BB		+	+	+	+	+	5	4	4
30	6D	20	BB		+	+	+	+	+	5	3	5
57	10D2	18	BB		+	+	+	+	+	5	4	4
18	4D	15	BB		+	+	+	+	+	5	3	6
41	8D1	12	BB		+	+	+	+	+	5	4	4
58	10D3	12	BB		+	+	+	+	+	5	4	4
23	5D1	11	BB		+	+	+	+	+	5	3	7
36	7D	10	BB		+	+	+	+	+	5	3	7
24	5D2	9	BB		+	+	+	+	+	5	3	6
42	8D2	8	BB		+	+	+	+	+	5	4	4

A = Speaker number B = Membership of the family C = Age D = Emigration background
E = Years of stay in the UK
GM = Grandmother M = Mother D = Daughter O = Other relative
FE = First-generation emigrant SE = Sponsored emigrant BB = British-born
a = Language choice patterns with family members b = Language choice patterns with non-family members

Appendix III. Social Network Scores

Table 10 Exchange networks (Total: 20 ties per speaker)
Male

A	B	C	D	E	Ethnic	Peer
25	6GF	73	SE	12	20	12
51	10GF	68	FE	25	16	8
1	1GF	66	SE	8	20	9
37	8GF	65	FE	30	14	10
26	6F	56	FE	31	17	10
45	9F	53	FE	27	15	12
32	7F	49	FE	23	12	7
10	3F	47	FE	29	18	9
39	8F	44	FE	30	14	11
53	10F	44	FE	25	15	10
5	2F	41	FE	20	16	8
15	4F	40	SE	16	2	11
20	5F	37	FE	17	15	9
2	1F	35	SE	12	16	9
47	9S1	24	BB		2	16
48	9S2	22	BB		3	12
28	6S1	22	BB		1	13
12	3S1	21	BB		5	15
13	3S2	19	BB		0	12
49	9S3	18	BB		0	13
34	7S1	18	BB		0	15
29	6S2	17	BB		0	14
43	8O	16	BB		0	17
55	10S	16	BB		0	12
7	2S1	15	BB		2	11
35	7S2	15	BB		0	15
22	5S	14	BB		2	12
8	2S2	12	BB		0	16
17	4S	11	BB		1	15
4	1S	10	BB		0	14

A = Speaker number B = Membership of the family C = Age D = Emigration background E = Years of stay in the UK
GF = Grandfather F = Father S = Son O = Other relative
FE = First-generation emigrant SE = Sponsored emigrant BB = British-born

Female

A	B	C	D	E	Ethnic	Peer
44	9GM	72	SE	18	20	10
9	3GM	70	SE	12	20	12
31	7GM	67	SE	6	20	14
14	4GM	65	FE	18	20	11
52	10GM	63	SE	23	20	9
38	8GM	61	FE	30	20	11
19	5GM	58	SE	10	20	12
27	6M	52	FE	31	17	12
46	9M	50	FE	27	18	14
54	10M	45	SE	21	18	13
11	3M	46	SE	26	20	11
33	7M	42	SE	20	15	10
40	8M	40	SE	22	18	11
6	2M	38	SE	17	20	12
16	4M	37	FE	18	6	10
21	5M	35	SE	15	20	11
3	1M	32	SE	12	18	13
50	9O	22	BB		2	14
56	10D1	21	BB		3	12
30	6D	20	BB		1	15
57	10D2	18	BB		2	15
18	4D	15	BB		0	17
41	8D1	12	BB		1	14
58	10D3	12	BB		1	12
23	5D1	11	BB		0	15
36	7D	10	BB		2	12
24	5D2	9	BB		1	15
42	8D2	8	BB		0	14

A = Speaker number B = Membership of the family C = Age D = Emigration background
E = Years of stay in the UK
GM = GrandMother M = Mother D = Daughter O = Other relative
FE = First-generation emigrant SE = Sponsored emigrant BB = British-born

Table 11 Interactive networks (percentage in brackets)
Male

A	B	C	D	E	Total	Ethnic		Peer	
25	6GF	73	SE	12	22	22	(100)	16	(72)
51	10GF	68	FE	25	27	17	(63)	14	(52)
1	1GF	66	SE	8	29	29	(100)	17	(59)
37	8GF	65	FE	30	30	15	(50)	15	(50)
26	6F	56	FE	31	29	17	(59)	16	(55)
45	9F	53	FE	27	24	10	(42)	12	(50)
32	7F	49	FE	23	33	16	(49)	16	(49)
10	3F	47	FE	29	29	15	(52)	15	(52)
39	8F	44	FE	30	27	3	(11)	13	(48)
53	10F	44	FE	25	28	5	(18)	14	(50)
5	2F	41	FE	20	32	7	(22)	15	(47)
15	4F	40	SE	16	27	6	(22)	26	(96)
20	5F	37	FE	17	31	6	(19)	16	(52)
2	1F	35	SE	12	28	5	(18)	14	(50)
47	9S1	24	BB		25	2	(8)	24	(96)
48	9S2	22	BB		19	0	(0)	18	(95)
28	6S1	22	BB		22	7	(32)	21	(96)
12	3S1	21	BB		18	0	(0)	18	(100)
13	3S2	19	BB		18	0	(0)	18	(100)
49	9S3	18	BB		25	0	(0)	25	(100)
34	7S1	18	BB		28	0	(0)	28	(100)
29	6S2	17	BB		22	2	(9)	22	(100)
43	8O	16	BB		22	0	(0)	22	(100)
55	10S	16	BB		16	2	(10)	20	(100)
7	2S1	15	BB		15	0	(0)	15	(100)
35	7S2	15	BB		18	0	(0)	18	(100)
22	5S	14	BB		16	1	(6)	16	(100)
8	2S2	12	BB		18	0	(0)	18	(100)
17	4S	11	BB		10	0	(0)	10	(100)
4	1S	10	BB		15	0	(0)	15	(100)

A = Speaker number B = Membership of the family C = Age D = Emigration background
E = Years of stay in the UK
GF = Grandfather F = Father S = Son O = Other relative
FE = First-generation emigrant SE = Sponsored emigrant BB = British-born

Female

A	B	C	D	E	Total	Ethnic		Peer	
44	9GM	72	SE	18	18	18	(100)	11	(61)
9	3GM	70	SE	12	15	15	(100)	10	(67)
31	7GM	67	SE	6	24	24	(100)	12	(50)
14	4GM	65	FE	18	27	27	(100)	14	(52)
52	10GM	63	SE	23	25	25	(100)	17	(68)
38	8GM	61	FE	30	22	22	(100)	11	(50)
19	5GM	58	SE	10	25	25	(100)	15	(60)
27	6M	52	FE	31	26	15	(58)	13	(50)
46	9M	50	FE	27	17	7	(41)	9	(53)
54	10M	45	SE	21	28	3	(11)	14	(50)
11	3M	46	SE	26	24	13	(54)	13	(54)
33	7M	42	SE	20	24	12	(50)	12	(50)
40	8M	40	SE	22	30	15	(50)	15	(50)
6	2M	38	SE	17	25	5	(20)	13	(52)
16	4M	37	FE	18	30	1	(3)	29	(97)
21	5M	35	SE	15	26	17	(65)	13	(50)
3	1M	32	SE	12	21	14	(67)	10	(48)
50	9O	22	BB		19	11	(58)	18	(95)
56	10D1	21	BB		23	13	(57)	22	(96)
30	6D	20	BB		26	3	(12)	26	(100)
57	10D2	18	BB		18	0	(0)	18	(100)
18	4D	15	BB		18	0	(0)	18	(100)
41	8D1	12	BB		24	1	(4)	24	(100)
58	10D3	12	BB		26	2	(8)	26	(100)
23	5D1	11	BB		25	0	(0)	25	(100)
36	7D	10	BB		22	2	(9)	22	(100)
24	5D2	9	BB		16	1	(6)	16	(100)
42	8D2	8	BB		20	0	(0)	20	(100)

A = Speaker number B = Membership of the family C = Age D = Emigration background
E = Years of stay in the UK
GM = Grandmother M = Mother D = Daughter O = Other relative
FE = First-generation emigrant SE = Sponsored emigrant BB = British-born

Table 12 'Passive' networks (Total: 10 ties per speaker)
Male

A	B	C	D	E	Ethnic
25	6GF	73	SE	12	10
51	10GF	68	FE	25	10
1	1GF	66	SE	8	10
37	8GF	65	FE	30	10
26	6F	56	FE	31	10
45	9F	53	FE	27	10
32	7F	49	FE	23	10
10	3F	47	FE	29	10
39	8F	44	FE	30	10
53	10F	44	FE	25	10
5	2F	41	FE	20	10
15	4F	40	SE	16	10
20	5F	37	FE	17	10
2	1F	35	SE	12	10
47	9S1	24	BB		7
48	9S2	22	BB		9
28	6S1	22	BB		6
12	3S1	21	BB		8
13	3S2	19	BB		8
49	9S3	18	BB		6
34	7S1	18	BB		5
29	6S2	17	BB		5
43	8O	16	BB		4
55	10S	16	BB		5
7	2S1	15	BB		6
35	7S2	15	BB		3
22	5S	14	BB		3
8	2S2	12	BB		5
17	4S	11	BB		6
4	1S	10	BB		4

A = Speaker number B = Membership of the family C = Age D = Emigration background
E = Years of stay in the UK
GF = Grandfather F = Father S = Son O = Other relative
FE = First-generation emigrant SE = Sponsored emigrant BB = British-born

Female

A	B	C	D	E	Ethnic
44	9GM	72	SE	18	10
9	3GM	70	SE	12	10
31	7GM	67	SE	6	10
14	4GM	65	FE	18	10
52	10GM	63	SE	23	10
38	8GM	61	FE	30	10
19	5GM	58	SE	10	10
27	6M	52	FE	31	10
46	9M	50	FE	27	10
54	10M	45	SE	21	10
11	3M	46	SE	26	10
33	7M	42	SE	20	10
40	8M	40	SE	22	10
6	2M	38	SE	17	10
16	4M	37	FE	18	10
21	5M	35	SE	15	10
3	1M	32	SE	12	10
50	9O	22	BB		8
56	10D1	21	BB		8
30	6D	20	BB		7
57	10D2	18	BB		5
18	4D	15	BB		5
41	8D1	12	BB		6
58	10D3	12	BB		5
23	5D1	11	BB		3
36	7D	10	BB		5
24	5D2	9	BB		4
42	8D2	8	BB		4

A = Speaker number B = Membership of the family C = Age D = Emigration background
E = Years of stay in the UK
GM = Grandmother M = Mother D = Daughter O = Other relative
FE = First-generation emigrant SE = Sponsored emigrant BB = British-born

References

Agar, M.H. (1980) *The Professional Stranger: An Informal Introduction to Ethnography.* New York: Academic Press.

Albert, M. and Obler, L.K. (1978) *The Bilingual Brain: Neuropsychological and Neurological Aspects of Bilingualism.* New York: Academic Press.

Allinson, R.E. (ed.) (1991) *Understanding the Chinese Mind.* Hong Kong: Oxford University Press.

Appel, R. and Muysken, P. (1987) *Language Contact and Bilingualism.* London: Edward Arnold.

Atkinson, J.M. and Drew, P. (1979) *Order in Court: The Organisation of Verbal Interaction in Judicial Settings.* London: Macmillan.

Atkinson, J.M. and Heritage, J. (eds) (1984) *Structures of Social Action: Studies in Conversation Analysis.* Cambridge: CUP.

Auer, P. (1981) Bilingualism as a members' concept. *Papière des SFB* 99, Konstanz, No. 54.

— (1984a) *Bilingual Conversation.* Amsterdam: John Benjamins.

— (1984b) On the meaning of conversational code-switching. In P. Auer and A. di Luzio (eds) *Interpretive Sociolinguistics* (pp. 87–112). Tübingen: Narr.

— (1988) A conversational analytic approach to code-switching and transfer. In M. Heller (ed.) *Code-switching: Anthropological and Sociolinguistic Perspectives* (pp. 187–213). Berlin: Mouton de Gruyter.

— (1990) A discussion paper on code alternation. In ESF (ed. a) pp. 69–87. Strasbourg: ESF.

— (1991) Bilingualism in/as social action: a sequential approach to code-switching. In ESF (ed.) Vol. 2. (pp. 319–52). Strasbourg: ESF.

Baetens Beardsmore, H. (1986) *Bilingualism: Basic Principles* (2nd edn). Clevedon, Avon: Multilingual Matters.

Baker, H.D.R. (1966) The five great clans of the New Territories. *Journal of the Hong Kong Branch of the Royal Asiatic Society* 6, 25–47.

— (1968) *A Chinese Lineage Village.* Stanford: Stanford University Press.

— (1979) *Chinese Family and Kinship.* New York: Columbia University Press.

Baker, H.D.R. and Honey, P.J. (1981) Background to the Chinese in Britain. In Nuffield Foundation (ed.) *Teaching Chinese Children.* London: CILT.

Barnes, J.A. (1954) Class and committees in a Norwegian Island Parish. *Human Relations* No. 7.

— (1969) Networks and political process. In J.C. Mitchell (ed.) *Social Networks in Urban Situations: Analyes of Personal Relationships in Central African Towns* (pp. 51–76). Manchester: Manchester University Press.

Barrera, M. (1981) Social support in the adjustment of pregnant adolescents. In B.H. Gottlieb (ed.) *Social Networks and Social Support* (pp. 69–96) Newbury Park, CA: Sage.

Baumann, R. and Sherzer, J. (eds) (1974) *Explorations in the Ethnography of Speaking.* Cambridge: CUP.

Beal, J. (1993) The grammar of Tyneside and Northumbrian English. In J. Milroy and L. Milroy (eds) *Real English: The Grammar of English Dialects in the British Isles* (pp. 187–213). Harlow: Longman.

Bell, A. (1984) Language style as audience design. *Language in Society* 13, 145–204.

Bentahila, A. and Davies, E. (1983) The syntax of Arabic-French code-switching. *Lingua* 59, 301–30.

Bernardó, D. and Rieu, B. (1973) Conflict linguistique et revendications culturelles en Catalogne Nord. *Les Temps Modernes,* nos. 324–6.

Bilton, T., Bonnett, K., Jones, P., Stanworth, M., Sheard, K. and Webster, A (1987) *Introductory Sociology* (2nd edn). London: Macmillan.

Blom, J.-P. and Gumperz, J.J. (1972) Social meaning in linguistic structures: Code-switching in Norway. In J.J. Gumperz and D. Hymes (eds) *Directions in Sociolinguistics: The Ethnography of Communication* (pp. 407–34). New York: Holt, Rinehart and Winston.

Boissevain, J. (1974) *Friends of Friends: Networks, Manipulators and Coalitions.* Oxford: Blackwell.

Bokamba, E.G. (1989) Are there syntactic constraints on code-mixing? *World Englishes* 8, 277–83.

Bortoni-Ricardo, S.M. (1985) *The Urbanization of Rural Dialect Speakers: A Sociolinguistic Study in Brazil.* Cambridge: CUP.

Bott, E. (1957) *Family and Social Network.* London: Tavistock (revised 2nd edn published in 1971).

Breitborde, L.B. (1983) Levels of analysis in sociolinguistic explanation: Bilingual code-switching, social relations, and domain theory. *International Journal of the Sociology of Language* 39, 5–43.

Briggs, C.L. (1986) *Learning How to Ask: A Sociolinguistic Appraisal of the Role of Interview in Social Science Research.* Cambridge: CUP.

Broady, M. (1955) The social adjustment of Chinese immigrants in Liverpool. *Social Review* 3, 65–75.

Brown, P. and Levinson, S.C. (1987) *Politeness: Some Universals in Language Usage.* Cambridge: CUP.

Bulmer, M. (ed.) (1982) *Social Research Ethics: An Examination of Merits of Covert Participant Observation.* London: Macmillan.

Butler, C. (1985) *Statistics in Linguistics.* Oxford: Basil Blackwell.

Chann, V.Y.F. (1988) Chinese language teaching. In CRE (ed.) *The Needs of the Chinese Community in Scotland and the North-East of England* (pp. 73–80). London: CRE.

Cheung, C.-H.W. (1975) The Chinese way: A social study of the Hong Kong Chinese community in a Yorkshire city. Unpublished MPhil. thesis, University of York, UK.

Chomsky, N. (1965) *Aspects of the Theory of Syntax.* Cambridge: MA: MIT Press.

Clyne, M.G. (1987) Constraints on code-switching: How universal are they? *Linguistics* 25, 739–64.

Cochran, M. (1990) Personal networks in the ecology of human development. In M.Cochran *et al. Extending Families: The Social Networks of Parents and their Children* (pp. 3–33). Cambridge: CUP.

Cohen, A.P. (ed.) (1982) *Belonging.* Manchester: Manchester University Press.

— (ed.) (1986) *Symbolising Boundaries: Identity and Diversity in British Culture.* Manchester: Manchester University Press.

Coupland, N., Coupland, J., Giles, H. and Henwood, K. (1988) Accommodating the elderly: Invoking and extending a theory. *Language in Society* 17, 1–41.

Coupland, N., Henwood, K., Coupland, J. and Giles, H. (1990) Accommodating troubles-talk. In G. McGregor and R.S. White (eds) *Reception and Response* (pp. 112–44). London: Routledge.

CRE (Commission for Racial Equality) (1979) *The Chinese in the UK Conference, 1978.* London: CRE for Chinese Action Group and Quakers Community Relations Committee.

— (1988) *The Needs of the Chinese Community in Scotland and the North-East of England.* London: CRE.

Cuff, E.C., Sharrock, W.W. and Francis, D.W. (1990) *Perspectives in Sociology* (3rd edn). London: Unwin Hyman.

Daniels, R. (1988) *Asian American: Chinese and Japanese in the United States since 1850.* Seattle: University of Washington Press.

DeCamp, D. (1971) Toward a generative analysis of a post-Creole speech continuum. In D. Hymes (ed.) *Pidginization and Creolization of Languages* (pp. 349–70). Cambridge: CUP.

Denison, N. (1972) Some observations on language variety and plurilingualism. In J.B. Pride and J. Holmes (eds) *Sociolinguistics* (pp. 65–77). Harmondsworth: Penguin.

Dikoter, F. (1990) Group definition and the idea of 'race' in modern China (pp. 1793–949). *Ethnic and Racial Studies* 13 (3), 420–32.

DiSciullo, A.-M., Muysken, P. and Singh, R. (1986) Code-mixing and government. *Journal of Linguistics* 22, 1–24.

Dorian, N.C. (1981) *Language Death: The Life Cycle of a Scottish Gaelic Dialect.* Philadelphia: University of Pennsylvania Press.

Duncan, S. (1969) Nonverbal communication. *Psychological Bulletin* 72, 118–37.

— (1972) Some signals and rules for taking speaking turns in conversations. *Journal of Personality and Social Psychology* 23, 283–92.

— (1973) Towards a grammar for dyadic conversation. *Semiotica* 9, 29–47.

Dunn, L.M. (1959) *Peabody Picture Vocabulary Test.* Tennessee: American Guidance Service.

Duranti, A. (1988) Ethnography of speaking: Towards a linguistics of the Praxis. In F.J. Newmeyer (ed.) *Linguistics: The Cambridge Survey Vol. IV. Language: The Socio-cultural Context* (pp. 210–28).Cambridge: CUP.

Eades, D. (1982) You gotta know how to talk: Information-seeking in Southeast Queensland Aboriginal society. *Australian Journal of Linguistics* 2, 61–83.

Eastman, C.M. (ed.) (1992) *Codeswitching.* Special issue of *Journal of Multilingual and Multicultural Development* 13, 1–2. Clevedon, Avon: Multilingual Matters.

Eckert, P. (1980) Diglossia: Separate and unequal. *Linguistics* 18, 1053–64.

Edwards, V. (1986) *Language in a Black Community.* Clevedon, Avon: Multilingual Matters.

Edwards, V. and Alladina, S. (1991) Many people, many tongues. In S. Alladina and V. Edwards (eds) *Multilingualism in the British Isles* Vol. 2. (pp.1–29). Harlow: Longman.

Edwards, W. (1990) Social network theory and language variation in Detroit. Paper presented at Sociolinguistics Symposium 8, Roehampton, London.

Eisenstadt, S.N. and Helle, H.J. (eds) (1985) *Macro-Sociological Theory: Perspectives on Sociological Theory* Vol. I. London: Sage.

Ellis, A. and Beattie, G. (1986) *The Psychology of Language and Communication.* London: Weidenfeld & Nicolson.

England, J. and Rear, J. (1981) *Industrial Relations and Law in Hong Kong.* Hong Kong: Oxford University Press.
Erbe, W. (1977) Gregariousness, group membership, and the flow of information. In S. Leinhardt (ed.) *Social Networks: A Developing Paradigm.* New York: Academic Press.
Ervin-Tripp, S.M. (1969) Sociolinguistics. In L. Berkowitz (ed.) *Advances in Experimental Social Psychology* Vol. IV (pp. 93–107). New York: Academic Press.
ESF (European Science Foundation Network on Code-Switching and Language Contact) (1990a) *Papers for the Workshop on Concepts, Methodology and Data.* Strasbourg: ESF.
— (1990b) *Papers for the Workshop on Constraints, Conditions and Models.* Strasbourg: ESF.
— (1990c) *Papers for the Workshop on Impact and Considerations: Broader Considerations.* Strasbourg: ESF.
— (1991) *Papers for the Symposium on Code-Switching in Bilingual Studies: Theory, Significance and Perspectives* 2 vols. Strasbourg: ESF.
Fairclough, N. (1988) *Language and Power.* London: Longman.
Fasold, R. (1984) *Sociolinguistics of Society.* Oxford: Blackwell.
— (1990) *Sociolinguistics of Language.* Oxford: Blackwell.
Ferguson, C.A. (1959) Diglossia. *Word* 15, 325–40. Reprinted in P. Giglioli (ed.) (1972) *Language and Social Context* (pp. 232–52). Harmondsworth: Penguin.
Fischer, C.S. (1982) *To Dell Among Friends: Personal Networks in Town and City.* Chicago: University of Chicago Press.
Fishman, J.A. (1963) Bilingualism with and without diglossia; Diglossia with and without bilingualism. *Journal of Social Studies* 23 (2), 29–38.
— (1964) Language maintenance and language shift as a field of inquiry. *Linguistics* 9, 32–70.
— (1965) Who speaks what language to whom and when. *La Linguistique* 2, 67–88.
— (1968) Sociolinguistic perspectives in the study of bilingualism. *Linguistics* 39, 21–48.
— (ed.) (1971) *Advances in the Sociology of Language* Vol. I. The Hague: Mouton de Gruyter.
— (1972) Domains and the relationships between micro- and macro-sociolinguistics. In Gumperz and Hymes (eds) *Directions in Sociolinguistics: The Ethnography of Communication* (pp. 435–53). New York: Holt Rinehart & Winston.
— (1976) The spread of English as a new perspective for the study of language maintenance and language shift. *Studies in Language Learning* 2, 59–104.
— (1980) Bilingualism and biculturalism as individual and as societal phenomena. *Journal of Multilingual and Multicultural Development* 1, 3–15.
— (1991) *Reversing Language Shift.* Clevedon, Avon: Multilingual Matters.
Freedman, M. (1958) *Lineage Organisation in Southeastern China.* London: Athlone Press.
— (1966) *Chinese Lineage and Society.* London: Athlone Press.
French, P. and Local, J. (1986) Prosodic features and the management of interruptions. In C. Johns-Lewis (ed.) *Intonation in Discourse.* London: Croom Helm.
Gal, S. (1979) *Language Shift: Social Determinants of Linguistic Change in Bilingual Austria.* New York: Academic Press.
— (1987) Codeswitching and consciousness in the European periphery. *American Ethnologist* 14 (4), 637–53.
— (1988) The political economy of code choice. In M. Heller (ed.) *Code-switching: Anthropological and Sociolinguistic Perspectives* (pp 245–54). Berlin: Mouton de Gruyter.

— (1989) Language and political economy. *Annual Review of Anthropology* 18, 345–67.

Gardner-Chloros, P. (1991) *Language Selection and Switching in Strasbourg*. Oxford: Clarendon Press.

Gardy, P. and Lafont, R. (1981) Diglossie comme conflit: L'exemple occitan. *Langages* 61, 75–91.

Garfinkel, H. (1967) *Studies in Ethnomethodology*. Englewood Cliffs, NJ: Prentice-Hall.

Garvey, A. and Jackson, B. (1975) *Chinese Children: Research and Action Project into the Needs of Chinese Children*. Cambridge: National Education Research Development Trust.

Gibbons, J. (1987) *Code-Mixing and Code Choice: A Hong Kong Case Study*. Clevedon, Avon: Multilingual Matters.

Giddens, A. (1984) *The Constitution of Society: Outline of the Theory of Structuration*. Cambridge: Polity Press.

— (1989) *Sociology*. Cambridge: Polity Press.

Giles, H. (1980) Accommodation theory: Some new directions. In S. De Silva (ed.) *Aspects of Linguistic Behaviour: A Festschrift in Honour of Robert Le Page*. Special issue of *York Papers in Linguistics*.

— (ed.) (1984) The dynamics of speech accommodation. *International Journal of the Sociology of Language* 46.

Giles, H. and Coupland, N. (1991) *Language: Contexts and Consequences*. Milton Keynes: Open University Press.

Giles, H. and Smith, P.M. (1979) Accommodation theory: Optimal levels of convergence. In H. Giles and R. St Clair (eds) *Language and Social Psychology* (pp. 45–65). Oxford: Blackwell.

Goffman, E. (1959) *The Presentation of Self in Everyday Life*. New York: Anchor Books.

— (1963) *Behaviour in Public Places*. Glencoe: Free Press.

Goodwin, C. (1981) *Conversational Organisation: Interaction between Speakers and Hearers*. New York: Academic Press.

Graddol, D., Cheshire, J. and Swann, J. (1987) *Describing Language*. Milton Keynes: Open University Press.

Granovetter, M. (1973) The strength of weak ties. *American Journal of Sociology* 78, 1360–80.

— (1982) The strength of weak ties: A network theory revisited. In P.V. Marsden and N. Lin (eds) *Social Structure and Network Analysis* (pp. 105–30). Beverly Hills, Calif.: Sage.

Greenfield (1972) Situational measures of normative language views in relation to person, place and topic among Puerto Rican bilinguals. In J. Fishman (ed.) *Advances in the Sociology of Language* Vol. II. The Hague: Mouton de Gruyter.

Grillo, R.D. (1989) *Dominant Languages*. Cambridge: CUP.

Grimshaw, A.D. (1987) Micro-/macrolevels. In H. von Ulrich, Ammon N. Dittmar and K.J. Mattheier (eds) *Sociolinguistics: An International Handbook of the Science of Language and Society* (pp. 66–77). Berlin: Mouton de Gruyter.

Grosjean, F. (1982) *Life with Two Languages*. Cambridge, MA: Harvard University Press.

Guimarães, L.L. (1972) Communication integration in modern and traditional social systems: A comparative analysis across twenty communities of Minas Gerais, Brazil. Unpublished PhD thesis, Michigan State University.

Gumperz, J.J. (1971) *Language in Social Groups*. Stanford: Stanford University Press.

— (1982) *Discourse Strategies*. Cambridge: CUP.

— (1992) Contextualization and understanding. In A. Duranti and C. Goodwin (eds) *Rethinking Context* (pp. 229–52). Cambridge: CUP.

Guttman, L. (1944) A basis for scaling quantitative data. *American Sociological Review* 9 (2), 140–50.

HAC (Home Affairs Committee, House of Commons) (1985a) *Chinese Community in Britain* (2nd Report). London: HMSO.

— (1985b) *Refugees and Asylum, with Special References to the Vietnamese* (3rd Report). London: HMSO.

Hamers, J.F. and Blanc, M.H.A. (1989) *Bilinguality and Bilingualism.* Cambridge: CUP.

Heath, J. (1989) *From Code-Switching to Borrowing: A Case Study of Moroccan Arabic.* London: Routledge.

Helle, H.J. and Eisenstadt, S.N. (eds) (1985) *Micro-Sociological Theory: Perspectives on Sociological Theory* Vol. II. London: Sage.

Heller, M. (1982) Negotiations of Language choice in Montreal. In J.J. Gumperz (ed.) *Language and Social Identity* (pp. 108–18). Cambridge: CUP.

— (ed.) (1988) *Codeswitching: Anthropological and Sociolinguistic Perspectives* Berlin: Mouton de Gruyter.

— (1990) The politics of code-switching: processes and consequences of ethnic mobilisation. In ESF (ed. c) (pp. 53–76).

Heritage, J. (1989) Current developments in conversation analysis. In D. Roger and P. Bull (eds) *Conversation: An Interdisciplinary Approach* (pp. 21–47). Clevedon, Avon: Multilingual Matters.

Højrup, T. (1983) The concept of life-mode: A form-specifying mode of analysis applied to contemporary western Europe. *Ethnologia Scandinavica,* pp. 1–50.

Hsu, F.L.K. (1971) *The Challenge of the American Dream: The Chinese in the United States.* Belmont, California: Wadsworth Publishing Company.

Hughes, A. and Trudgill, P. (eds) (1987) *English Accents and Dialects* (2nd edn). London: Edward Arnold.

Hyltenstam, K. and Obler, L.K. (eds) (1989) *Bilingualism Across the Lifespan.* Cambridge: CUP.

Hymes, D. (1974) *Foundations in Sociolinguistics.* Philadelphia: University of Pennsylvania Press.

Jackson, B. and Garvey, A. (1974) The Chinese children of Britain. *New Society* 30, 9–12.

Jacobson, R. (ed.) (1990) *Codeswitching as a World-Wide Phenomenon.* New York: Peter Lang.

Jones, D. (1979) The Chinese in Britain: Origins and development of a community. *New Community* 7 (3), 397–402.

Jones, I. (1979) Some cultural and linguistic considerations affecting the learning of English by Chinese in Britain. *English Language Teaching Journal* 34, 55–61.

Jorgensen, D.L. (1989) *Participant Observation.* Newbury Park: Sage.

Joshi, A.K. (1985) Processing of sentences with intrasentential code-switching. In D. Dowty *et al.* (eds) *Natural Language Processing: Psychological, Computational and Theoretical perspectives* (pp. 190–205). Cambridge: CUP.

Kendon, A. (1977) *Studies in the Behaviour of Social Interaction.* Lisse: Peter de Ridder.

— (1990) *Conducting Interaction: Patterns of Behaviour in Focused Encounters.* Cambridge: CUP.

Kerswill, P. (1985) A sociolinguistic study of rural immigrants in Bergen, Norway. Unpublished PhD thesis, University of Cambridge.

Knorr-Cetina, K. and Cicourel, A.V. (eds) (1981) *Advances in Social Theory and Methodology: Towards an Integration of Micro- and Macro-sociologies.* Boston: Routledge & Kegan Paul.

Kremnitz, G. (1981) Du 'bilinguisme' au 'conflit linguistique'. *Langages* 61, 63–73.

Kwong, P. (1979) *Chinatown, New York: Labor and Politics 1930–50.* New York: Monthly Review Press.

Labov, W. (1966) *The Social Stratification of English in New York City.* Washington, DC: Centre for Applied Linguistics.

— (1972a) *Sociolinguistic Patterns.* Philadelphia: Pennsylvania University Press.

— (1972b) *Language in the Inner City.* Philadelphia: Pennsylvania University Press.

— (1972c) Some principles of linguistic methodology. *Language in Society* 1, 97–154.

— (1981) Field methods used by the project on linguistic change and variation. Sociolinguistic Working Paper 81. Austin, TX: South Western Educational Development Laboratory.

Labrie, N. (1988) Social networks and code-switching: A sociolinguistic investigation of Italians in Montreal. In N. Dittmar and P. Schlobinski (eds) *The Sociolinguistics of Urban Vernaculars: Case Studies and Their Evaluation* (pp. 217–32). Berlin: Mouton de Gruyter.

Lambert, W.E. (1955) Measurement of the linguistic dominance of bilinguals. *Journal of Abnormal and Social Psychology* 50, 197–200.

— (1964) Evaluational reactions of bilingual and monolingual children to spoken languages. *Journal of Abnormal and Social Psychology* 69, 89–97.

— (1969) Psychological studies of interdependencies of the bilingual's two languages. In J. Puhvel (ed.) *Substance and Structure of Language.* Los Angeles: University of California Press.

Lau, S.-K. (1981) Utilitarianistic familism. In A.Y.C. King and R.P.L. Lee (eds) *Social Life and Development in Hong Kong* (pp. 195–216). Hong Kong: The Chinese University Press.

— (1982) *Society and Politics in Hong Kong.* Hong Kong: The Chinese University Press.

Lavandera, B. (1978a) The variable component in bilingual performance. In J. Alatis (ed.) *International Dimensions of Bilingual Education* (pp. 391–411). Washington DC: Georgetown University Press.

Le Page, R.B (1978) Projection, focussing, diffusion, or steps towards a sociolinguistic theory of language. *Society for Caribbean Linguistics Occasional Paper* No.9. School of Education, University of the West Indies, St Augustine, Trinidad. Reprinted in *York Papers in Linguistics* 9 (1980).

Le Page, R.B. and Tabouret-Keller, A. (1985) *Acts of Identity.* Cambridge: CUP.

Levinson, S.C. (1983) *Pragmatics.* Cambridge: CUP.

Li, C.N. and Thompson, S.A. (1987) Chinese. In Comrie (ed.) *The World's Major Languages* (pp. 811–33). London: Croom Helm.

Li, P.S. (1988) *The Chinese in Canada.* Toronto: Oxford University Press.

Li Wei (1988) Audience design and language choice in a Chinese student community in Britain. Paper presented to Sociolinguistics Symposium 7, York (UK).

— (1992) A social network perspective on language shift and reversing language shift: The example of a Chinese community school in Newcastle upon Tyne. Paper presented to Sociolinguistics Symposium 9, Reading UK.

— (1993) Mother tongue maintenance in a Chinese community school in Newcastle upon Tyne. *Language and Education* 7 (3), 199–215.

— (1994) Network analysis. In H. Goebl *et al.* (eds) *Contact Linguistics: An International Handbook of Contemporary Research.* Berlin: Mouton de Gruyter.

Li Wei, L. Milroy, and Pong, S.C. (1992) A two-step sociolinguistic analysis of code-switching and language choice: The example of a bilingual Chinese community in Britain. *International Journal of Applied Linguistics* 2 (1), 63–86.

Li, W.L. (1982) The language shift of Chinese Americans. *International Journal of the Sociology of Language* 38, 109–24.

Linguistic Minorities Project (1985) *The Other Languages of England.* London: Routledge.

Lippi-Green, R.L. (1989) Social network integration and language change in progress in a rural alpine village. *Language in Society* 18 (2), 213–34.

Local, J.K. (1986) Patterns and problems in a study of Tyneside intonation. In C. Johns-Lewis (ed.) *Intonation in Discourse* (pp. 181–98). London: Croom Helm.

— (1992) Continuing and restarting. In P. Auer and A. Di Luzio (eds) *The Contextualization of Language* (pp. 273–96). Amsterdam: John Benjamins.

Local, J.K., Kelly, J. and Wells, W.H.G. (1986) Towards a phonology of conversation: Turn-taking in Tyneside English. *Journal of Linguistics* 22, 411–37.

Local, J.K., Wells, W.H.G. and Sebba, M. (1984) Phonology for conversation: Phonetic aspects of turn delimitation in London Jamaican. *Journal of Pragmatics* 9, 309–30.

Lüdi, G. (ed.) (1987) *Devenir bilingue — parler bilingue.* Tübingen: Niemeyer.

Luke, K.K. and Richards, J.C. (1982) English in Hong Kong: Functions and status. *English World-Wide* 3 (1), 47–64.

McClure, E. (1977) Aspects of code-switching in the discourse of bilingual Mexican-American children. In M. Saville-Troike (ed.) *Linguistics and Anthropology* (pp. 93–115). Washington DC: Georgetown University press.

McClure, M. and McClure, E. (1988) Macro- and micro-sociolinguistic dimensions of codeswitching in Vingard, Romania. In M. Heller (ed.) (pp. 25–52). Berlin: Mouton de Gruyter.

McCracken, G.D. (1988) *The Long Interview.* Newbury Park, CA: Sage.

McGregor, G. and Li Wei (1991) Chinese or English? Language choice amongst Chinese students in Newcastle upon Tyne. *Journal of Multilingual and Multicultural Development* 12 (6), 493–510.

Mackey, W. F. (1962) The description of bilingualism. *Canadian Journal of Linguistics* 7, 51–85.

McKinnon, K. (1977) *Language, Education and Social Processes in a Gaelic Community.* London: Routledge.

— (1984) Power at the periphery: The language dimension and the case of Gaelic Scotland. *Journal of Multilingual and Multicultural Development* 5 (6), 491–511.

Macphedran, G. (1989) Banana split. *The Listener* 28 September.

Maehlum, B. (1990) Codeswitching in Hemnesberget — Myth or reality? *Tromsø Studies in Linguistics* 11, 338–55 Oslo: Novus Press.

Martin-Jones, M. (1984) The newer minorities: Literacy and educational issues. In P. Trudgill (ed.) *Sociolinguistic Patterns in British English* (pp. 425–48). London: Arnold.

— (1989a) Language, power and linguistic minorities: The need for an alternative approach to bilingualism, language maintenance and shift. In R.D. Grillo (ed.) *Social Anthropology and the Politics of Language* (pp. 106–25). London: Routledge.

— (1989b) Language education in the context of linguistic diversity. In J. Esling (ed.) *Multicultural Education and Policy.* Toronto: Ontario Institute for Studies in Education.

— (1991) Sociolinguistic surveys as a source of evidence in the study of bilingualism. *International Journal of the Sociology of Language* 90, 37–55.

Martin-Jones, M. and Romaine, S. (1985) Semilingualism: A half-baked theory of communicative competence. *Applied Linguistics* 7, 26–38.

May, J.P. (1978) The Chinese in Britain, 1860–1914. In C. Holmes (ed.) *Immigrants and Minorities in British Society.* London: Allen and Unwin.

Mayer, P. (1961) *Townsmen or Tribesmen*. London: Tavistock.

Milardo, R.M. (1988) Families and social networks: An overview of theory and methodology. In Milardo (ed.) *Families and Social Networks* (pp. 13–47). Newbury Park, CA: Sage.

Milroy, J. (1992) *Linguistic Variation and Change*. Oxford: Blackwell.

Milroy, J. and Milroy, L. (1977) Speech community and language variety in Belfast. Report to SSRC (HR3771).

Milroy, J. and Milroy, L. (1978) Belfast: Change and variation in an urban vernacular. In P. Trudgill (ed.) *Sociolinguistic Patterns in British English* (pp. 19–36). London: Arnold.

Milroy, J. and Milroy, L., *et al.* (1983) Sociolinguistic variation and linguistic change in Belfast. Report to SSRC (HR5777).

Milroy, J. and Milroy, L. (1985) Linguistic change, social network and speaker innovation. *Journal of Linguistics* 21, 339–84.

— (1991) *Authority in Language* (2nd edn). London: Routledge.

— (1993) Mechanisms of change in urban dialects: The role of class, social network and gender. *International Journal of Applied Linguistics* 3 (1), 57–78.

Milroy, L. (1982) Social network and linguistic focusing. In S. Romaine (ed.) *Sociolinguistic Variation in Speech Communities* (pp. 141–52). London: Edward Arnold.

— (1985) What a performance! Some problems with the competence-performance distinction. *Australian Journal of Linguistics* 51, 1–17.

— (1987a) *Language and Social Networks* (2nd edn). Oxford: Blackwell.

— (1987b) *Observing and Analysing Natural Language*. Oxford: Blackwell.

Milroy, L. and Milroy, J. (1992) Social network and social class: Towards an integrated sociolinguistic model. *Language in Society* 21, 1–26.

Milroy, L. and Li Wei (1990) A sociolinguistic investigation of language shift in Chinese communities in the North-East of England. End of Award Report to ESRC (R000 22 1074).

— (1991) A social network perspective on code-switching and language choice: The example of the Tyneside Chinese community. In ESF (ed.) Vol. I. (pp. 233–52). An updated version is to appear in L. Milroy and P. Muysken (eds) *One Speaker Two Languages: Cross-disciplinary Perspectives on Code-switching*. Cambridge: CUP.

Milroy, L., Li Wei and Moffatt, S. (1991) Discourse patterns and fieldwork strategies in urban settings. *Journal of Multilingual and Multicultural Development* 12, 287–300.

Mitchell, J.C. (1969) The concept and use of social networks. In J.C. Mitchell (ed.) *Social Networks in Urban Situations: Analyses of Personal Relationships in Central African Towns* (pp. 1–50). Manchester: Manchester University Press.

— (1986) Network procedures. In D. Frick (ed.) *The Quality of Urban Life* (pp. 73–92). Berlin: Mouton de Gruyter.

— (1987) *Cities, Society, and Social Perception: A Central African Perspective*. Oxford: OUP.

Moerman, M. (1988) *Talking Culture: Ethnography and Conversation Analysis*. Philadelphia: University of Pennsylvania Press.

Moffatt, S. (1990) Becoming bilingual: A sociolinguistic study of the communication of young mother-tongue Panjabi-speaking children. Unpublished PhD thesis, University of Newcastle upon Tyne.

Moreno, J. (1953) *Who Shall Survive? Foundations of Sociometry, Group Psychology and Sociodrama*. New York: Beacon House.

Muysken, P. (1990) Ten remarks from the perspective of grammatical theory. In ESF (ed. a) (pp. 15–30). Strasbourg: ESF.

214 THREE GENERATIONS, TWO LANGUAGES, ONE FAMILY

— (1991) Needed: A comparative approach. In ESF (ed.) pp. 253–72.

Myers-Scotton, C. (1990) Intersections between social motivations and structural processing in code-switching. In ESF (ed. b) (pp. 57–81). Strasbourg: ESF.

— (1991) Whither code-switching? Prospects for cross-field collaboration: Production-based models of code-switching. In ESF (ed.) (pp. 207–31). Strasbourg: ESF.

— (1992) Codeswitching as socially-motivated performance meets structurally-motivated constraints. In M. Putz (ed.) *Thirty Years of Linguistic Evolution Amsterdam* (pp. 417–28). John Benjamins. Strasbourg: ESF.

Ng, A.K.T. (1982) Learning of Chinese by Chinese immigrant children. Unpublished BPhil. thesis, School of Education, University of Newcastle upon Tyne.

Ng, K.C. (1968) *The Chinese in London.* Oxford: OUP.

Ng, R.C.Y. (1986) My people: The Chinese community in the North-East. *Multilingual Teaching* 4, 30–3.

— (1988) The needs of the Chinese community in the North-East. In Commission for Racial Equality (ed.) *The Needs of the Chinese Community in Scotland and the North-East of England* (pp. 18–22). London: CRE

Ninyoles, R. (1969) *Conflicte Lingüistica Valéncia.* Valencia: Eliseu Climent Editor.

Norman, J. (1988) *Chinese.* Cambridge: CUP.

Nortier, J.M. (1990) *Dutch-Moroccan Arabic Code-Switching Among Moroccans in the Netherlands.* Dordrecht: Foris.

Nuffield Foundation (1981) *Teaching Chinese Children.* London: CILT.

O'Neill, J.A. (1972) The role of family and community in the social adjustment of the Chinese in Liverpool. Unpublished MA thesis, University of Liverpool.

Osbourne, M.E. (1983) *Southeast Asia: An Introductory History* (2nd edn). Sydney: George Allan & Unwin.

Pieke, F. (1988) The social position of the Dutch Chinese. *China Information* 3 (2), 12–23.

Pfaff, C. (1979) Constraints on language mixing. *Language* 55, 291–318.

Pomerantz, (1984) Agreeing and disagreeing with assessments: Some features of preferred/dispreferred turn shapes. In J.M. Atkinson and J. Heritage (eds) *Structures of Social Action: Studies in Conversation Analysis* (pp. 57–101). Cambridge: CUP.

Pong, S.C. (1991) Intergenerational variation in language choice patterns in a Chinese community in Britain. Unpublished MPhil. thesis, University of Newcastle upon Tyne.

Poplack, S. (1980) Sometimes I'll start a sentence in Spanish Y TERMINO EN ESPANOL: Towards a typology of code-switching. *Linguistics* 18, 581–618.

— (1981) Syntactic structure and social function of code-switching. In R. Duran (ed.) *Latino Discourse and Communicative Behaviour* (pp. 169–84). New Jersey: Ablex.

— (1983) Intergenerational variation in language use and structure in a bilingual context. In C. Rivera (ed.) *An Ethnographic/Sociolinguistic Approach to Language Proficiency Assessment* (pp. 42–70). Clevedon, Avon: Multilingual Matters.

— (1988) Contrasting patterns of code-switching in two communities. In M. Heller (ed.) (pp. 215–44). Berlin: Mouton de Gruyter.

— (1990) Variation theory and language contact. In ESF (ed. a) (pp. 33–65). Strasbourg: ESF.

Poplack, S. and Sankoff, D. (1984) Borrowing: The synchrony of integration. *Linguistics* 22, 99–135.

Poplack, S., Sankoff, D. and Miller, C. (1988) The social correlates and linguistic processes of lexical borrowing and assimilation. *Linguistics* 26, 47–104.

Poplack, S., Wheeler, S. and Westwood, A. (1989) Distinguishing language contact phenomena: Evidence from Finnish-English bilingualism. In K. Hyltenstam and L.K. Obler (eds) (pp. 132–54). Cambridge: CUP

Preston, D.R. (1989) *Sociolinguistics and Second Language Acquisition.* Oxford: Blackwell.

Punch, M. (1986) *The Politics and Ethics of Fieldwork.* Beverly Hills, California: Sage.

Ramsey, S.R. (1987) *The Languages of China.* Princeton, NJ: Princeton University Press.

Redding, S.G. (1990) *The Spirit of Chinese Capitalism.* Berlin: Mouton de Gruyter.

Reid, E. (1978) Social and stylistic difference in the speech of children: Some evidence from Edinburgh. In P. Trudgill (ed.) *Dialects in Contact* (pp. 158–72). Oxford: Blackwell.

Rickford, J.R. (1987) The haves and have nots: Sociolinguistic surveys and the assessment of speaker competence. *Language in Society* 16, 149–78.

Rin, H. (1982) The synthesizing mind in Chinese ethno-cultural adjustment. In G. De Vos and L. Romanucci-Ross (eds) *Ethnic Identity: Cultural Continuities and Change* (pp. 137–55). Chicago: University of Chicago Press.

Rivera, C. (ed.) (1983) *An Ethnographic/Sociolinguistic Approach to Language Proficiency Assessment.* Clevedon, Avon: Multilingual Matters.

Romaine, S. (1980) Stylistic variation and evaluative reactions to speech. *Language and Speech* 23, 213–32.

— (1982) *Socio-Historical Linguistics: Its Status and Methodology.* Cambridge: CUP.

— (1984) The status of sociological models and categories in explaining linguistic variation. *Linguistische Berichte* 90, 25–38.

— (1986) The syntax and semantics of the code-mixed compound verb in Panjabi-English bilingual discourse. In D. Tannen and J. Alatis (eds) *Languages and Linguistics* (pp. 35–50). Washington DC: Georgetown University Press.

— (1989) *Bilingualism.* Oxford: Blackwell.

Roper, S. (1988) The needs and means for action. In CRE (ed.) *The Needs of the Chinese Community in Scotland and the North-East of England* (pp. 2–6). London: CRE.

Rowe, L.A. (1988) An Investigation into the Spoken English of Six Chinese Second Language Learners. Unpublished B.Phil. dissertation, School of Education, University of Newcastle upon Tyne.

Rubin, J. (1968) *National Bilingualism in Paraguay.* The Hague: Mouton.

Russell, J. (1982) Networks and sociolinguistic variation in an African urban setting In R. Romaine (ed.) *Sociolinguistic Variation in Speech Communities* (pp. 125–40). London: Edward Arnold .

Ryan, B.F., Joiner, B.L. and Ryan, T.A., Jr. (1985) *Minitab Handbook* (2nd edn). Boston: PWS Publishers.

Sachdev, I., Bourhis, R.Y., D'Eye, J. and Phang, S.-W. (1990) Cantonese-Chinese vitality in London, England. *Journal of Asian Pacific Communication* 1, 209–27.

Sachdev, I., Bourhis, R.Y., Phang, S.-W. and D'Eye, J. (1987) Language attitudes and vitality perceptions: Intergenerational effects amongst Chinese Canadian communities. *Journal of Language and Social Psychology* 6, 287–307.

Sacks, H. and Schegloff, E.A. (1979) Two preferences in the organisation of reference to persons in conversation and their interaction. In G. Psathas (ed.) *Everyday Language: Studies in Ethnomethodology* (pp. 15-21). New York: Irvington.

Sacks, H., Schegloff, E.A. and Jefferson, G. (1974) A simplest systematics for the organisation of turn-taking in conversation. *Language* 50, 696–735.

Sankoff, D. and Mainville, S. (1986) Code-switching of context-free grammars. *Theoretical Linguistics* 13, 75–90.

Sankoff, D. and Poplack, S. (1981) A formal grammar of code-switching. *Papers in Linguistics* 14 (1), 3–45.

Sankoff, D., Nait M'Barek, M. and Montpetit, C. (1987) VSO/SVO bilingual syntax. NWAVE XVI, Austin, Texas.

Sankoff, D., Poplack, S. and Vanniarajan, S. (1991) The empirical study of code-switching. In ESF (ed.) (pp. 181–206). Strasbourg: ESF.

Sankoff, G. (1972) Language use in multilingual societies: Some alternative approaches. In J.B. Pride and J. Holmes (eds) Sociolinguistics (pp. 33–51). Harmondsworth: Penguin.

Saville-Troike, M. (1989) The Ethnography of Communication: An Introduction (2nd edn). Oxford: Basil Blackwell.

Schatz, H. (1989) Code-switching or borrowing? English elements in the Dutch of Dutch-American immigrants. ITL 83–4, 125–62.

Schegloff, E.A. (1972) Sequencing in conversational openings. In J.J. Gumperz and D. Hymes (eds) Directions in Sociolinguistics: The Ethnography of Communication (pp. 346–80). New York: Holt, Rinehart and Winston.

— (1984) On some gestures' relation to talk. In J.M. Atkinson and J. Heritage (eds) Structures of Social Action: Studies in Conversation Analysis. Cambridge: CUP.

— (1992) In another context. In A. Duranti and C. Goodwin (eds) Rethinking Context (pp.191–228). Cambridge: CUP.

Schegloff, E.A., Jefferson, G. and Sacks, H. (1977) The preference for self-correction in the organization of repair in conversation. Language 53, 361–82.

Schegloff, E.A. and Sacks, H. (1973) Opening up closings. Semiotica 7 (4), 289–327.

Schiffrin, D. (1987) Discourse Markers. Cambridge: CUP.

Schmidt, A. (1985) Young People's Dyirbal. Cambridge: CUP.

Schmidt-Rohr, G. (1932) Die Sprache als Bildnerin der Völker. Jena.

Schooling, S. (1990) Language Maintenance in Melanesia. Dallas, TX: Summer Institute of Linguistics .

Scotton, C.M. (1976) Strategies of neutrality: Language choice in uncertain situations. Language 52 (4), 919–41.

— (1980) Explaining linguistic choices as identity negotiations. In H.Giles W.P. Robinson and P.M. Smith (eds) Language Social Psychological Perspectives (pp. 359–66). Oxford: Pergamon.

— (1982) The possibility of code-switching: Motivation for maintaining multilingualism. Anthropological Linguistics 24, 432–43.

— (1983) The negotiation of identities in conversation: A theory of markedness and code choice. International Journal of the Sociology of Language 44, 115–36.

— (1986) Diglossia and code-switching. In J.A. Fishman et al. (eds) The Fergusonian Impact Vol. 2. (pp. 403–417). Berlin: Mouton de Gruyter.

— (1987) Differentiating borrowing and code-switching. In K. Ferrara et al. (eds) Linguistic Change and Contact: Proceedings of the NWAV 16 (Austin, Texas).

— (1988) Code-switching as indexical of social negotiations. In M. Heller (ed.) (pp. 151–86). Berlin: Mouton de Gruyter.

Sebba, M. and Wootton, A.J. (1984) Conversational code-switching in London Jamaican. Paper presented at Sociolinguistic Symposium 5, Liverpool.

Shang, A. (1984) The Chinese in Britain. London: Batsford.

Singh, R. (1985) Grammatical constraints on code-mixing. Canadian Journal of Linguistics 30 (1), 33–46.

Silverman, D. (1985) Qualitative Methodology and Sociology: Describing the Social World. Aldershot: Gower.

So, J.L.W. (1989) Meeting their needs: An analysis of the language needs of the Chinese women in Newcastle as a basis for English language courses. Unpublished BPhil. thesis, School of Education, University of Newcastle upon Tyne.

Social Services Department, City of Newcastle upon Tyne, Ethnic Minorities Team Report (1985-88) *Community Services*.

Spolsky, B. (1988) Bilingualism. In F.J. Newmeyer (ed.) *Linguistics: The Cambridge Survey* Vol. IV *Language: The Social-cultural Context* (pp. 100–18). Cambridge: CUP.

Spradley, J.P. (1979) *Ethnographic Interview*. New York: Holt, Rinehart & Winston.

— (1980) *Participant Observation*. New York: Holt, Rinehart & Winston.

Sridhar, S. and Sridhar, K. (1980) The syntax and psycholinguistics of bilingual code-mixing. *Canadian Journal of Psychology* 34, 407–16.

Sung, B.L. (1967) *Mountain of Gold: The Chinese in America*. New York: Macmillan.

Surra, C.A. (1988) The influence of the interactive network on developing relationships In R.M. Milardo (ed.) *Families and Social Networks* (pp. 48–82). Newbury Park, CA: Sage.

Swann Committee: Committee of Inquiry into the Education of Children from Ethnic Minority Groups (1985) *Education for All*. London: Her Majesty's Stationery Office.

Tay, M.W.J. (1989) Code-switching and code-mixing as a communicative strategy in multilingual discourse. *World Englishes* 8, 407–17.

Taylor, J.G. and Turton, A. (eds) (1988) *Southeast Asia*. Basingstoke: Macmillan Education.

Taylor, M.J. (1987) *Chinese Pupils in Britain: A Review of Research into the Education of Pupils of Chinese Origin*. Windsor: NFER-Nelson.

Torres, L. (1989) Code-mixing and borrowing in a New York Puerto Rican community: A cross-generational study. *World Englishes* 8, 419–22.

Treffers-Daller, J. (1990) Towards a uniform approach to code-switching and borrowing. In ESF (ed. b) (pp. 259–79). Strasbourg: ESF.

Trudgill, P. (1974) *The Social Differentiation of English in Norwich*. Cambridge: CUP.

— (1983) *On Dialect*. Oxford: Blackwell.

— (ed.) (1984) *Language in the British Isles*. Cambridge: CUP.

— (1986a) *Dialects in Contact*. Oxford: Blackwell.

— (1986b) The apparent time paradigm: Norwich revisited. Paper presented to Sociolinguistic Symposium 6, University of Newcastle upon Tyne.

Tsow, M. (1984) *Mother-Tongue Maintenance: A Survey of Part-time Chinese Language Classes*. London: CRE.

Vaid, J. (ed.) (1986) *Language Processing in Bilinguals: Psycholinguistic and Neuropsychological Perspectives*. Hillsdale, NJ: Lawrence Erlbaum.

Vallverdú, F. (1970) *Dues ilengües: Dues funcions?* Barcelona: Edicions 62.

Wald, B. (1981) Topic and situation as factors in language performance. NCBR Working Paper California: National Centre for Bilingual Research.

Wardhaugh, R. (1987) *Languages in Competition*. Oxford: Blackwell.

Warren, C.A.B. (1988) *Gender Issues in Field Research*. Beverly Hills, Calif.: Sage.

Watson, J.L. (1975) *Emigration and the Chinese Lineage: The Mans in Hong Kong and London*. Berkeley, CA: University of California Press.

— (1977) The Chinese: Hong Kong villagers in the British catering trade. In J.L. Watson (ed.) *Between Two Cultures: Migrants and Minorities in Britain* (pp. 181–213). Oxford: Blackwell.

— (1982) Chinese kinship reconsidered: Anthropological perspectives on historical research. *The China Quarterly* 92, 589–622.

Weinreich, U. (1953) *Languages in Contact*. The Hague: Mouton de Gruyter.

Wells, G. (1985) *Language Development in the Preschool Years*. Cambridge: CUP.

Wells, J.C. (1982) *Accents of English: The British Isles* (Vol. 2). Cambridge: CUP.

Whyte, W.F. (1984) *Learning From the Field.* Beverly Hills: Sage.
Williams, G. (1979) Language group allegiance and ethnic interaction. In H. Giles and B. Saint-Jacques (eds) *Language and Ethnic Relations.* Oxford: Pergamon.
— (1987) Bilingualism, class dialect, and social reproduction. *International Journal of the Sociology of Language* 66, 85–98.
Williams, G. and Roberts, C. (1982) Institutional centralisation and linguistic discrimination. In G. Braga and M. Civell (eds) *Linguistic Problems and European Unity.* Milan: Franco Angeli Editore.
Williams, I.M.O. (1980) Functions of code-switching as a communicative strategy in a Spanish–English bilingual classroom. Unpublished PhD thesis, Kent State University.
Williams, J. and Snipper, G. (1990) *Literacy and Bilingualism.* New York: Longman.
Wong, F.-M. (1979) Family structure and processes in Hong Kong. In Lin, Lee, and Simonis (eds) *Hong Kong: Economic, Social and Political Studies in Development* (pp. 95–121). White Plains, NY: M.E.Sharpe.
Wong, L. Y.-F. (1992) *Education of Chinese Children in Britain and the USA.* Clevedon: Multilingual Matters.
Woods, A., Fletcher, P. and Hughes, A. (1986) *Statistics in Language Studies.* Cambridge: CUP.
Woolard, K. (1985) Language variation and cultural hegemony: Towards an integration of linguistic and sociolinguistic theory. *American Ethnologist* 12 (4), 738–48.
Woolford, E. (1983) Bilingual code-switching and syntactic theory. *Linguistic Inquiry* 14 (3), 519–36.
Wu, Y.-L. and Wu, C.-H. (1980) *Economic Development in Southeast Asia: The Chinese Dimension.* Stanford, CA: Hoover Institution Press.
Yum, J.O. (1988) The impact of Confucianism on interpersonal relationships and communication patterns in East Asia. *Communication Monographs* 55, 374–88.
Zentella, A.C. (1981) Hablamos los dos. We speak both. — Growing up bilingual in el barrio. Unpublished PhD thesis, University of Pennsylvania.
Zhu, G. (1991) A historical demography of Chinese migration. *Social Sciences in China* 12 (4), 57–84.

Index